BLACK IMAGE
EDUCATION COPES WITH COLOR

BLACK IMAGE
EDUCATION COPES WITH COLOR

ESSAYS ON THE BLACK EXPERIENCE

Edited by

Jean Dresden Grambs
University of Maryland

John C. Carr
University of Maryland

with

James A. Banks
University of Washington

Phyllis Franklin
University of Miami

Barbara Glancy
University of Maryland

Juel M. Janis
Director of Head Start
Dade County, Florida

WM. C. BROWN COMPANY PUBLISHERS
Dubuque, Iowa

Printed in the United States of America

Acknowledgments

Chapter 2. A book review of Dharathula H. Millender's *Crispus Attucks, Boy Of Valor* by Jean D. Grambs, *Harvard Educational Review* 38 (Summer, 1968): 605-611. Copyright © 1968 by President and Fellows of Harvard College.

A book review of William Katz's *Eyewitness: The Negro in American History* by Larry Cuban, *Harvard Educational Review* 38 (Summer, 1968): 611-617. Copyright © 1968 by President and Fellows of Harvard College.

A letter to the Editor from James A. Banks with replies from Larry Cuban and Jean D. Grambs, *Harvard Educational Review* 39 (Winter, 1969): 155-161. Copyright © 1969 by President and Fellows of Harvard College.

Chapter 4. Adapter and reprinted with the permission of the publisher from "Instructional Materials for the Disadvantaged Child," in *Reaching the Disadvantaged*, edited by A. Harry Passow (New York: Teachers College Press), 1970.

Chapter 8. Reprinted with the permission of the publisher from *Social Education* 34 (May, 1970): 549-552.

Chapter 9. Excerpted from "The Need for Positive Racial Attitudes in Textbooks," in *Racial Crisis in American Education*, edited by Robert L. Green (Chicago: Follett Educational Corporation, 1969): 177-183. Reprinted by permission of the publisher.

Appendix One: Adapted from *Children's Interracial Fiction: An Unselective Bibliography* by Barbara Jean Glancy (Washington, D.C.: American Federation of Teachers, 1969). Reprinted by permission of the publisher.

Appendix Two: Expanded and adapted from "A Bibliography of Research and Commentary on Textbooks and Related Works" by Barbara Finkelstein, Loretta Golden, and Jean D. Grambs, *Social Education* 33 (March, 1969): 331-336. Reprinted by permission of the publisher.

Contents

Preface

This is a book about books: textbooks and other books designed for young people from pre-school through twelfth grade. It is a book that attempts to examine the ways in which the values of the readers of those books may be influenced by the things which appear between their covers—print and pictures. Specifically, as its title suggests, this is a book about the way in which black people in the United States have been—are—depicted in the information sources and literature which are most generally available to those of school age.

For some reason, perhaps because books of all kinds, but particularly textbooks, are so familiar a part of the classroom that they are easily overlooked, the role of these ubiquitous materials in creating attitudes and transmitting values has not been explored with the degree of care that it deserves. Because education is not a neutral activity, neither are its tools. Values are implicit in all literary and graphic materials, and it is the concern of *Black Image* to examine the values transmitted by them.

The view of the authors of the following chapters is that education in the United States is philosophically committed to teaching for a changing society as well as transmitting traditional information and values. This book is specifically directed at teachers, librarians, supervisors, administrators and laymen active in book selection for young people since it is they who largely control the opportunity for change. In order to perform their tasks adequately, these leaders must be able to determine and examine the "hidden messages" in instructional materials and literature which pass into the hands of millions of young people as "recommended" or "required" reading. If *Black Image* is helpful to the general reader, who may exercise his prerogative of exerting individual pressure, it may aid in further education for change.

It is not necessary to read *Black Image* all the way through from chapter to chapter, although this method may prove instructive. It is hoped, however, that the reader, curious about the matters considered here, will be able to turn to the particular chapter (or appendix) of his concern and be able to read it as an entity. The book begins with an introduction to the problem of the writer versus the censor, thereby introducing the context in which the black image in America has come to be —is—in written and illustrated form. The issue of historical realities and philosophies regarding blacks is next considered, followed by an examination of the way in which young people's literature finds its way to the public. The next four chapters are concerned with ways in which instructional materials, elementary and secondary, convey the realities of American society. Chapter four, specifically, is devoted to an examination of elementary school social studies textbooks and other instructional materials; chapter five examines secondary-school history, government, and sociology texts; chapter six is concerned with materials about black history produced by school personnel; while chapter seven considers the role of blacks in literature anthologies. Chapter eight discusses how children's literature can be used to improve racial understanding. The final chapter raises the question, "Will things be different—and better—in the future?" The book is concluded with two bibliographies, one of over 200 books for young people, ages four to sixteen (plus), and the other listing research and commentary on the subjects of textbooks and other literary media.

CHAPTER 1

Storytellers and Gatekeepers

Juel Janis *and* **Phyllis Franklin**

All societies possess their own way of transmitting the dominant ideals and values of their culture. In nonliterate societies, this information is preserved in the ritual and mythology of the tribe and taught through oral repetition. A child learns to follow appropriate patterns of behavior and to cherish certain values in an informal way—by listening to legends told by his society's storyteller. In literate societies, some of this information is transmitted by the school, where the child learns much of what is expected of him in a more formal way—by reading books, the medium of the literate society's storyteller. In either kind of society, however, the effect is the same. The storyteller contributes to the socialization process.

All societies also possess ways of protecting their dominant values and ideals, and they develop ways of insuring that the young shall be properly prepared for life in their society. There are, accordingly, in addition to the storytellers who pass on traditions, those who act as gatekeepers of information, or if you will, as guardians of the culture's values. Together the storyteller and the gatekeeper determine the kind of values that the young are to learn. In nonliterate societies there is rarely disagreement over what information shall be passed on. To question traditional customs and beliefs would be unthinkable, and so the role of the gatekeeper is often synonymous with that of the storyteller.

In literate societies, especially those embracing a variety of people with different customs, beliefs, and traditions, the question of what shall be passed on represents a more complex problem, and, the greater the diversity of the people, the more difficult the problem becomes. In such a society, storytellers and gatekeepers are no longer likely to be the same. In fact, as a society advances and as its traditions and ideals multiply, the number of gatekeepers who are not storytellers increases, and the importance of the storyteller decreases. For instance, involved in the preparation of the modern schoolbook there is not only the author (or storyteller) but also those who influence the content of his books, those who sell his work, and those who finally select and purchase his wares. Under these conditions, the storyteller may be little more than a puppet, subject to the pressures exerted by the other gatekeepers, his role limited to the simple expression of his storytelling skill.

Like other literate societies, one of the ways in which America transmits its own cultural values is through its schoolbooks. And therefore, it seems important that those involved in education be aware of the activities of the storytellers, who are at least partially responsible for the kinds of values and traditions transmitted to the young. And it also seems important to be aware of the activities of the gatekeepers, for if the storyteller and his story do, as we believe, influence the socialization process, then those who influence his work also help determine the way in which a child learns about his society.

While few would deny the important role books play in the shaping of a child's mind, little has been done to study the extent and the nature of this influence. It would not be fair to say that twentieth century educators have ignored the importance of schoolbooks, but they have been concerned primarily with *how* a child learns rather than with *what* he learns. Though there is a vast amount of literature devoted to the learning process, the major concern of these studies has been with the Law of Effect rather than with a Law of Affect. This lack of emphasis on content, however, is understandable when we consider the general direction that American education has taken since the turn of the century. The scientific study of education naturally stressed the importance of methods and techniques, and the progressive education movement, with its emphasis on experience and the use of many kinds of instructional materials, also directed attention to method and made the role of the single classroom text less important.

Nevertheless, the assumption that the spoken and printed word does function as a part of this process has been used by so prominent a sociologist as David Riesman, who, in his now classic study *The Lonely*

Crowd, explored, as one aspect of character formation, the influence of different kinds of stories and different modes of storytelling upon the development of different kinds of character.[1] He concluded that although print alone cannot determine the direction of social values, it can "powerfully rationalize the models which tell people what they ought to be like,"[2] and often, the printed story can "reinforce . . . social pressures" without the softening influence that direct contact with the storyteller provides.[3]

In the light of Riesman's observations, the general lack of interest on the part of educators in the specific effects that books have on children is particularly difficult to understand. It seems fair to regard the schoolbook as an important part of the socialization process, for the schoolbook, whether textbook or fiction, provides the child with a recurrent storytelling experience, an experience of unusual significance according to Riesman because the normally important relationship between the storyteller and the reader "becomes a special case in situations in which the child is the reader. By teaching children to read, a gain is made in the efficiency of the socialization process."[4]

Why schoolbooks, as conveyors of cultural values, have been ignored is unclear. Obviously it is difficult to separate the effect of what a child reads from the numerous forces which help him to define his world. Another, less obvious, though perhaps more significant explanation of this neglect, may be due to the fact that many educators assume that the values a child finds in his schoolbooks are merely a reflection of societal values and as such do not merit special scrutiny. An examination of several historical studies of children's books makes this assumption questionable. This is not to suggest that schoolbooks have failed to mirror the general beliefs of their time. Actually, they have done this very well. But it seems to have been only the popular beliefs and a single aspect of the multiple American experience that has been reflected.

A few years ago, threatened perhaps by ominous warnings that the American textbook would soon fade into oblivion, the American Textbook Publishers Institute and the National Education Association issued a report extolling the role of the textbook in American education. The report noted that among the textbook's many virtues was the fact that

---

1. David Riesman, *The Lonely Crowd* (New Haven: Yale University Press, 1950), pp. 84-112.
2. *Ibid.,* p. 91.
3. *Ibid.,* p. 98.
4. *Ibid.,* p. 93.

it had served to bridge the gap between peoples and nations[5] and assisted in unifying societies of men by giving them common goals and common traditions.[6] The evidence at hand simply fails to support this contention for either contemporary textbooks or those published in earlier decades.

Judging from the evidence reported in several studies of nineteenth century texts, it is obvious that these books not only failed to use material which might "bridge the gap between people and nations," but instead presented supranationalistic materials which actually served to broaden this gap. These texts may have unified members of the dominant majority, but they did so only by ignoring or belittling the customs and traditions of minority group members.

forces influencing textbook content

Religion was undoubtedly one of the dominant forces in nineteenth century American life, and the texts of this period quite naturally reflected this influence. The textual material used in the first half of the nineteenth century was almost exclusively of a religious nature—pro-Protestant and anti-Catholic.[7] Ruth Elson, in her book *Guardians of Tradition; American Schoolbooks of the Nineteenth Century,* says that "In this period true religion is patently limited to Protestantism. Catholicism is depicted not only as a false religion, but as a positive danger to the state; it subverts good government, sound morals, and education."[8] After 1850, the more obvious religious concepts disappeared but references to proper morals reflected Protestant values and remained as the dominant theme in all textbooks.[9]

The goals of the nineteenth century American schoolbooks were aimed not only at the transmission of factual and useful information but also at the development of moral virtue. And the storyteller did his best

---

5. *Guidelines for Textbook Selection* (Washington, D. C.: National Education Association, 1967), p. 10.
6. *Ibid.,* p. 11.
7. Ruth Miller Elson, *Guardians of Tradition; American Schoolbooks of the Nineteenth Century* (Lincoln: University of Nebraska Press, 1964).
8. *Ibid.,* p. 47.
9. *Ibid.* See also Charles Carpenter, *History of American Schoolbooks* (Philadelphia: University of Pennsylvania Press, 1963); John Nietz, *Old Textbooks* (Pittsburgh: University of Pittsburgh Press, 1961); Richard D. Mosier, *Making the American Mind; Social and Moral Ideas in the McGuffey Readers* (New York: King's Crown Press, Columbia University, 1947).

to inculcate the proper kind of values. The character traits praised in these books were those of the Protestant work ethic—thrift, industry, honesty, hard labor, and pride in acquisition. The desire for learning was considered a virtue only when the knowledge was useful. Elson considers that as a result of the utilitarian needs first of the frontiersman and later the businessman, "anti-intellectualism" as a force in American life was "thoroughly embedded in the schoolbooks . . . read by generations of pupils since the beginning of the Republic."[10]

In their attitudes toward racial and ethnic differences, the nineteenth century storytellers also expressed the views of the majority. As David B. Tyack has noted, "Americanism was defined in such a way that it could fit only the white, middle-class, Protestant, native-born citizen."[11] These books often referred to the Negro "race" as "ignorant and degraded," while Caucasians were described as "the most noble of the five races of men." American Indians were characterized as "savage, barbarous, warlike, and rude"; Mexicans were said to "have all the bad qualities of the Spaniards"; and Asiatics were described as "heavy, morose, treacherous, furiously passionate, unsocial and unfriendly to people of other nations." By contrast, Europeans were most always depicted in a favorable manner: "intelligent," "brave," "industrious," "of good stature, shape, and complexion."[12]

What these textwriters chose to omit reveals as much about their attitudes as what they chose to include. Tyack's suggestion that these omissions represented attempts by the authors to disguise the real world seems an unfair interpretation of motive, but it is true that while America was moving toward an urbanized and industrial society its "schoolbooks painted a sentimental picture of rural bliss," and it is also true that while industrial violence abounded "they ignored the conditions of labor and described unions as the evil plots of foreigners, anarchists, and Communists."[13]

Elson reports similar kinds of omissions, noting that reform movements which might have had profound social or political effects were either ignored or derided. She points out that "While Jeffersonian and Jacksonian democracy agitated the adult world, the child was taught the necessity of class distinctions." In place of the social philosophies of Jef-

10. Elson, *Guardians of Tradition; American Schoolbooks of the Nineteenth Century,* p. 230.
11. David B. Tyack, *Turning Points in American Educational History* (Waltham, Mass.: Blaisdell Publishing Co., 1967), p. 183.
12. Nietz, *Old Textbooks,* pp. 216-220.
13. Tyack, *Turning Points in American Educational History,* p. 184.

ferson and Jackson, the schools of "Hamilton and Daniel Webster governed the minds of the children."[14] With some wryness, she summarizes the basic attitudes of these texts toward controversial subjects:

> Women in the United States have already been awarded all the rational liberty suitable to their natures . . . Dissatisfaction with their status is both unwomanly and ungrateful . . . The child . . . must be tolerant of other religions, but he should not recognize them as equal to Protestantism on pain of subversion of both church and state. He should be moved emotionally by the inhumanity of war, but he should admire without reserve the exploits of military heroes and be happy to sacrifice his life in any war in which his country is engaged. Before the Civil War he may pity the slave, but he must stay away from the abolitionist movement. After the Civil War he can look back to the evils of slavery now safely buried in the past, but he need not concern himself with the freedman; . . . He must revere values already established in American society by his schoolbooks rather than attempt to institute new ones or expand the old.[15]

A selective education of this type would seem to have had several general effects. First, it would seem to perpetuate only the most popular and conservative values of the period; second, because these values were repeated from generation to generation, this kind of education might have acted as a solidifying force giving added credibility and reinforcement to these traditions. We are inclined to agree with Elson's conclusion that although these "schoolbook authors consider[ed] themselves guardians of liberty, they can be more accurately described as guardians of tradition."[16]

In retrospect, it appears that the strongly conservative tone of these early textbooks, written in a period of relative stability, created no serious problems. For most of the century, a child's adult life could be expected to follow a pattern strikingly similar to that of his parents. Schoolbooks which emphasized their ideals and values easily prepared a child for the role he was to play in their world. To this extent, books preserving only the conservative traditions posed no serious social problem.

recent efforts to influence textbook content

This no longer seems to be the case. The twentieth century has been a period of rapid social change, and our society grows increasingly more complex, embracing a multitude of interests. It would seem that text-

---

14. Elson, *Guardians of Tradition,* p. 340.
15. *Ibid.,* p. 341.
16. *Ibid.,* p. 340.

books which present a restrictive view of such a diverse society would reduce the possibility of educating children who will be capable of behavior that is both intelligent and flexible. To the degree that schoolbooks do influence a society's values and beliefs by reinforcing and giving validity to them, it is apparent that in a period such as the present, instructional materials which offer the student a unidimensional understanding of his society may serve a dysfunctional purpose in the socialization process.

Because of the power of traditional nineteenth century institutions, there were few organized minority interest groups able to affect the content of schoolbooks. The philosophy of textbook authors remained largely unchallenged, and they functioned as both storytellers and gatekeepers. In the twentieth century, however, the philosophy of textbook authors has been consistently challenged by many different groups of gatekeepers. Despite this fact, there has been little effort to examine the effect of such challenges. But if one is concerned about the transmission of values, it does seem important to understand the kind of influence that modern gatekeepers exert on the stories told by modern storytellers.

This relationship is not a simple one, for in our complex society, gatekeepers are no longer synonymous with storytellers. Perhaps the most obvious, certainly the most vocal, gatekeepers are the representatives of various interest groups. Although the earliest significant effort to influence textbook content actually took place in the nineteenth century, (both before and after the Civil War, when partisans of the North and the South attempted to see their own versions of the conflict reflected in their children's texts), it was not until after 1918 that attempts to influence textbook content became a significant force. After World War I there was a "rash of textbook criticism," ranging from charges by some critics that the treatment of the American Revolution in United States history books reflected pro-British sentiments to charges by others that textbooks "did not place enough emphasis on military history to make good soldiers out of children" or even that they "credited Columbus, instead of Leif Ericson, with the discovery of America."[17]

In the twenties, other groups with other interests and objectives made their own attempts to influence textbook content. Some organizations wished to have books published that would teach history from a world point of view and stress the "peace-loving qualities of America's heroes." Organized labor wished to see "that the cause of labor was given favorable treatment in the school texts" and was able to persuade pub-

17. Jack Nelson and Gene Roberts, Jr., *The Censors and the Schools* (Boston: Little, Brown and Co., 1963), pp. 27-30.

lishers to allow their manuscripts to be read prior to publication "so that they could benefit by criticism in advance of publication." In 1928, the Federal Trade Commission exposed a large scale effort to influence textbooks when they revealed that public utility companies had worked with school superintendents and publishers in order to promote their "own interpretation of history."[18] According to Nelson and Roberts, in their book *The Censors and the Schools,* the utility companies, concerned over what they believed was a trend toward the municipal ownership of utilities, conducted several textbook studies and concluded that these books contained unfair and misleading statements about their companies. They then decided to have "new books specially written for the nation's classrooms."[19] As a result of public indignation aroused by the F.T.C. report, there were few reported attempts to influence directly the content of texts for several years.

Textbook criticism did not erupt again on a nationwide scale until the end of the 1930's after some high school texts had begun to reflect the newer attitudes of American historians toward the American past. This time the target of the attack, led by the Advertising Federation of America, the American Legion, and the National Association of Manufacturers, was Dr. Harold Rugg, a Columbia University professor who had written a popularly acclaimed social studies textbook series. These groups charged that his texts "were laced with anti-business sentiment and economic-determinist and socialistic theories."[20] The effectiveness of their attack is demonstrated by the fact that the sales of his texts in 1938 totaled 289,000, but six years later, despite the fact that they had initially been acclaimed by educators throughout the country, sales had "dwindled ninety per cent to 21,000 copies."[21] This dramatic drop seems to reflect the sensitivity of educators to political pressure exerted by these special interest groups, who sponsored numerous public hearings in order to discredit the texts.

From the late thirties to the mid-fifties textbook censors were relatively quiet. However, the firing of Sputnik and the reports of the brainwashing of American soldiers during the Korean War prompted a concerned college professor to charge that American history texts were brainwashing American high school students. Professor E. Merrill Root, along with the Daughters of the American Revolution and an organiza-

---

18. *Ibid.,* p. 31.
19. *Ibid.,* p. 32.
20. *Ibid.,* p. 37.
21. *Ibid.,* p. 39.

tion called America's Future, were certain that a communist conspiracy lurked behind the pages of most of America's history textbooks.

In his book, *Brainwashing in the High Schools,* Root asserted that the American soldier's susceptibility to brainwashing attempts during the Korean War was due largely to the fact that history textbooks had failed to instill a proper reverence for American heroes or an adequate love of country.[22] He charged these texts with emphasizing the "seamy side" of American life and with picturing America "as a foul continental slum."[23] Furthermore, he claimed that these 1950 texts failed to give "Radical conservatism . . . a chance to speak; it is not even admitted to exist. . . . It is not a matter of *dis*proportion; it is a matter of *no* proportion."[24] The Daughters of the American Revolution have made similar charges, asserting that most history texts treat America's Christian heritage sparingly, fail to challenge the welfare state, stress such ideas as tolerance, social acceptance, and mental health, and discuss the atomic bomb so as to instill attitudes of fear, compromise, and surrender in America's future citizens.[25]

Although attacks by right-wing organizations were widely publicized, it is difficult to determine the effectiveness of these efforts. One of the more obvious effects may be seen in the extreme caution with which textbook publishers approached controversial subjects during the 1950's. Nelson and Roberts have pointed out that such topics as birth control, evolution, sex education, and minority groups were all considered taboo subjects by most publishers. Furthermore, they note that the literature circulated by the American Textbook Publishers Institute tended to go even further: in a pamphlet entitled *Textbooks are Indispensable,* the Institute is quoted as advising publishers to "try to avoid statements that might prove offensive to economic, religious, racial or social groups or any civic, fraternal, patriotic or philanthropic societies in the whole United States."[26]

A similar approach is reflected in book selection policies of public libraries. Charles Morgan, Jr. cites the following excerpt from a policy

22. E. Merrill Root, *Brainwashing in the High Schools; An Examination of Eleven American History Textbooks* (New York: The Devin-Adair Co., 1959).
23. *Ibid.*, p. 153.
24. *Ibid.*, p. 247.
25. National Defense Committee, Daughters of the American Revolution, "Textbook Study 1958-1959," Washington, D. C.
26. Nelson and Roberts, *The Censors and the Schools,* p. 181.

statement of one of America's outstanding public libraries with respect to controversial books:

> The library may . . . decide to exclude sensational, violent, or inflammatory books, and those that contain demonstrably false statements and undocumented accusations. . . .
>
> The library may exclude from its collection a majority of the books presenting views that are regarded by a consensus of responsible opinion—civic, scientific, religious, and educational—as unsound, and have been so regarded for over a period of years.[27]

Moreover, recent studies of the way American history textbooks have presented such topics as the American Revolution, the War of 1812,[28] the Civil War,[29] World War I,[30] and the Cold War,[31] indicate that the "average high school student is often reading not the results of careful historical research and evaluation, but propaganda."[32]

The advent of the Black Revolution in the last decade also sparked a number of carefully researched studies which document the failure of American schoolbooks to give favorable treatment not only to the black man but to other minority groups as well.[33] As Hillel Black, author of *The American Schoolbook*, facetiously noted: "Until the 1960's . . . No

---

27. Charles Morgan, Jr., "Freedom to Read and Racial Problems," *American Library Association Bulletin* 59 (June, 1965): 488-489.
28. Ray Allen Billington, et al., *The Historian's Contribution to Anglo-American Misunderstanding; Report of a Committee on National Bias in Anglo-American History Textbooks* (New York: Hobbs, Dorman & Co., Inc., 1966); Harold J. Noah, Carl E. Prince, and C. Russell Riggs, "History in High School Textbooks: A Note," *School Review* 70 (1962): 415-436.
29. Noah, passim. See also discussions by Irving Sloan, *The Negro in Modern American History Textbooks* (n.p.) American Federation of Teachers, AFL-CIO, 1966; Kenneth Stampp, et al., *The Negro in American History Textbooks* (Sacramento: California State Department of Education, June, 1964).
30. Billington, *The Historian's Contribution*, passim.
31. Noah, "History in High School Textbooks," passim.
32. *Ibid.*, p. 432.
33. There are many studies which deal with this problem. See The American Council of Education's *Intergroup Relations in Teaching Materials*, Washington, D.C.: American Council on Education, 1949; Lloyd Marcus' *The Treatment of Minorities in Secondary School Textbooks*, New York: Anti-Defamation League of B'nai B'rith, 1961; Irving Sloan's *The Negro in Modern American History Textbooks* (n.p.), American Federation of Teachers, AFL-CIO, 1966; Kenneth Stampp, et al., *The Negro in American History Textbooks*, Sacramento: California State Department of Education, June, 1964; and *A Report on the Treatment of Minorities in American History Textbooks*, published by the Michigan Department of Education, 1968.

Negro child ever romped with Spot, no Negro child ever performed a scientific experiment, no Negro child was ever portrayed as reading a book, hitting a baseball, playing a musical instrument."[34] And, even in the early sixties most American history textbooks "typically presented . . . material which glossed over the hardships of slavery, ignored the positive gains achieved during the Reconstruction Era, included pictures of blacks which only depicted slave life, and omitted any discussion of the problems of discrimination encountered by blacks over the last half century."[35]

The overall effect of such accounts, as Noah, Prince, and Riggs point out in their report "History in High School Textbooks," is that the material contained in high school history textbooks "tends to be black and white, stereotyped, suitable for perpetuating the myths which pass for history but unable to provide students with contrasting interpretations of events and policies."[36] (Chapter five treats this topic in more detail.)

In considering the various criticisms leveled at schoolbooks within the past twenty-five years, it appears that for the conservative, American textbooks have not been faithful to America's heritage because they have deviated from the older moral, religious, and nationalistic emphasis, accepted cultural pluralism and religious diversity, reduced emphasis on military exploits, and given increasing attention to concepts of brotherhood and peace. For the liberal, the text's failure to deal in a meaningful way with controversial issues, its all-white, Anglo-Saxon bias, its tendency to interpret the rise of communism as a conspiracy "moving by stealth, beards and bombs to accomplish its nefarious purposes,"[37] all bespeak a simplistic approach to important topics, which they believe gives a child an inadequate and distorted understanding of the realities of the present world.

internal gatekeepers: school selection committees

Interest groups, however, serve only as external gatekeepers. That is, they are able to react to the issue of what books a child will use only after the material has actually been purchased by a particular school system. The pressure they exert must be exerted unofficially after the books

---

34. Hillel Black, *The American Schoolbook* (New York: William Morrow & Co. Inc., 1967), p. 106.
35. Juel Janis, "Educating for Social Stupidity." See chapter five.
36. Noah, "History in High School Textbooks," p. 432.
37. *Ibid.*, p. 431.

have been selected and purchased by the internal gatekeepers—those individuals who serve on textbook selection committees within the educational establishment, who officially decide which books will be placed on the approved purchasing list for their school district or, in some cases, their state. (It should be noted that there is a circular effect operating here, in that these internal gatekeepers are, of course, influenced by the external gatekeepers.)

Generally, in the eastern, mid-western, and western states schoolbooks are selected by district textbook selection committees while in most of the southern and southwestern states textbooks are selected through state textbook selection committees. Throughout the country these committees are made up of teachers, supervisors, and administrators. In the south and southwestern states these individuals are appointed by the State Board of Education after the recommendation of the State's Commissioner of Education, while in the other states these appointments are made by local Boards of Education in response to the recommendations of the District School Superintendent.[38] A publisher has almost no chance of selling his books to individual schools if the state or the district committees have not included them on their approved book lists.

The formality of these appointment procedures clearly indicates the importance that society attaches to these internal gatekeepers. This same formality might lead one to think that only those with some special competence would be asked to serve on such committees and that committee members would be given clearly defined criteria upon which to base their selections. Too often this is not the case. In the first place, a report in *School Management* has raised a question about the ability of many members of textbook selection committees to select texts. Few teachers, the report points out, are properly trained to evaluate textbooks. In the second place, in many cases, textbook selection committee members do not have written criteria for assessing books.[39]

Unfortunately, even in places where such criteria exist, they tend to deal primarily with the physical rather than the substantive aspects of

---

38. See Hillel Black, ed., "Survey of Textbook Purchasing Practices," *School Management* 10 (March, 1966):138-166; William H. James and Harold H. Eibling, "Is Your District Using the Right Textbook?" *School Management* 8 (October, 1964): 79-86; "Textbook Selection: Whose Job?" *School Management* 8 (April, 1964): 74-78, 130-134; *Guidelines for Textbook Selection, op. cit.;* "NEA Research Memo," NEA Research Division (Washington, D.C.: National Education Association, November, 1963).
39. "Textbook Selection: Whose Job?" pp. 74-78, 130-134.

the text.* Too often committee members using these criteria involve themselves in a consideration of the size of the print, the strength of the binding, and the quality of the illustrations. Rarely are the committee members provided with any tangible guidelines which might help them to deal with the significance of the ideas, the philosophy of the authors, the validity of the presentation, the treatment of controversial issues, or the capability of a text to develop a student's ability to think.

These points are not completely neglected, but they are not dealt with in a meaningful way. Invariably, for example, in considering the competency of a textbook's author, these evaluation sheets pose two questions for the textbook selection committee member: (1) "How satisfactory are the qualifications of the authors?" and (2) "Are they active in teaching?" It is difficult to understand why an affirmative answer to the last question should add or, for that matter, subtract from a book's worthiness. Moreover, asking about author qualifications without establishing adequate criteria for judging these qualifications can easily result in a situation wherein this term becomes synonymous with "well-known" or "popular." Other guides, such as those of Idaho and Louisville, Kentucky, are quite elaborate and well developed.

In terms of content, the emphasis of these evaluation forms is usually upon such points as "interest level," "subject organization," and "teacher aids." Attempts to rate a text's presentation in terms of subject matter are often dealt with only in a very general way: "Is the content designed to promote the objectives of the course?" "Is the subject matter meaningful . . .?" Interestingly, in the spring of 1969 of thirty-four state and city school superintendents asked for information regarding their "guidelines for the adoption and retention of social studies textbooks," only one noted that his school system was using evaluative criteria suggested by the American Historical Association Committee for the selection of American history textbooks.** This is unfortunate because the members of this committee have developed what seem to be very helpful criteria. Not only do they list those issues that they believe should be included in any contemporary American history textbook, but they also provide the teacher with specific examples of typical phrases and chapter titles which they believe indicate a slanted interpretation of certain historical events. Obviously, the use of such criteria in the evaluation pro-

---

*The following comments are based upon an examination of textbook evaluation guidelines used by twenty-eight school systems.
**The request for this information was made by Jean D. Grambs, College of Education, University of Maryland. The Cleveland school system reported that it was using these criteria.

cess provides the textbook committee member with a far more sensitive and informed guide to textbook evaluation than the vague criteria used by school systems—if they use them at all. One wonders whether the failure of most school systems to use such criteria is due to a reluctance by committee members to employ criteria established by an outside professional organization, or simply due to the fact that it is easier to rely upon the advice of book company representatives.

In a report on textbook selection procedures in *School Management*, Lee Deighton, President of the Macmillan Publishing Company, stated: "I've often said that someone ought to train teachers in textbook selection, but few districts usually do. Usually, if anyone gives teachers an inkling of how to analyze a book, it's the book salesman and not always adequately in the amount of time they have."[40] Mr. Deighton's statement implies that given sufficient time, book salesmen could do an adequate job of helping a teacher to evaluate a textbook. But, such a situation obviously creates certain problems in obtaining an objective evaluation since the goals of a textbook salesman are, certainly, quite different from the goals of an educator.

This dependency by the purchaser upon the recommendations of the representative of a commercially merchandised item is not, of course, unusual. Doctors quite frequently report that their major source of information regarding a particular drug is obtained from a representative of the pharmaceutical house which manufactures the drug. Considering the busy schedule of both doctors and teachers, it is not surprising that they have allowed themselves to be sold products in this way. Nevertheless, while the doctor can rely to some extent upon the Food and Drug Administration to establish certain quality controls over the product, educators have no comparable protection.

Textbook publishing in America is big business. In 1960, "some fifty-odd publishers [had] sold some $230 million worth of elementary and high school textbooks—almost $100 million more than they had sold in 1954."[41] The textbook salesman is, of course, interested in making sales, and the publisher who employs him wishes to capture the largest possible market. In neither case can their primary concern be for the nature of the book's content except insofar as it appeals to the purchaser.

The purchaser's needs may, and often do, however, influence textbook content. For example, until recently, the first question the Chairman of the Louisiana State Textbook Selection Committee used to ask a text-

40. "Textbook Selection: Whose Job?" p. 76.
41. Martin Mayer, "The Trouble with Textbooks," *Harpers* 225 (July, 1962): 65-71.

book publisher's representative was "'You got any niggers in your book?'" His "'No, sir'" reply insured this representative a probable sale for his company in this state.[42]

As if to compound the inadequacies of selection procedures involved in the initial choice of a text, most school districts have "no specific systems designed to insure that textbooks are reviewed regularly and effectively." In a report made on this subject in 1964, James and Eibling noted that "unless somebody raises a question, a textbook—once adopted—is liable to be continually reordered until it is no longer in print."[43]

Perhaps the most graphic way of portraying the kind of peculiar situation that can develop out of the haphazard activities of various gatekeepers acting in conjunction with publishers bent on a very legitimate profit is to observe the process of textbook selection in a particular place. Black, in a revealing chapter entitled "Texas King Censor," presents a fascinating case study of how the individuals involved in this process are able to influence textbook content.

In Texas, like most other southern states, the state's public school textbooks are selected by a committee of teachers, administrators, and supervisors. No publisher can hope to have his books accepted by this committee unless he is willing to revise his textual material to meet their demands. The stipulations regarding revisions are quite explicit. According to Black:

> Under Texas law every publisher who submits a textbook for adoption must sign a contract in which he agrees to "make revisions in content as the State Board of Education may direct, authorize, and demand." If the publisher fails to make the changes, his textbook will automatically be rejected and he will be penalized $2,500. According to Texas authorities, few publishers have failed to make the alterations demanded by the state's officials.[44]

Furthermore, it appears that "Texas is the only state that insists upon approving the political affiliation of the books' authors."[45] As recently as 1968, under the list of "Special Provisions" for textbook selection there is a passage which specifies that "Authors of all textbooks and teaching aids offered for adoption under this proclamation shall sign the non-subversive oath. . . ."[46] In order to cover all possible contingencies, there is, as

42. Black, "Survey of Textbook Purchasing Practices," p. 121.
43. James and Eibling, "Is Your District Using the Right Textbook?" p. 80.
44. Black, "Survey of Textbook Purchasing Practices," pp. 147-148.
45. *Ibid.*, p. 148.
46. See mimeographed description of textbook selection procedures (May, 1968), available from Texas Education Agency, Austin, Texas.

Black noted, "even a provision for dead or missing authors." Should such an event occur, then it is "up to the publisher to swear that the textbook represents the work of a loyal citizen."[47]

The state selection committee exercises considerable control over the content of materials used in Texas, since all of the state approved textbooks "are paid for with state funds, [and] the local schools invariably choose from among those books" selected by the committee with the approval of the State Board of Education.[48] However, this committee also exerts control over the content of materials which reach school children far beyond the boundaries of Texas.

Texas, the largest of the southern states which adopts books for statewide use, quite naturally offers a very lucrative market for the textbook publisher. It is so important a market that the publisher is not only willing to make the changes suggested by the selection committee but, because it is less costly to issue a single edition, he sells the Texas-approved text throughout the nation. Black notes that while most of the revisions consist of correcting factual errors, a number of changes alter the tone and character of a text. One publisher's agent diligently searches galley proofs for "controversial material." But despite such preliminary screening by the publisher, the committee still requests changes, which, according to Black, "reflect the political hue of the state."[49] For example, in one case " 'all references to and works by' " such "alleged 'subversives' " as Pete Seeger and Langston Hughes were removed from the seventh- and eighth-grade vocal music books.[50] In another instance, substantive changes were made in a biology text's treatment of evolution so as to prevent a "misleading picture of biology's most basic theory."[51] And in still another text, a reference to the United Nations, which expressed a belief in all nations working together for the peaceful solution of problems, was deleted and replaced by a passage which loses this tone of brotherhood by emphasizing instead the importance of the United States in the United Nations.[52]

Clearly, internal gatekeepers can be very important in determining textbook content. The Texas textbook selection committee has been effective in eliminating material relating to such topics as biology, history, and social reform. It is surprising, and perhaps ironic, that none of the

---

47. Black, "Surveys of Textbook Purchasing Practices," p. 148.
48. *Ibid.*, p .147.
49. *Ibid.*, p. 150.
50. *Ibid.*, pp. 48-149.
51. *Ibid.*, pp. 153-154.
52. *Ibid.*, p. 149.

individuals in this fifteen-member group in 1968 had degrees in any of these subjects.[53] Such changes seem to reflect the views of powerful interest groups in a politically conservative state rather than the views of experts legitimately concerned with correct information. And yet this committee has been successful in persuading textbook publishers to make changes in their books, and these changes now appear in texts read by school children from Maine to California.

For many political scientists who are even slightly cynical, such a state of affairs surely reinforces their contention that power struggles within a society or among societies actually are struggles to determine whose version of reality will prevail. What passes for history may have little or no relation to the reality of past events, for the recording of history, according to such a view, is merely the recording of what those in power believe. Viewed from this perspective, the fact that a small group in just one part of the country was able to have its version of reality accepted in textbooks and then used throughout the nation can be explained merely by assuming that this group reflected the beliefs and values of the most powerful interest groups in the nation.

While such an explanation is surely credible, is it entirely acceptable? Perhaps an equally plausible explanation is that some groups in our society have been more keenly aware than others of the significant role that gatekeepers and storytellers play in the socialization process. In particular, educators, perhaps because of their concern with methods and measurement rather than with content, may have allowed these interest groups to influence the content of educational materials by default, abdicating part of their responsibilities as gatekeepers to the special interests, who, by definition, lack a balanced view of the goals of education and the relationship of these goals to the welfare of society as a whole.

But is this explanation acceptable; that is, are we willing to continue to accept such a situation? Given the multiplicity of the American experience, the diversity of the American people, and the pressing need for a flexible approach to modern problems, do we wish to accept a version of reality fostered by only a single interest group? If we are truly concerned with giving young people a more comprehensive view of their society, if we are concerned with change, or at least with learning to live with change, who is better equipped than the educator to participate both as a storyteller and a gatekeeper?

However, it would be unrealistic to suppose that this role would ever be the exclusive prerogative of the educator. On the contrary, when

---

53. See "Appointment of 1968 State Textbook Committee," Austin, Texas: Texas State Board of Education, May, 1969, mimeo.

the educator becomes an active gatekeeper, he joins the ranks of those in other interest groups who are actively attempting to determine which of society's values and beliefs shall be passed on to succeeding generations. But his role as gatekeeper is a special one, for he comes to the task with a very special qualification. He is concerned with more than the attainment of his own personal interests; he is also concerned with attaining the larger, more idealistic goals of education.

summary

The essence of the democratic process is the competition among various groups to cast the existing political structure in their own image and, thereby, to further their own goals and aspirations. At the heart of this system is the notion that only if the total electorate remains politically aware and informed will it be possible to prevent any one special interest group from having its particular philosophy prevail. This is one classic truth of the American political process. Thus, this nation's cohesiveness in the future would seem to depend not upon the dominance of the view of any one group but upon the ability of different groups to participate in the decision-making process.

If educators accept this and participate more actively as storytellers and gatekeepers, they will find themselves using materials that represent not single versions of reality but instead reveal the heterogeneous nature of society. This means that both educators and lay leaders in education will have to learn to live with controversy. They may even come to recognize that controversy is not always bad. Harold Full, in his recent book *Controversy in American Education,* points out that controversy can assist in maintaining a balance in society insofar as it allows for the "intellectual expression of . . . conflicts, anxieties, and hostilities [thereby serving] to ease these tensions by permitting the peaceful processes of discussion and debate to minimize the danger of open strife and rebellion."[54]

To admit diversity and participate in controversy, then, and to make it possible for the young to participate also, may allow the educator to best fulfill a very basic social goal of education—the preservation of his society's values and ideals.

---

54. Harold Full, *Controversy in American Education* (New York: The Macmillan Co., 1967), p. 1.

CHAPTER 2

Black vs. Negro History: What Are the Issues?

Jean Dresden Grambs, Larry Cuban,
and **James A. Banks**

introduction

Is there a difference between Negro history and a history of the Negro? Is there an appreciable difference when one or the other is written by a black or a non-black? Can only a Negro provide authentic insight? What, if any, are the differences between the perceptions of a "Negro" and a "Black?"

The following chapter, which includes an exchange of letters (all of which appeared originally in issues of the *Harvard Educational Review*), focuses primarily upon Negro versus Black History; questions of what is "authentic history" are also raised. Questions are also implicit regarding the kind of history young people may find profitable: at what age, and in what context.

This chapter raises many questions important to educators: What should be taught in the area of history? Who should decide what should be taught, and, in the context of minority group experience, who is the "better" judge?

The questions are raised primarily about historical writing for children. The issue of Black History and/or Black Studies is also currently of great concern to educators and historians at the secondary and college level. For the reader who is primarily concerned with the issues raised as they relate to other levels of instruction, there is a brief bibliography of articles and essays devoted to a discussion of these issues at the end of this chapter.

The significance of the questions raised in the following chapter, and in the bibliographical references, is not merely academic. An increasing number of school systems, writers, and publishers are moving into the area of black studies. As Mrs. Janis discusses in chapter six, school system efforts to "do their own thing" in writing black or Negro history guides achieved varied degrees of success. Reading the following chapter, one may gain some insight into the issues which must be resolved before an adequate and appropriate black history can be written.

CRISPUS ATTUCKS, BOY OF VALOR. by Dharathula H. Millender. *Indianapolis: Bobbs-Merrill, 1965. 200 pp.*
JEAN DRESDEN GRAMBS*

It is not usual to accord a lengthy review to a book written for fourth or fifth grade students in American schools. This is unfortunate. Public and school libraries have shelves of such books; the market is good and is growing with each new injection of federal money.

One portion of this market, growing faster than any other, are books which have anything to do with Negroes, today or yesterday. The volume reviewed here is a "natural" for enjoying a wide and profitable market; for young children, it is a book about a Negro whose name occurs in American revolutionary history, but is not controversial. Thus, we are teaching Negro history and can tell Black Power leaders to hush.

Many educators, white and Negro, are justly critical of American history for its continuing distortions of the history and influence of Negroes, both individually and as a major ethnic group. We are naturally eager that these distortions be corrected, the blank places filled in, and the appropriate data reported accurately. In an effort to overcome the ignorance of Negro and white teachers and historians, new books and articles devoted to Negro history, African history, or biographies of Negroes are appearing at a great rate. It is to be hoped that librarians and educators will see to it that these volumes take their place with other works on American history, and that the data reported become a standard part of students' historical study of America from the very earliest

---

*Minor technical corrections have been made in this section since its initial printing.

grades. Hopefully, too, textbooks will reflect balanced versions of the African, British, and Spanish Caribbean backgrounds of American Negroes, a more realistic view of the demeaning aspects of slave life prior to the Civil War, a reasonable as well as accurate discussion of the Reconstruction period, and a balanced report of the struggle by Negroes and other ethnic minority groups to gain full access to the privileges and responsibilities of American citizenship.

The contribution of *Crispus Attucks, Boy of Valor*, however, is a major disservice to these commendable goals. Works of this kind give history a bad name in education and they also give to the Negro a dubious role in American life. To change our sentimental view of the past it is one thing to present authentic, historic material, but it it quite another matter to twist or invent material. That the Negro has been ignored or lied about in American history does not justify our telling other historical lies to repair the damage. Unfortunately, that is exactly what occurs in this "biography" of Crispus Attucks.

Despite the absence of historical data regarding Attucks' life, the author does not hesitate to "reconstruct" a complicated family, complete with conversations purporting to show how happy the slaves were with their New England masters.

Historical reviews of Attucks' life indicate no authentic data, other than an advertisement to pay a reward for his capture as an escaped slave, his appearance and sudden death in front of the Boston Customs House on March 5, 1770, and disputed, contradictory evidence at the trial of the British soldiers involved.

Questions may be asked, too, about the kind of "history" which has Attucks' father recounting to his son his own life in Africa.

'. . . Tell me about your father.'
'Well, my father was known best for his efforts to make the people of his kingdom prosperous. He encouraged them to be farmers and to trade with other people . . .

My father told his people that they needed to go to school in order to learn how to be prosperous or successful. Our schools were different from the schools in this country, but they were suited to the needs of our people. They taught our people how to read and write our own language. We had doctors and scientists, too, and many other kinds of workers . . . Then one day my father was killed and I was sold as a slave.'

'How awful, Father!'

'No, not awful, son. Anyone captured during a war was thought of as a slave. That's the way things were in those days. Slaves were the property of the chief of a tribe or the head of a family, and could be kept or sold as the owner wished. Most of them became trusted members of the tribe or family and were free to carry on many activities. But others were sold and taken to other countries. I was one of these.'

'What happened to you?'

'I was sold to some traders from the West Indies, who brought me here.'

The father goes on to explain how the family became the property of Colonel Buckminster. Crispus is hesitant to accept their condition of servitude, but his father remonstrates:

'Not many slaves have their own cottages,' Prince [Attucks' father] explained. 'I have my own plot of ground just as I might have had in Africa, though not as large. You have always been happy here and you can keep on being happy. The important thing is that you are my son and I'm proud of you . . .' (pp. 33-35).

Where are the horrors of the Middle Passage? What about the less than gentle slave trading resorted to by African tribal chiefs?

What a delightful picture of the life of slaves in colonial Massachusetts! One wonders what kind of "history" Millender is writing, and for whom? Such a benign picture would warm the hearts of book selection committee members from Texas to Mississippi.

No footnotes or lists of references indicate the sources from which this "biography" has been "reconstructed." It appears that the author has done some study of the lives of Indians, colonial customs, and the incidents leading up to the Boston Massacre, but what is "true" and what has been fabricated by the author cannot be untangled. To pretend that this book provides an authentic story of the life of Crispus Attucks is to mislead in the grossest possible fashion.

Concluding the book, Mrs. Millender states:

Much has been written about the beginnings of the American Revolution. Strangely enough, few United States history books have ever given sufficient attention or credit to Crispus Attucks, the first to fall for American Independence. (p. 187)

What the author fails to point out, as we will document below, is that Crispus Attucks became a martyr of the American Revolution by an accident of history.

It is true that Mrs. Millender is not alone in desiring a larger-than-life role for her "hero." Unfortunately, other historians have similarly distorted the role of Attucks. According to C. Eric Lincoln:

Crispus Attucks, a Negro sailor who sought to rally the confused Americans in the face of the British fire, was the first to give his life for America.[1]

---

1. C. Eric Lincoln, *The Negro Pilgrimage in America* (New York: Bantam Books, 1967), p. 18.

Another eminent Negro Historian, John Hope Franklin, also falls into the chauvinistic trap:

Attucks could hardly be described as a saucy boy. Nor was he deserving of the other harsh things John Adams had to say about those who fell in the Boston Massacre. He was more than forty-seven years old and had made his living during the twenty years after he ran away from his Framingham master by working on ships plying out of Boston harbor. As a seaman he probably [sic] felt keenly the restrictions which England's new navigation acts imposed. He now undertook [sic] to make the protest in a form that England would understand. Attucks' martyrdom is significant not as the first life to be offered in the struggle against England. . . . The significance of Attucks' death seems to lie in the dramatic connection which it pointed out between the struggle against England and the status of the Negroes in America. Here was a fugitive slave who, with his bare hands, was willing to resist England to the point of giving his life. It was a remarkable thing, the colonists reasoned, to have their fight for freedom waged by one who was not as free as they.[2]

On what basis Franklin dismisses John Adams' comments and produces his own probabilities is not discernable from the information he provides.

Benjamin Quarles, still another black historian, does not allow his blackness to distort his historical appraisal:

John Adams later [after the event] observed that the men who lost their lives that night were 'the most obscure and inconsiderable that could be found upon the continent.' His remark had some justification. Crispus Attucks, 'the first to defy, and the first to die,' was a Negro of obscure origin, with some admixture of Indian blood. Presumably he had been a slave . . . Attucks' obscurity prior to the Boston Massacre was in dramatic contrast to his role on that occasion . . .

Whatever Attucks actually did that night, his prominent role in the Boston Massacre owed much to John Adams, who, as counsel defending the British soldiers, chose to make him the target. . . . It was Attucks 'to whose mad behavior, in all probability, the dreadful carnage of that night is chiefly to be ascribed.'[3]

Quarles argues that there is little historical evidence that Attucks was motivated by patriotic principles, and that in all likelihood—as John Adams in the defense of the British soldiers states—Attucks was merely part of an unruly and drunken mob enjoying the prospect of goading the nervous British. Yet, he continues, it is historically *possible* that he was

2. John Hope Franklin, *From Slavery to Freedom*, 2nd ed. (New York: Alfred A. Knopf, 1965), p. 127.
3. Benjamin Quarles, *The Negro in the American Revolution* (Durham: University of North Carolina Press, 1961), pp. 5-6.

influenced, as were other Bostonians, by anti-British sentiment. But *all of this is inference,* as Quarles observes.[4]

In his collection of first-hand accounts of Negro historical events, Katz summarizes in his own words the events of the mob action which resulted in the Boston Massacre by reporting:

> A group of Boston patriots met a company of British soldiers, but this time the usual name-calling, scuffling, and throwing of snowballs ended in bloodshed.
>
> The leader of the crowd of Boston men and boys was Crispus Attucks, a tall runaway slave who had become a seaman. When Attucks waved his cordwood club and urged the crowds forward, someone gave the order to fire and the British muskets cut down Attucks and four other Bostonians.[5]

The actual "eyewitness" account, however, does not quite jibe with the above summary. Katz quotes an observer, also a Negro, who stated in court:

> . . . a stout (heavy set) man with a long cordwood stick, threw himself in, and made a blow at the officer; I saw the officer try to ward off the stroke, whether he struck him or not I do not know; the stout man then turned around, and struck the grenadier's gun at the captain's right hand, and immediately fell in with his club, and knocked his gun away, and struck him over the head, the blow came either on the soldier's cheek or hat. This stout man held the bayonet with his left hand, and twitched it and cried kill the dogs, knock them over; this was the general cry; the people then crowded in, and upon that the grenadier gave a twitch back and relieved his gun, and he up with it and began to pay away on the people.[6]

From the eyewitness account, it sounds as though Attucks was foolhardy in the extreme; had the soldier not retrieved his bayonet and fired, it is likely that he would have been the one killed. Katz, the summarizer, should re-read Katz, the documentarian. There is absolutely no supporting evidence that Attucks was a "patriot," except in the sense that he was the first man to fall, mortally wounded, in a brawl with British soldiers in Boston in 1770. This fact, however, does not qualify him *as an individual,* Negro or white, for elevation to the Hall of Fame.

By contrast, the classic history of the United States of Charles and Mary Beard provides this comment, and only this comment, on the Boston Massacre:

---

4. *Ibid.,* p. 8.
5. William L. Katz, *Eyewitness: The Negro in American History* (New York: Pitman Publishing Co., 1967), p. 44.
6. *Ibid.,* p. 56.

. . . school children (of Boston) now emulated their elders by jeering at soldiers and officers; indeed, one of the first Americans killed in the conflict was a school boy shot by an informer who resented childish ridicule.

This affair was shortly followed by the 'Boston Massacre' of March, 1770, starting in comedy as some youths threw snowballs and stones at a small body of British regulars and ending in tragedy with the killing and wounding of several citizens.[7]

In writing her fantasy biography of Crispus Attucks for children, Mrs. Millender has him attending the trial of a man named Richardson, who shot the taunting schoolboy. Nothing in the historical record would indicate that Attucks would do such a thing, particularly since his official status as a runaway slave would make such public appearance dangerous. Courthouses, in those times, were not large and impersonal places; a person of Attucks' appearance would have certainly drawn comment, whereupon his former master could have had him seized; thus the author ignores the very real "probabilities" of history in order to invent those more suited to her purpose of inflating an individual tragedy to the level of heroic martyrdom.

A more recent "popular" history of the United States summarizes the Boston Massacre in these terms:

> The Townshend Acts bore most heavily on Massachusetts, and for its protests against them that colony's General Court was dissolved in 1768. Violence broke out soon after when a mob attacked some customs agents trying to collect Townshend duties from John Hancock's sloop, *Liberty*. This prompted the governor to ask for troops. On March 5, 1770, a snowball attack on some of the soldiers brought the unfortunate order to fire, and after the melee four [sic] Bostonians were lying dead.
>
> New England seethed over the "Boston Massacre;" but when the new Lord North Ministry repealed all duties but that on tea, quiet seemed to have been restored . . .[8]

The charge that the Beards and William Miller, being white, are thus insensitive to the role of the Negro is worthy of further examination since one may pick up any current American history textbook and find similar quotations. Few general histories today do an adequate job of placing the Negro in perspective *throughout* our history. Indeed, one could cite the absence of Crispus Attucks in "white" history books, and school textbooks. Suffice it to say that, historically, those who died pro-

---

7. Charles and Mary Beard, *The Rise of American Civilization,* rev. ed. (New York: Macmillan Co., 1934), p. 221.
8. William Miller, *A New History of the United States* (New York: George Braziller, Inc., 1958), p. 102.

vided a rallying cry for the American patriots. Yearly, the anniversary was

> duly observed . . . in a public ceremony, which took on a ritualistic pattern. Bells would toll during the day, and at night lighted transparencies depicted the soldiers and their victims, giving a substance of sorts to the "discontented ghosts, with hollow groans" summoned to solemnize the occasion. The highlight of the evening was a stirring address by a leading citizen which, as the contemporary historian David Ramsay observed, "administered fuel to the fire of liberty, and kept it burning with an incessant flame." The propaganda value of the Boston Massacre cannot be minimized. . . .[9]

The necessary question remains: must we make a hero out of Crispus Attucks? At a critical point in American colonial history, a traumatic event occurred whose propaganda value, as Professor Quarles indicates, played a useful role in rallying wavering colonial sentiments and stiffening the resistance to British rule.[10]

One small nagging question might occur to the careful reader: what about those other Bostonians killed along with Attucks? John Adams, in supporting the defense witness who stated that it was to Attucks' "mad behavior, in all probability, the dreadful carnage of that night is chiefly to be ascribed," added ". . . a Carr from Ireland and an Attucks from Framingham, happening to be here, at the head of such a rabble of negroes, etc. etc. etc., as they can collect together, and then there are not wanting persons to ascribe all their doings to the good people of the town."[11] No one, however, in writing the history of the Irish in America makes much claim for Patrick Carr for having lost his life in the same fracas. The backgrounds and forebears of the others who died have faded into the fogs of history. Why such efforts to resurrect Crispus Attucks?

Perhaps the important point is that when Negroes have appeared in these smaller but critical points in American history they have somehow become "whitewashed." The impression conveyed to the innocent and the ignorant is that Negroes appear in American history as slaves, over whom the states quarreled and therefore had a bloody and unnecessary war, and who then, after living in animal conditions for decades, once more have become visible and voluble on the American scene.

A reasonable request might be, then, to "color them black" when, indeed, black faces appear as they do throughout our history. But is it

---

9. Quarles, *op. cit.*, p. 7.
10. Charles H. Welsey, "Editorial," Negro History *Bulletin,* 30, No. 3, March 1967, p. 4.
11. Thomas J. Fleming, "The Boston Massacre," *American Heritage,* XVIII, No. 1, December 1966, pp. 6-11ff.

necessary to go further and create heroes out of non-heroes, black, white, or in-between? The life of Crispus Attucks by Mrs. Millender is only one in a series of over one hundred titles published by the Bobbs-Merrill Company. One can justly ask what kind of historical authenticity guides the production of these volumes, and what kind of publishing responsibility is demonstrated?

At a time when authentic history is more essential than ever, we must refrain from creating non-history. We, who tittered over the revisions of Russian history to discredit Stalin and Khruschev, have perhaps some housecleaning to do at home.

Future historians can, however, at least settle the problem of Crispus Attucks by turning to the definitive discussion of the incident in a recent essay by Thomas J. Fleming, who persuasively argues that the true import of the event was not who did or did not provoke the bloodshed, but that a bloody confrontation had indeed taken place, and furthermore, that men who were to play leading roles in the American Revolution took opposing sides in the trial of the British soldiers: Samuel Adams and the Liberty Men against his cousin John Adams and the rule of law and reason. John Adams, reviled by other Bostonians for taking on the defense of the British, won the case through his skill with courts and procedures, and thus gained time for the coming revolution to mature. He and Sam Adams became friends though they never agreed on tactics. In the end, Fleming observes:

> That John [Adams] won the larger place in history should not be surprising to anyone who penetrates beyond the patriotic myth to the interior drama of this great but little-understood trial.[12]

Are these subtleties of history too difficult for little children? Must we instead give them fantasy? I for one would opt for genuine make-believe, the great myths and fairy tales, the sagas and ballads, Paul Bunyan and Ulysses. Let youth, in all good time, ponder some of these obscure and dramatic by-ways of authentic history, from which lasting ethical and moral insights may, in all truth, also be gained.

EYEWITNESS: THE NEGRO IN AMERICAN HISTORY, by William L. Katz, *New York: Pitman Publishing Co., 1967. 554 pp.*
LARRY CUBAN

Booker T. Washington is an Uncle Tom; Nat Turner is a Freedom Fighter; Abraham Lincoln is a white supremacist, and the first President

---

12. *Ibid.*, p. 111.

of the United States is just another honkie. Mali, Songhay, and Timbuktu are enshrined; and hog maws, chittlings and black-eyed peas are ennobled. Here is the stuff of Black History. Heroes, all black, struggle for freedom, while villains, all white, oppress for profit. Ignored facts are dusted off and celebrated, while previously scorned items are converted into virtues and extolled.

Black History, a tool used by race-conscious activists who wish to create a sense of peopleness between and among black people here and abroad, bursts with righteousness, pride, and outrage.

Negro History, on the other hand, straightens out distortions and carefully plugs up the enormous gaps of information about people of color in this nation. Restraint and balance mark this approach. Injustice is soberly catalogued. Negro inventors, soldiers, and artists enter into their proper chronological niche to tell Americans that this nation is indebted to the invisible man. Negro History, in short, speaks to the mind of white men and middle- and upper-income Negroes of the above thirty-five generation. Black History speaks to the souls of black men, especially to those of the young.

The dichotomy, of course, is not without cracks; leakage turns up all the time. But the differences between the two histories in style, content, and audience mirror the larger conflicts over the why's of racial consciousness among black Americans. The Olympic Boycott, the Black Power debate, I.S. 201, student uprisings at the public school and university levels—all have in common a striving for racial we-ness interwoven with the push and pull of assimilation or ethnic identity. "I'm real torn up," a southern Negro school teacher said, "between what my head knows is right and what people say my skin should tell me to believe."[13]

When the issues telescope to education, the distinction between the two histories gains in importance. Much of the heated dialogue over who should teach black children, the question of integrated or segregated content, and the confusing flood of books and materials pumped out annually can be filtered out roughly between one or the other.

What sense, for example, is one to make out of the complex tangle of opinions of who should teach black children history? To most whites and Negroes the answer turns on the competency of the teacher, regardless of race. But to Black History advocates, concerned less with input of information and more with redefining blackness in a positive light, only a black man can teach the subject. For as one student put it: "If you

---

13. Robert Coles, *Children of Crisis* (Boston: Little, Brown, 1967), p. 160.

wanted to learn how to be a carpenter, you get apprenticed to a carpenter, not a bricklayer."[14]

A controversy rages over the use of segregated or integrated content; i.e. a course on Black History or one on U.S. History with emphasis on the role of the Negro. Those who urge inclusion of ethnic material into the appropriate slot fall into the camp of Negro History. If, for example, there is a unit on the westward movement, Jim Beckwourth (fur trapper), Nat Love (Deadwood Dick of the 1880's), and the Indian pacification efforts of the ninth and tenth cavalry units must be given their fair share of text and photographs. Those, however, who demand a separate course stressing African civilizations, oppression and liberation of the race in this country, and Black culture—art, music, language, food, etc.— clearly fall into the group desiring a heightened racial awareness.

Turning to books and curriculum materials, the same dichotomy applies. Books that glorify Crispus Attucks, who is, at best, a shadowy historical figure, are part of the effort to create a pantheon of black heroes that children can point to with pride. Since movements need heroes— martyrs, preferably—Attucks, Nat Turner, Peter Salem, Malcolm X, regardless of their authenticity in historians' eyes, can be used to counter white propaganda and convince black people that they counted years ago and they count now.

To evaluate such books solely by the canons of historical "objectivity" and accuracy, as Negro History devotees of both races often do, is missing the point, I think; the purpose of such books is to build black counterparts to the Nathan Hales and Molly Pitchers of the past. That shadowy white heroes have been manufactured and legends perpetuated in the name of patriotism should give pause to the critics who attack books without considering their purpose and audience. The basic issues are whether black mythology will compete with the white mythology commonly called "social studies," and whether mythology—white or black —belongs in the public schools at all.

Black History advocates, a minority within a minority and often without resources, have produced, not unexpectedly, the least amount of publishable materials—the few coming from SNCC, Freedom Schools, local Afro-American associations, and the like. The supporters of Negro History have managed to secure the ear of many publishers and, at the same time, insert a hand into the federal pocketbook through the recent-

14. Miriam Wasserman, "The Loud, Proud, Black Kids." *The Progressive*, April 1968, p. 38.

ly-introduced bill for the establishment of a Commission on Negro History. As a result, in the past few years, materials ranging from straight textual narrative—Rayford Logan and Irving Cohen, *The American Negro* (New York: Houghton-Mifflin, 1965) or Mabel Morsbach, *The Negro in American Life* (New York: Harcourt, Brace and World, Inc., 1966)— to very competent and creative efforts have begun to penetrate some, but by no means most, classrooms. An example of the latter effort is William Loren Katz's *Eyewitness: The Negro in American History* and its companion *Teachers' Guide to American Negro History* (Quadrangle Books, 1968, 192 pp.).

Aiming at the teacher of the conventional United States History course at the secondary level, Katz combines narrative with original sources in a unit by unit approach that is closely keyed to the chronological pattern followed by most history teachers. With the *Teachers' Guide* . . . which includes sample units, bibliography, audio-visual aids, and other numerous suggestions, Katz has outflanked those members of Boards of Education, social studies supervisors and history teachers who complain about the lack of ethnic instructional materials usable in the classroom. None can gripe now that such materials are unavailable; Katz has finally gutted that complaint. Probably other excuses will be fabricated, but Mr. Katz has done students and teachers a great service by producing a comprehensive text and source material that require little change on the part of the teacher and the least revision of a U.S. History course. This raises other problems, however, that will be dealt with later.

Eyewitness is superior to many of its competitors in a number of ways. First, the book permits people to speak in their own words to students rather than telling them what others did or said. Long introductions giving the historical context, but running in too many cases to over half of a chapter, precede abundantly human documents seldom seen in collections for students. In the chapter on the English colonies, the topic perhaps most boring to high school students, Katz included, among others, accounts of Gustavus Vasa, an African abducted into bondage, a slave revolt, and an eloquent epitaph to a slave. Elsewhere many other excerpts such as "Fighting Off a Bandit Ambush," and "A Negro in the CCC" add to instructional materials that crucial human element so necessary for contact and interaction between students, materials, and teacher.

Second, there is a rich diversity of sources, far different from the usual potpourri of laws, judicial decisions, and political speeches often found in current histories of the Negro. Anything dealing with Negro Americans related to the particular period of study becomes a source;

letters, diaries, poems, testimony, leaflets, and photographs create a lively blend of material.

Third, the volume uses liberal selections of paintings, prints, and photographs, some seen for the first time in schoolbooks. Few publishers or historians, for that matter, go to the trouble of digging out valuable sources such as these. Nonverbal material imaginatively used (and the possibilities were hardly touched in *Eyewitness*) can increase immeasurably the impact of the excerpts and the main points of the volume.

The reservations I have about the book deal not with the specific content, which I recommend highly, but with the issues that prompted the author and publisher and others like them to make certain decisions in putting together a volume such as *Eyewitness*. There are three major issues.

Is history the best vehicle for capturing the meaning of the Negro experience? The content of most schoolbooks on the Negro often pursues the Estevanico-to-Martin Luther King chronology, or the flip-side of the Columbus-to-Eisenhower record. These texts are highly factual. Gaps of information are filled and distortions are straightened out—processes that are essential, if for no other reason than to cleanse the sorry record of publishers. But what is missing from the deluge of facts is the meaning of the Negro experience in America: three centuries of corrosive and oppressive relations between the races, with continual and persistent protests by black people. Yet only a few facets of this experience are ever touched upon or examined in depth. The reason is that such analysis requires strong, and sometimes negative, points of view about the character of America, and evidence indicates that while facts comfort, points of view can disturb. Conventional textbooks have points of view, often implicit and innocuous, that are acceptable to the main stream of white America. But by sticking to the facts of the historical record, these texts sap the anger, the tragedy, and the healthy responses of being black in white America and leave only the white man's perception of the Negro experience: a striving for integration. While valid, this perception is only a fraction of the historical record. There is much more.

For example, the topic of racial attitudes—their origin, perpetuation, influence on behavior and modification—is something that kids of both races are vitally interested in and can deal with. But where can it fit into the conventional history of the Negro? Where does the question of assimilation and ethnic pride enter? And what about the issue of identity, black or white? History, as presently defined in most schools, simply doesn't have the elasticity to treat these and other questions in depth. What is needed is some homework on how Black History activists have formulated the history of the Negro in broader terms, leaning heavily on personal experiences and borrowing extensively from the social sciences.

To the degree that analysis replaces proselytizing, this formulation has great relevance for writers, educators, and students of both races. But when analysis is subordinated to exhortation, the audience narrows, the tone turns theological, and the classroom becomes a meeting hall. When this occurs the losers are those who seek truth, and the winners are those who need to believe. Yet, and this is the important point, the kinds of content that Black History proponents have pursued I feel, has great promise for capturing the meaning of the Negro experience and providing a broader base for its study in the public schools.

What is the best stategy for introducing instructional materials on the Negro into the classroom? At present, two routes have been taken. Producing textbooks with high multiethnic visibility, such as Franklin, May, and Caughey, (sic) *Land of the Free* (New York: Benziger Bros., 1966), guarantees some penetration of content, since most teachers follow a text. This approach introduces problems of motivation and learning, however, because it stresses the accumulation of information, much of it irrelevant.

The other route is through supplementary units and books such as Richard Wade, *The Negro in American Life* (New York: Houghton-Mifflin, 1965), Larry Cuban, *The Negro in America* (Chicago: Scott, Foresman, 1964), the Logan and Cohen and Morsbach books, units by Educational Development Corporation, and American Education Publications. Although some of these emphasize original sources combined with different teaching stategies, they present problems. They require additional funds, since their material is supplementary; teachers need careful preparation to use these materials effectively; and their inherently segregated treatment of race raises many objections.

Aside from cost, *Eyewitness* overcomes two of the objections by integrating racial content extremely well into the conventional course offering and thereby permitting teachers to handle the ethnic content pretty much as they would the rest of the course. Nevertheless, in meeting these objections, another trap appears. By choosing what is essentially a conservative strategy, as so many publishers do, at a time when the teaching of history is shifting slightly from an approach stressing information to one stressing skills of inquiry, proponents of Negro History find themselves a step behind the best in curricular change. A few, like EDC, AEP and the Scott, Foresman book, try to avoid this trap.

An even more serious consideration confronting all supplementary materials is the large attitudinal burden that ethnic history carries. In other words, what everyone is after—once distortions and omissions are corrected—is a change of attitudes, based upon information. Yet without any systematic effort to modify teachers' perceptions and educate them in the use of racial-content materials, it is fraudulent to think that students will shift in their attitudes—much less change their behavior—simply on the basis of reading something, "discussing" it, and spilling out the facts on a test. Such deception continues, nourished by publisher blurbs and liberal rhetoric.

Will studying Negro or Black History, then, improve the self-concept and instill pride? The only answer has to be that no one knows. No evidence has been produced to demonstrate any direct results from exposure to racial content. That no evidence exists, of course, does not mean improved self-concept and pride are not produced; absence of imprecise instruments or inferior methodology may well explain the lack of evidence. Furthermore, self-concept has yet to be defined with sufficient precision to indicate whether instructional materials can have the differential impact that boosters promise for them. But to promise that returns in increased ego strength will result if certain printed materials are used —the claim of some publishers—either borders on ignorance or is another instance of academic hustling.

In other words, there are two drawbacks to creating a course or writing a book for the express purpose of instilling pride or improving self-image: it inflates the influence of words beyond reasonable bounds and, more important, it dictates selection of content that accentuates only the positive, only the success story, only the victory. And this is propaganda. I don't know if it works but I do know that its place is in the storefront, not the classroom; its teacher is a true believer, not an inquirer; and it can be taught only by the race-conscious black man, not a white man.

Instructional materials, then, are limited tools for the job of attitudinal and behavioral change. The only legitimate goals of such content, I think, are to prepare materials that correct errors of fact, are free of stereotypes and accurately describe the Negro's role in the American past, and, to get students to analyze the meaning of the black American's experience in this country. Academics in curriculum development, supported lustily by commercial publishers, have watered their stock abundantly, promising dividends that will seldom materialize. Far more attention and money have to focus upon the craftsmen who use those tools.

And this is the rub. Much time, energy, and money are spent in recruiting scholars and teachers to produce ethnic materials for thousands of teachers. But these teams know full well that any piece of material lives or dies in the hands of the teacher and that there is no such thing as a teacher-proof unit or book. Yet try to convince those with money for developing materials that their grants would be more wisely spent in creating constituencies for racial content by spending it on imaginative in-service training programs, workshops, and the like that prepare teachers with the skills to develop their own materials and choose wisely from commercially-produced units.

Here again the activists who preach Black History rightly see the person who teaches as being far more important than the materials he uses. Advocates of Negro History, on the other hand, emphasize materials as if they will magically change attitudes or absolve educators from obligations. Obviously, it is not an either/or proposition, but there is much to be learned from the unorthodox, intuitional growth of the Black History movement.

Much of it, I feel, should be treated outside the public school, as CORE and the NAACP have done in Cleveland or as many spontaneous Afro-American associations have done in storefronts across the country. But wherever it is located, educators, academics, and writers who are concerned about the growing tide of racial awareness among youth have much to learn from the style and substance of Black History. If they ignore what's happening, they will miss another opportunity to revitalize what happens in school.

The dichotomy of Negro and Black History will not be easily resolved by the schools until the larger question of melting pot or salad bowl is resolved. And that question has fundamental implications for the very nature of the educational system. Turning out bigger and better texts or creating new courses only mirrors the ferment in the nation and, at best, deals lightly with the advance guard of a deeper, developing struggle over the role of the school in the lives of children. Perhaps the issues will not be examined by schoolmen, since they are disturbing. And, perhaps, the choice between Negro History or Black History will become only a matter of taste. If this happens, children of both races will be losers.

VARIETIES OF HISTORY: NEGRO, BLACK, WHITE.
JAMES A. BANKS

To the Editors:

In a provocative review of Katz, *Eyewitness: the Negro in American History* (Summer, 1968), Larry Cuban makes a distinction between

"Black History" and "Negro History." In Black History, "Heroes are all black and struggle for freedom. Villains are all white and oppress for profit. . . . Ignored facts are dusted off and celebrated, while previously scorned items are converted into virtues and extolled." Booker T. Washington is portrayed as an Uncle Tom; Abraham Lincoln as a white supremacist. Black History ". . . bursts with righteousness, pride and outrage." While Black History distorts, Negro History ". . . corrects distortions and fills in the enormous gaps of information about people of color . . . Restraint and *balance* mark this approach . . ." Ethnic content, Cuban argues, should offer a *balanced* view that ". . . correct errors of *fact* . . . and accurately describe the Negro's role in the American past . . ." (All italics in this letter are mine.)

In the same issue Jean D. Grambs reviews a recent biography of Crispus Attucks and raises issues similar to those discussed by Cuban. Like a growing number of white "liberal" educators, these authors are alarmed by what they perceive as attempts by black militants to "distort" history by glorifying the black man's past in order to imbue pride in black students. Grambs accuses Millender, the black author of Attucks' biography, of telling "historical lies to repair the damage" done by previous distortions of black history. Grambs maintains that "appropriate data" should be reported "accurately" and that textbooks should reflect "*balanced* versions" of black history. She writes, ". . . it is one thing to present *authentic* historic material, but it is quite another matter to twist or invent material." The author posits her own canons of historical objectivity and uses her standards to ascertain the "accuracy" of the treatments of Attucks given by two black historians. She argues that Benjamin Quarles *accurately* portrays Attucks because he depicts him as a shadowy historical figure. "Quarles," writes Grambs, "unlike some of his colleagues, does not let being Negro distort his historical appraisal." The author vehemently attacks John Hope Franklin, an eminent historian, for falling into the "chauvinistic trap" and portraying Attucks as a significant historical personality.

Cuban and Grambs err when they assume that there is such a phenomenon as an unbiased, objective, and balanced written history. Both believe that the historian, by carefully gathering data, can derive historical statements which are balanced, factual and without distortions. This assumption emanates from a confusion of *historical facts* with *past events*. These two authors imply that historical facts are hard and stable, waiting to be uncovered by the studious, objective historian. Grambs argues that Quarles portrays Attucks as he really was, while Franklin distorts the *real* Attucks. The Boston Massacre is a *past event*. It has taken place and will never occur again; neither Quarles nor Franklin will ever be able to observe Attucks' participation in that historic battle; neither can go back in time. Even if they could they would probably perceive Attucks' role differently. Thus, the historian can never deal with actual past events, but must deal with *statements about events* written by biased individuals with divergent points of view. Moreover, the historian necessarily and inevitably reflects his own biases in his attempts to reconstruct the past. Using various sources to find out about past events, the historian *must* select from the statements which he uncovers those which he wishes to report and regard as factual. The historian can never discover all of the "facts" about a past event; his selection and interpretation are greatly influenced by his personal bias, cultural environment and his reasons for writing. His statements are actually symbols for past events, and it is difficult to argue that symbols are true or false. As Becker notes, "The safest thing to say about a symbol is that it is more or less appropriate."[15]

We cannot, like Cuban and Grambs, contend that any versions of history are "balanced" and without distortions, because historical facts are products of the human mind and are not identical with past events. The most we can say about any version of history is that its statements are regarded as factual by a greater number of historians than other statements which comprise other varieties of history. The versions of history accepted as most factual by historians vary greatly with the times, the culture, and the discovery of artifacts and documents. The present heavily influences how historians view the past. Becker, the noted historian, writes: "The past is a kind of screen upon which we project our vision of the future; and it is . . . a moving picture, borrowing much of its form and color from our fears and aspirations."[16] Commager, like Becker, argues that we look at the past through our own eyes, " . . . judging it by our own standards, recreating it by our own words or reading back into the language of the past our own meaning."[17]

Implicit in Cuban's argument is the belief that statements which constitute Negro History are more widely regarded as factual by white, liberal historians than the statements which constitute Black History. He

---

15. Phil L. Synder, ed., *Detachment and the Writing of History: Essays and Letters of Carl L. Becker* (Ithaca, N.Y.: Cornell University Press, 1958), p. 47.
16. *Ibid.*, p. 59.
17. Henry S. Commager, *The Nature and the Study of History* (Columbus: Charles E. Merrill, 1965), p. 46.

assumes that because these statements are more widely accepted by "established" white historians they more accurately describe past events than statements which constitute Black History. Similarly, Grambs believes that Attucks is a shadowy historical figure because he is described as such by most established, white historians. We cannot accept consensus within the community of white, established historians as adequate evidence for historical accuracy. This is true not only because there is rarely agreement among historians on controversial issues, but because historians in different countries and in different times regard highly conflicting statements as factual.

Grambs reveals her cultural and personal biases when she accepts Quarles' interpretation of Attucks and rejects Franklin's. Which historian's portrayal of Attucks is more congruent with the actual past is a moot question. Provided that she diligently searched all available data, carefully considered all points of view, and reached her conclusion through critical reflection, Grambs is justified in regarding Attucks as an insignificant figure; but she is not justified in contending that her conclusion is the "right" conclusion and that Quarles' view of Attucks is more accurate than Franklin's. She can only argue that she *believes* that Quarles' portrayal is more accurate. We must grant Cuban the right to prefer Negro History to Black History, but he cannot claim that the statements which make up Negro History more accurately reflect past events than statements which are products of the human mind; both reflect the historians' personal biases, cultural backgrounds and purposes for writing.

The writers of Negro History attempt to construct history which reflects the opinions of established historians (most of whom are white); writers of Black History write history primarily to imbue pride in black students; writers of white schoolbook history write to glorify the United States and to develop patriotism in white children. Because of the tenuous nature of history, we are more justified in questioning the aims of these different varieties of history than we are in challenging the accuracy of the statement which they promulgate. Since black people are vehemently complaining about the treatment of the Negro in schoolbooks, which were written by white established historians and educators, we cannot assume that the professional white historian has fewer biases than the black militant historian.

Cuban and Grambs, and other educators who are alarmed over recent attempts to create a black version of history, grossly misinterpret the proper role of history in the public school. These educators assume that there is *an* "accurate" version of history, and that it is the role of the teacher to help youngsters become effective consumers of this authentic and balanced history. Actually, the role of the school, as Bolster says, is to help students ". . . create their own accounts of the past and to put their conclusions against those of other writers of history."[18] As I have argued elsewhere, by approaching the study of history in this way, students will realize that there are alternative ways of looking at identical events and situations; consquently, their reasoning and critical powers will be strengthened.[19]

In writing their own accounts of history, students should determine for themselves which versions of history are more accurate and balanced. *To do this, they must be exposed to all types and varieties of history, including Negro History, Black History and White Schoolbook History.* Students should also be exposed to different versions of history because thinking occurs when students are forced to consider conflicting interpretations and points of view. To ban any version of history from the public school is to deny the student academic freedom. Students should not have to go to the storefront school to encounter versions of history which conflict with *the* version endorsed by established institutions.

By reading historical documents, examining historical artifacts, reading accounts of history written by others, and writing their own versions of history, students will discover that written history is at best accounts of events from particular points of view. The conclusions which students derive about the accuracy of historical statements, and the versions of history which they construct will be greatly influenced by their own personal biases and cultural environment. We cannot confiscate the student's right to reach his own conclusions regarding the accuracy of historical statements and to construct his own accounts of history. Rather, we should encourage students to carefully consider all points of view and to responsibly defend their own judgments. If a student concludes that Crispus Attucks is a significant historical figure, we cannot accuse him of falling into a "chauvinistic trap." If we disagree with his conclusions the most we can do is to encourage him to begin inquiry anew, for the ultimate goal of social education is to help students develop a commitment to inquiry and not to make them unthinking consumers of any version of history.

---

18. Arthur S. Bolster, Jr., "Review of History and the Social Sciences: New Approaches to the Teaching of Social Studies" by Mark M. Krug, *Harvard Educational Review* 38 (Summer, 1968):599.
19. See James A. Banks and Ermon O. Hogan, "Inquiry: A History Teaching Tool," *Illinois Schools Journal* 48 (Fall, 1968); eprinted in *Readings on Elementary Social Studies: Emerging Changes,* edited by Jonathan C. McLendon, William W. Joyce, and John R. Lee, pp. 332-337 (Boston: Allyn and Bacon, 1970.)

Mr. Cuban replies:

Mr. Banks went hunting for elephant and, I fear, bagged only a mouse and that with buckshot.

Considering his lucid historiographical explanation about the nature of history and bias in historians, I plead guilty to imprecision in language. I probably shouldn't have used the phrase "Black History" as a counterpoint to Negro History which, at the time, seemed a convenient and stylistic shorthand for a point I wanted to make. Instead I should have used "Black Consciousness" which would have been closer to what I was after. Because of my imprecision, the door was opened for Banks to lecture me on the meaning of my implied assumptions on history as he perceived them and the futility of objective history. It was kind of him, but unnecessary. It seems that Banks had on his agenda the putting down of white "liberal" educators, a group that—to my knowledge—exists only in someone's imagination.

Interestingly enough, Mr. Banks ends his letter with a ringing challenge for educators to teach students (of both races, I presume) the skills of inquiry through analysis and use of conflicting sources—a position that I endorse heartily and have implemented in my classroom for the past decade. Rather than considering how Banks and I view history and its instruction, I prefer to deal with what I considered were the main points of my book review, points which Mr. Banks consistently ignored.

The Negro History vs. Black History dichotomy is simply shorthand for the longtime integrationist vs. nationalist differences that have split Negro leadership, intellectuals, culture, economics, and politics for the past two centuries in this country. I was not saying that Negro History is more acceptable than Black History (integrationist as opposed to nationalist). Clearly, black historians of either bent have written fine history—Carter Woodson, John Hope Franklin, Vincent Harding, Harold Cruse, to name only a few. But the point is *not* whether an historian can deal with his biases (as Banks would define the issue); rather, toward what ends is the history they and others produce directed?

Consider what two black writers have said on this issue. Michael Thelwell of the University of Massachusetts writes:

> Black necessity has less to do with manufacturing a history than with the excavation, articulation and legitimization of what has been ignored or misrepresented in our history.
> (*Partisan Review*, Fall 1968, p. 404.)

On the other hand, James Garrett, of Federal City College, notes:

> Nation building, then, must be the end product of black studies and the beginning of a lasting and meaningful black peoplehood.
> (*New York Times*, November 17, 1968.)

The directions implied here—one, historical search by black intellectuals to uncover what white middle-class historians have avoided or ignored and, at the same time, to establish the integrity of what is found; the other, a selected use of the past to weld a race consciousness—suggest the broad spectrum of disagreement among black intellectuals (as, indeed, among any ethnic grouping) as to the uses of the past.

I was trying to deal with these diverse aims and uses as they have been translated by publishers and educators. Not once did Banks pick apart my "provocative" assertions about these aims. Three of these points bear repeating:

    a. History doesn't teach identity; people and experiences do. No evidence exists which proves that self-image results from courses, materials, or good intentions.

    b. If history is used to build black identity, its place is outside the public school. It belongs in a parochial education.

    c. If educators, militants, and assorted "liberal" friends believe the teaching of black consciousness belongs in the public schools to improve self-image, then black mythology would replace the infant efforts recently begun to uproot the corrupt white mythology that so obviously failed in building a white American identity. Banks' recipe for inquiry does not square with the true believers who are compelled to tell the "truth" about the past and build black identity. He just can't have it both ways.

Yet, why doesn't Mr. Banks question these assertions? I don't know. He chose to catch me up on imprecise definitions—which I concede. I would have preferred if he addressed himself to more basic issues that demand far more clarification than my limited efforts.

Dr. Grambs replies:

Mr. Banks' letter commenting on book reviews by Larry Cuban and myself blurs the issues which I was trying to present.

First, for the record: I made careful inquiries of both black and white authorities regarding the known "facts" about Crispus Attucks. On this basis I questioned the rather extenuating inferences John Hope Franklin makes as against the more restrained comment by Benjamin Quarles. I am sure I would have been quite satisfied with Quarles' position even if I had not known his color, and indeed I read his history and found it attractive quite some time before I knew he was black. The point is that Quarles finds it unnecessary to go beyond what other (white and black) scholars believe to be the admissable and relevant facts; Franklin does feel so inclined. And so does Mr. Katz, whom I also cited for some loose handling of the data, but whom Mr. Banks forgets about (because Katz is white? Is he?) in his concern over my presumed white bias. What does Mr. Banks assume my color to be? And, even if he knew, are my arguments thus contaminated? Tomorrow we may find a lost document which will reveal that, *in fact*, Crispus Attucks was a descendant of an African Prince and was a secret agent of Sam Adams. But until tomorrow comes, until that document is revealed, if it in fact exists, I do insist that historians have an obligation to state the facts *as they know them*, make clear the basis *in fact* for the inferences they may draw, and let the hypotheses follow.

Second, I wanted in my review to draw attention to what I consider negligent publishing and writing; namely the third grade "history" written by Dharathula Millender. I would find Mr. Banks' suggestions for incorporating historiography into the study of history quite valuable, but at third grade? I would think that one can begin to develop a healthy skepticism about information sources (such as TV commercials) by third grade or even sooner, but one is dealing in rather more complicated intellectual processes when one instructs third graders in history. As I said, I would prefer true mythology at this age, rather than pretend history. Certainly Mr. Banks would not encourage extensive exposure of young minds to a fictionalized history which would suggest that slavery was a rather benign and happy institution—or would he?

Third, I am not alarmed at the appearance of "black history." I do not, however, condone the creation of black non-heroes, as Larry Cuban appears to be doing in his review. Just because whites manufactured a Nathan Hale or a Molly Pitcher seems a poor reason for "allowing" blacks to have a Crispus Attucks. Presumably, when black history "matures," he will go the way of Betsy Ross. This seems to be a patronizing acceptance of myth for history, and I do not think blacks need either the patronage or the mythology.

It is unfortunate that criticism of the chauvinism of Black History makes one open to the charge of white bias. Is criticism of chauvinistic French history to be denied me because I am an American? Are we to let what appears to be biases of perception by whatever group, of whatever color, or nationality, (or sex) go un-remarked? On the one hand, Mr. Banks protests that criticism of differing historical interpretations appears to imply an idea of absolute historical "truth," but on the other hand, he wants students to have a hand in comparing different versions of past events. Toward what end? To proving all historians are liars? Or that the study of history is, indeed, a waste of time since it is only "my" version of "the facts" versus "yours"?

I would support historiography as a very enlightening approach to teaching history, not because it might lead to a nebulous "commitment to inquiry," but because it might lead to an insight into the twisted motives and perverse passions of the human heart and mind. Students could learn that even as we make history we distort it; even as we read it, we learn only what is comforting or agreeable. Historiography is excellent medication for the diseases of provincialism and chauvinism, and needed by all of us in this ailing and troubled world.

Black Studies: A Brief Bibliography

Banks, James A. *Teaching the Black Experience: Methods and Materials.* Palo Alto, Calif.: Fearon Publishing Company, 1970.

———. "Developing Racial Tolerance with Literature on the Black Inner-City," *Social Education* 34 (May, 1970): 549-552.

Bibliographic Survey: The Negro in Print. Negro Bibliographic and Research Center, Inc., 117 R Street, N. E., Washington, D. C. 20002.

The Black Arts Magazine. Concept East Publishing Co., 401 East Adams Street, Detroit, Michigan 48226.

Black Dialogue Magazine. Post Office Box 1019, New York, New York 10027.

The Black Scholar: Journal of Black Studies and Research, published by Black World Foundation, Box 906, Sausalito, California 94965.

"Black Studies in American Education," *Journal of Negro Education* (Yearbook Issue) 39 (Summer, 1970): 189-273. See also Fall, 1969 issue of same journal.

Black Theater. Room 103, 200 West 135th Street, New York, New York 10030.

Black World (formerly *Negro Digest*). Monthly devoted to articles and reports, including Black Studies, 1820 S. Michigan Ave., Chicago, Illinois 60616.

Blassingame, John. "Black Studies: An Intellectual Crisis," *The American Scholar* 38 (Autumn, 1968): 548-561.

———. " 'Soul' or Scholarship: Choices Ahead for Black Studies," *Smithsonian* 1 (April, 1970): 58-65.

Childs, Charles. "Black Studies at Cornell: The Troubled Path to Understanding," *Life* 68 (April 17, 1970): 56-60.

CLA Journal: Official Publication of the College Language Association. Morgan State College, Baltimore, Maryland 21212.

Crowley, Richard. "Black Identity and the Broader Vision in Lyric Poetry," *Maryland English Journal* 7 (Spring, 1969): 12-16.

Directory of Black Literary Magazines. Negro Bibliographic and Research Center, Inc., 117 R Street, N. E., Washington, D. C. 20002.

Fenton, Edwin. "Crispus Attucks is Not Enough: The Social Studies and Black Americans," *Social Education* 33 (April, 1969): 396-400.

Freedomways. 799 Broadway, New York, New York 10003.

Fry, William A. "A Black Foot is in the Door," *Maryland English Journal* 8 (Fall, 1969): 33-39.

Gilman, Richard. "White Standards and Negro Writings," essay review of *Soul on Ice* by Eldridge Cleaver. *New Republican* 58 (March 9, 1968): 25-30.

Hare, Nathan. "Teaching of Black History and Culture in the Secondary Schools," *Social Education* 33 (April, 1969): 385-389.

Journal of Black Studies. Sage Publications, 275 South Beverly Drive, Beverly Hills, California 90212.

Lamon, Gwendolyn. "The Black Image Past and Present," *Maryland English Journal* 8 (Fall, 1969): 40-48.

Lewis, W. Arthur. "The Road to the Top is Through Higher Education Not Black Studies," *New York Magazine* (May 11, 1969): 34-53.

"Minority Culture in the Curriculum," *The Bulletin of the National Association of Secondary School Principals* 54 (April, 1970): 1-129.

Munro, John U. "Black Studies, White Teachers, and Black Colleges," *Teaching Forum* 3 (April, 1970): 3-9.

Onyewu, Nicholas D.U. "The Teaching of African Politics," *Black World* 19 (August, 1970): 37-48.

Pickens, William G. "Teaching Negro Culture in High Schools—Is It Worthwhile?" *Journal of Negro Education* 34 (Spring, 1965): 106-13.

Porter, Dorothy B. *The Negro in the United States.* Washington, D. C.: Government Printing Office, 1970.

Robinson, Armstead, et al., eds. *Black Studies in the University: A Symposium.* New Haven, Conn.: Yale University Press, 1969.

Stanford, B. D. "Affective Aspects of Black Literature," *English Journal* 59 (March, 1970): 371-4.

Studies in Black Literature. Department of English, Mary Washington College, Fredericksburg, Virginia 22401.

Viewfinder. Grambling College, Grambling, Louisiana 71245.

"What White Students Think of Black Studies: Special Report From the U.S. Campus," *Life* 68 (May 8, 1970): 34.

Whittemore, Reed. "Black Studies in Glass Houses," a review of *Amistad I*, edited by John A. Williams and Charles F. Harris, *New Republic* 162 (May 9, 1970): 25-27.

CHAPTER 3

Why Good
Interracial Books
Are Hard to Find

Barbara J. Glancy

introduction

"I'd be most happy to have my children read about black young-sters, but I just can't find any good books." This statement, and variations on the same theme, have been heard frequently at institutes, conferences, and teachers' meetings where the focus has been on improvement of intergroup relations. As a matter of fact, individuals who make such a complaint have a sound basis for doing so. Relatively few children's books of literary quality exist which have black characters.

The reasons for the scarcity of these books are examined by Barbara Glancy in the following chapter. The publishing market for children's books operates in an intricate and far from rationalized system. Books have to have authors, and authors have to present material to publishers which publishers believe will find a market and make a profit. Critics and reviewers assess books which, for one reason or another, they believe should be drawn to the attention of a given audience—teachers, librarians, parents, booksellers. To facilitate book acquisition, bibliographies are put together by specialists—librarians, curriculum personnel, educators—who, of course, have their own selective bias.

The result, as Mrs. Glancy points out, is that not only are many books for children never reviewed, but many good ones—in her opinion, are ignored. The reviewer or bibliographer may omit the fact that characters written about or depicted in illustrations are black. The potential reader or purchaser is, therefore, unaware of the race of the characters in the story.

The data which Mrs. Glancy provides is only one example of the selective perception which operates in the subjective area of book publishing and book evaluation. The issues she raises about "invisible characters" in "invisible" or out-of-print books, can also be applied to books about many other touchy or taboo areas. This study serves to alert the teacher or librarian to the limitation of the sources of information utilized for learning what books are available on any subject.

Militant demands for children's books which deal with blacks make it imperative to recognize this particular segment of the population when selecting books for children, yet many problems exist for the teacher or librarian who wants to buy such books.

The first and most obvious problem arises from an inadequate supply of books about American blacks. Nancy Larrick's survey of books published from 1962 through 1964 indicated that only forty-four books of fiction and nonfiction for children included American blacks in post-World War II settings and that twelve of these were picture books with no written mention of race.[1] Dorothy Sterling, considering books published between 1960 and 1966, found only forty-two books which mentioned blacks.[2] One has only to consider the fact that about 3,000 children's books are published annually to realize how truly inadequate the supply of books about blacks has been. Surely Sterling's complaint that there are "hardly enough titles to fill a five-foot shelf when what we need is a fifty-foot shelf"[3] is a justifiable one.

the role of the publisher

The existence of so few titles seems to be, at least in part, due to publishers' concern for sales receipts. In the early fifties and before, few books for children included blacks in either text or illustrations. Larrick

1. Nancy Larrick, "The All-White World of Children's Books," *Saturday Review* 48 (September 11, 1965): 64.
2. Dorothy Sterling, "The Soul of Learning," *English Journal* 57 (February 1968): 171.
3. ——."Negroes and the Truth Gap," *Interracial Books for Children* 1 (Winter 1967): 5.

reports an analysis made by Golden Press of their own previously published books to see where they might have naturally included black characters, such as in scenes of downtown Chicago or in professional football. They acknowledged that they had missed many such opportunities.[4] The editor of Hastings House recalls that an author was asked to change the race of characters in a particular book because the publisher feared that the presence of black characters might hurt sales.[5] Such fears have not been without justification. Larrick relates an experience of the Albert Whitman Company:

> Carolin Rubin, editor of Albert Whitman, tells of three books brought out in the 1950's: *Denny's Story,* by Eunice Smith, which shows Negro children in illustrations of classroom activity; *Fun for Chris,* by Blossom Randall, with Negro and white children playing together; and *Nemo Meets the Emperor,* by Laura Bannon, a true story of Ethiopia. "The books won favorable comment," writes Mrs. Rubin, "but the effect on sales was negative. Customers returned not only these titles but all stock from our company. This meant an appreciable loss and tempered attitudes toward further use of Negro children in illustrations and text."[6]

By 1963, however, interracial books that had received an initially negative reception in the South enjoyed improved sales when reviews were favorable.[7] Certainly, this seems to indicate the general direction of change as far as both publishers' attitudes and public sentiment are concerned. A well-known writer notes that a publisher eager for her books once rejected three because they dealt with controversial racial topics. She now believes that the lack of interracial books is due to the fact that not enough manuscripts of publishable quality are submitted.[8] Jean Karl, an editor who has published several notable books with black characters, and Joan Lexau, who has recently written four interracial books, express a similar opinion.[9] There was an average of eleven interracial books published per year from 1951 through 1963 and an average of forty-one a year from 1964 through 1967.

Although the changing sentiments of publishers and the general public have become increasingly favorable to the publication and recep-

4. Larrick, "The All-White World of Children's Books," p. 84.
5. Jean Poindexter Colby, "How to Present the Negro in Children's Books," *Top of the News* 21 (April 1965): 193.
6. Larrick, "The All-White World of Children's Books," p. 65.
7. *Ibid.,* p. 84.
8. "A Letter to the Council from Phyllis A. Whitney," *Interracial Books for Children* 1 (Summer 1966): 5.
9. Jean Karl, "An Editor's Point of View: Enough for All," *ibid.,* pp. 1, 7; Joan M. Lexau, "What Other People are Thinking," *ibid.,* No. 2-3, p. 8.

tion of interracial books, there are still problems involved in connecting prospective purchasers and readers with the kinds of books they want.

the role of book reviewers

Because many reviewers fail to note the race of characters in their reviews, it is now more often the book reviewer who stands between the publisher and the public. Two of the three reviews of Ezra Jack Keats' book, *The Snowy Day,* included in *Book Review Digest,* illustrate this point.

> . . . story of three- or four-year old boy, who wakes to the miracle of a snowy day, goes out to play, makes a snowman, tries to bring in a snow-ball, loses it, . . . goes to sleep in sorrow, and wakes to the joy of another snowy day. (*Sat. R.*)

> Part water-color, part collage, the sensitive, spacious pictures have rare mood and beauty. A new author-artist to watch. E. M. Graves. *Commonweal* 77:205 (N 16 '62) 30W.

> It is refreshing to have a natural story in which only the illustrations show that Peter is a Negro child. Recommended with enthusiasm. M. B. Bell.[10]

As Augusta Baker points out, at a time when buyers are diligently searching for books portraying minority group members, it is a disser-vice to overlook race in reviews, even if race is not an issue in the plot.[11]

Traditionally, most writers, publishers, and critics have been in-clined to think in terms of an all-white world, and this has been the world they let children see. Now, faced with a somewhat different view of the world, they must decide what perceptions of a multi-ethnic world are acceptable to themselves and to their public. As Otto Klineberg has so aptly put it, we are used to indirectly teaching children that "Life is Fun in a Smiling, Fair-Skinned World,"[12] and it is apparently difficult to resist applying at least part of this ideal to the interracial book, there-by creating, as Larrick notes, plots for Negro boys and girls that are too gentle and unrealistic.[13]

The following excerpts from reviews and annotations illustrate the dilemma of reviewers and writers, as they subjectively perceive a multi-

---

10. *Book Review Digest,* 1963, p. 549.
11. George Woods, "To Mississippi in the Interests of Children and Books," *Wilson Library Bulletin* 41 (June, 1967): 1030.
12. Otto Klineberg, *Saturday Review* 46 (February 16, 1963): 75-77, 87.
13. Larrick, "The All-White World of Children's Books," p. 64.

ethnic world in life and in books. One reviewer notes that "except for a complete absence of violence,"[14] one interracial book is realistic. Another reviewer lauds an "unstated approach . . . to race relations" as sound.[15] A third says "that a book for teenage boys . . . is no place for a glib treatment of a highly complex problem."[16] It is apparent that some reviewers criticize as unrealistic interracial books that fail to deal with racial problems. Others fault books with racial problems and laud those that ignore race but are "interracial."

Perhaps a better way of pointing out the dilemma inherent in book reviews in the sensitive area of race relations is to compare different reviews of a single book. The following excerpts are from *Book Review Digest:*

> Baum, Betty, *A New Home for Theresa.* il. by James Barkley. . . .

> The story of a young black girl, orphaned in Harlem, then placed in a foster home—a beautiful, clean, airy, but to Theresa, frightening place [in an integrated development in Queens]. Adapting, Theresa learns to love her foster parents [the Chintons], her new schoolmates (black and white), and her new life.   (*N.Y. Times Bk. R.*)

> The Chintons' discussions, the attitudes of the teachers and the children in the new school, the advice of the social worker who placed Theresa: all these begin to change her. When the long-building confrontation between the black and white pupils erupts, Theresa is strong enough to act as a leader. The variety and challenge of Theresa's life come through clearly in both the text and the many illustrations. A book well worth reading and then discussing in the middle grades.   J. H. Clarke.

> A sympathetic story which conveys sentiments and moods in the Afro-American population. . . . [Theresa] wants to please [her foster parents], but finds herself torn between her foster mother's determination to resist social integration and her foster father's desire for peaceful mixing with all the neighbors in their housing project. The book's message is unity, hammered home as good whites and good blacks join forces . . . Although marred by some ridiculous lines . . . this message book about the problems connected with integration is an equally valid depiction of the predicament of any girl who has been transplanted from familiar surroundings and is trying to make new friends and learn new ways. Madalynne Schoenfeld.

> Fine things are in this book. That a ghetto child can't believe black people own anything beautiful is heartbreaking, and true. Mrs. Baum reveals Theresa's fears and insecurities to readers, and then lays them to

---

14. *Virginia Kirkus' Service, Inc.* 32 (July 15, 1964).
15. *Ibid.*, 33 (February 15, 1965).
16. Robert Daley, "Hard to Tackle," *New York Times* (November 18, 1956), p. 30.

rest with skill. The portrait of Theresa's foster mother shows added inspiration: a frightened black, proud but timid, whose final awareness of the need to be more trusting of all people is wonderfully written. Unfortunately, the rest of the book isn't. Mrs. Baum has Theresa recall and use Martin Luther King's methods of nonviolence to put down a school bully and his white gang. It isn't believable. And she is unable to characterize members of a large cast as individuals, which may cause confusion.   John Neufeld. (*N.Y. Times Bk. R.*)[17]

If the varied perspectives of book reviewers create one kind of problem for the prospective book buyer, no reviews at all create an entirely different set of problems. With so many children's books published annually, the reader or book buyer is increasingly at the mercy of those who decide which books shall even *be* reviewed. More than one-third of the books concerning Negroes published between 1962 and 1964 were either negatively reviewed or not reviewed at all.[18] One researcher notes that one-fourth of all children's books receive no reviews.[19]

An analysis of books not reviewed in the aforementioned major publications indicated that the lack of a review did not necessarily mean that a book lacked value. For example, Helen Wells' *Escape by Night*, and Hagler's book, *Larry and the Freedom Man*, were not reviewed by those periodicals and are now out of print.[20] Until 1969 no other children's interracial books dealt with blacks' involvement in the Underground Railroad or the story of slavery with the slave emerging as a full-bodied character. Both books were overlooked by all the journals covered by *Book Review Digest*.

the role of sales

Other books, even though reviewed and often reviewed favorably, were out-of-print and out of sight in 1967. This author's research shows that over a third of the interracial fiction published between 1951-1963 was out-of-print by 1967; about half of these had been reviewed. Why should Hunt's *Ladycake Farm*, a 1952 farm story of a black family meet-

---

17. *Book Review Digest, 1969* 65: 24.
18. Larrick, "The All-White World of Children's Books," p. 64.
19. Mabel Louise Galloway, "The Extent and Nature of Reviews of Juveniles in Eight Journals and Newspapers," as reported in *Dissertation Abstracts* 19: 2679.
20. Helen Wells, *Escape by Night* (New York: John O. Winston, Co., 1953), (out-of-print); Margaret Hagler, *Larry and the Freedom Man,* illus. by Harold Berson (New York: Lothrop, Lee, and Shepard Co., Inc., 1959), (out-of-print).

ing racial hatred by grinning until their tormenters tire, be in print to-day?[21] And why should *Kenny,* a sensitive 1957 story about the black author-artist, E. Harper Johnson, which relates the initial reluctance of a black American engineer's son to associate with the African boys his age when his father takes a foreign job, be out-of-print although it received as many favorable reviews as *Ladycake Farm?*[22] Certainly Kenny's discovery of the bonds that unites people of different cultures is a more relevant book for today's youngsters.

Dorothy Sterling, in reference to her biography of Robert Smalls, wonders why her story of this heroic black sold so poorly in comparison with her other publications on less vital subjects.[23]

> Although reviewers seemed to find it well-written and researched, only 11,255 copies of it have been sold in 8 1/2 years. In the first six months of 1966, when the Education Act provided funds for school librar-ies, it sold 926 copies. During the same six months, a book I wrote on mosses, ferns, and mushrooms sold more than 3,000 copies. Can we per-mit our children to grow up knowing more about mushrooms than they do about their fellow Americans?[24]

There is some indication that we are beginning to think that it is im-portant for our children to learn not only about mushrooms but also about their fellow Americans. A few interracial books out-of-print in 1967 are now being reprinted either by their original publishers, by pa-perback companies, or by one of the reprint companies.[25] One of these is *Masquerade,* the story of a girl who passes for white. Another, *Banners at Shenandoah,* concerns a Union soldier spying behind Confederate lines who is aided by freedmen and black Underground Railroad con-ductors. Sterne's story based on an actual slave revolt of the Middle Passage, *The Long Black Schooner: The Voyage of the Amistad,* is the third.

---

21. Mabel Leigh Hunt, *Ladycake Farm,* illus. by Clothilde Embree Funk (Philadelphia: J. B. Lippincott Company, 1952).
22. E. Harper Johnson, *Kenny,* illus. by the author (New York: Henry Holt and Company, 1957).
23. Dorothy Sterling, *Robert Smalls, Captain of the Planter* (New York: Dou-bleday & Co., Inc., 1958).
24. Sterling, "Negroes and the Truth Gap," p. 4.
25. Dorothy Gilman Butters, *Masquerade* (Philadelphia: Macraw Smith Co., 1961), (out-of-print, republished 1967); Bruce Catton, *Banners at Shen-andoah* (New York: Doubleday & Co., Inc., 1955), (out-of-print, reprinted in paper by Bantam Press, 1965); Emme Sterne, *The Long Black Schoo-ner: The Voyage of the Amistad,* illus. by Earl H. Pringle (New York: Al-laddin, 1953), (out-of-print, available American Publishers, since going out-of-print).

But other good books are still out-of-print. Among them, for example are Steinman's book of black involvement on the Underground Railroad and Weiss' pleasant story of interracial friendships.[26]

the role of library selection tools

Many other factors, in addition to a book's being in print, either enable or limit book purchasers in their search for the kind of books they want. A book's success often depends on whether or not it is included in such standard library references as *Children's Catalog, A Basic Book Collection for Elementary Grades, A Basic Book Collection for Junior High Schools, Subject Index to Books for Primary Grades,* and *Subject Index to Books for Intermediate Grades.*[27] These reference books play a critical role in book selection. The author of a 1965 dissertation on "Minority Americans in Children's Literature" surveyed all the current editions of the above catalogs plus their annual supplements in order to find fiction published between 1945 and 1964 which portrayed contemporary American blacks and other minority group members. He found *sixteen* books about blacks and most of these were about teenagers.[28]

Even if the recommended books in library references were adequate, one wonders if libraries would purchase an adequate number of interracial books. An American Library Association publication has deplored the tendency of libraries to stock their shelves in the fashion of

26. Beatrice M. Steinman, *This Railroad Disappears*, illus. by Douglas Gorsline (New York: Franklin Watts, Inc., 1958), (out-of-print); Harvey Weiss, *Paul's Horse Herman*, illus. by the author (New York: G. P. Putnam's Sons, 1958), (out-of-print).
27. Mary K. Eakin, comp., *Subject Index to Books for Intermediate Grades*, 3rd ed. (Chicago: American Library Association, 1963); Mary K. Eakin and Eleanor Merritt, comps., *Subject Index to Books for Primary Grades*, 3rd ed. (Chicago: American Library Association, 1967); Miriam Snow Mathes, ed., *A Basic Book Collection for Elementary Grades*, 7th ed. (Chicago: American Library Association, 1960); Eloise Rue, comp., *Subject Index to Books for Intermediate Grades*, 2d ed. (Chicago: American Library Association, 1963); Margaret V. Spengler, ed., *A Basic Book Collection for Junior High Schools*, 10th ed. (Chicago: American Library Association, 1960); Dorothy Herbert West and Rachel Shor and Estelle A. Fidell, eds., *Children's Catalog*, 10th ed. (New York: The H. W. Wilson Company, 1966; supplements 1967-70); Rachel Shor and Estelle A. Fidell, *Junior High School Library Catalog*, 2nd ed. (New York: H. W. Wilson Co., 1970).
28. David K. Gast, "Minority Americans in Children's Literature," *Elementary English* 44 (January 1967): 12-23.

supermarkets: token selections for the special groups while the bulk of their selections is for the average American. The American Library Association has urged libraries to analyze their own clientele and then select books specifically for them,[29] but unless the standard reference works begin to publish special supplements listing books for special groups it will remain difficult to locate enough appropriate books.

the role of teachers' selection tools

Teachers as well as librarians have a tremendous impact on whether interracial books become available to children. Elementary teachers, many of whom are required to take Children's Literature, will frequently use texts, such as those of Arbuthnot, and Huck and Young. Arbuthnot's 1964 edition lists only thirty books pertaining to the American black in addition to referring to Augusta Baker's excellent but now out-of-print bibliography of *Books About Negro Life for Children*.[30] Only seven of the books Arbuthnot cited, however, were published after 1950. Huck and Young's 1968 text includes about the same number, but most of the books are newer and more deal with the realities of discrimination.[31] Although there is an appendix listing other bibliographies appropriate for finding books about the black and other minorities, some of the already meager number of books of fiction are recommended with reservations. The burden is again, therefore, upon the teacher or librarian to search for more interracial books.

special bibliographies

A number of specialized booklists have been compiled in order to supplement the standard library reference lists. Each fall, the District of Columbia school system circulates "Recent Books of Significance for Human Relations and Cultural Appreciations," a mimeographed list, to its libraries.[32] In 1966, when black pupil enrollment exceeded 90 percent,

29. Charles Morgan, Jr., "The Freedom to Read and Racial Problems," *Freedom of Inquiry: Supporting the Library Bill of Rights* (Chicago: American Library Association, Conference on Intellectual Freedom, 1965), p. 32.
30. May Hill Arbuthnot, *Children and Books* (Glenview, Ill.: Scott, Foresman and Company, 1964).
31. Charlotte S. Huck and Doris A. Young, *Children's Literature in the Elementary School* (New York: Holt, Rinehart and Winston, 1968).
32. Department of Library Science, Public Schools of the District of Columbia, "Booklist II," September 19, 1966. (Mimeographed).

this list of fifty-four titles contained only twenty-eight books about black people. Eleven of the fifteen books of fiction included in this number that were about American blacks were nonracial problem books; the remaining twenty-six titles concerned other minorities, handicapped children, a "bird born without wings," and stories set in foreign lands. If predominantly black schools overlook so many good books with or without racial problems how much attention would these books get in schools elsewhere? There still seems to be a problem of being either unable or else unwilling to find sufficient numbers and kinds of interracial books.

An Office of Economic Opportunity booklet includes forty-four books about blacks out of approximately 1,000 titles that are recommended. The annotations of Keats' Whistle for Willie, "Tender story about a little boy who learns to whistle," and Faulkner's Melindy's Medal, "Enjoying the bright roominess of the new apartment in the housing project and winning a medal at school makes Melindy's eighth year especially happy," illustrate the color-blind approach often used.[33] Furthermore, many of the already limited selections were by this time passé.

While not all young disadvantaged readers are black, a sizeable percentage are. The rationale implicit in many of these bibliographies, both for blacks and for a more inclusive group of disadvantaged youngsters, is that learning about the unique characteristics and problems of other people, or even animals, enables a child to understand and cope with prejudice.*

Unfortunately, the problems of race are sufficiently unique and psychologically devastating that the "animal or strange-people" approach is inadequate. Part of the reason for both the color-blind reviews and this oblique approach to prejudice is our nation's discomfort over proof of prejudice.

Some bibliographies deal exclusively with books about black people.** One very subjective bibliography lists only eighty-five titles of fiction and nonfiction, with annotations that are often distorted. The author attributes a prejudiced remark made by one of the characters in Baum's

33. Children's Services Division of the American Library Association, Selected Lists of Children's Books and Recordings (Washington, D.C.: Office of Economic Opportunity, 1966), pp. 3, 24.

*Huck and Young's 1961 edition of Children's Literature in the Elementary School includes the story of a spotted and a white rabbit who encounter prejudice and a a furry elephant who achieves acceptance among a herd of mammoths in their section "Books Help Children Accept Differences: Differences in Racial Background" on pp. 259-60. These items were fortunately dropped from the 1968 edition.

**An annotated bibliography of bibliographies pertinent to interracial books will follow this chapter.

book, *Patricia Crosses Town,* to the author.[34] "Chapter six has reference to 'all of them are good at that'—meaning cleaning and implying that this is the type of work Negro mothers do."[35] However, the statement occurs in chapter ten as part of the dialog of one of the mean white children that Pat overhears in her new school; Pat's teacher, several classmates, and the author concur in their disapproval of the remark.[36] On the same page, this bibliographer lauds Cobb's *Swimming Pool,* a pallid story of prejudiced children resolving their differences,[37] even though many of the characters in this book had spoken of "niggers and kikes."[38] Throughout this bibliography, the editor reflects a distaste for books dealing with poverty.

Three bibliographies published in 1967 do much better.[39] *Bibliography of Materials By and About Negro Americans for Young Readers,* a U.S. Office of Education research contract, contains sixty-three titles of fiction and 311 of nonfiction.* An NAACP booklet is devoted primarily to textbooks but includes about eighty interracial storybooks as well, with many of these quite recent. Another outstanding bibliography, *We Build Together,* provides a balanced overview, listing about 250 titles of various types of books and, in addition, reviewing the interesting history of the black in children's books.

No bibliographies, however, can keep current unless they are re-edited annually. Because of the recent growth in the numbers and kinds of interracial books, current information is especially desirable. Since bibliographies are generally selective—with no information on which

---

34. Dharathula H. Millender, *Real Negroes, Honest Settings, Children's and Young People's Books About Negro Life and History* (Chicago: American Federation of Teachers, AFL-CIO, 1967), p. 27. (Hereinafter referred to as *Real Negroes*).
35. *Ibid.*
36. Betty Baum, *Patricia Crosses Town,* illus. by Nancy Grossman (New York: Alfred A. Knopf, 1965), p. 110.
37. Millender, *Real Negroes,* p. 27.
38. Alice Cobb, *Swimming Pool,* illus. by Joseph Escourido (New York: Friendship Press, 1957).
39. Office of Education, Bureau of Research, *Bibliography of Materials By and About Negro Americans for Young Readers* (Atlanta, Georgia: Atlanta University, 1967); NAACP Education Department, *Integrated School Books: A Descriptive Bibliography of 399 Pre-School and Elementary School Texts and Story Books* (New York: NAACP, 1967); and Charlemae Rollins, ed., *We Build Together* (Champaign, Ill.: National Council of Teachers of English, 1967).

*The title of the bibliography is somewhat misleading because the books do not all have black authors.

books were rejected rather than overlooked—even annual supplements would shed light on only those books about the black which fit the editor's particular perception of life. Two possible solutions would be annual, unselective, annotated bibliographies, more comprehensive supplemental bibliographies by the major library reference publishers, or centers where all of the pertinent books are made available so that the selector or buyer could knowingly pick what he wants from the total available supply.

A Bibliography of Bibliographies

(A list of bibliographies of interracial books, books by and about Negroes, and related topics of interest)

American Association of School Librarian's Committee on Treatment of Minorties in Library Books and Other Instructional Materials in *School Libraries* 19 (Winter 1970): 49-57.

American Friends Service Committee. *Books are Bridges.* New York: Anti-Defamation League of B'nai B'rith, 1957. Entries are annotated, classified by subjects, priced and assigned to age levels. Books about various groups that stress likenesses with high literary qualities are chosen.

Baker, Augusta. *Books About Negro Life for Children.* New York: New York Public Library. Revised edition, 1966.

Bibliographic Survey: The Negro in Print. Washington, D.C.: Negro Bibliographic and Research Center, quarterly. Four or five pages devoted to "Young Readers." Other minority groups also included.

Chapman, Abraham. *The Negro in American Literature and a Bibliography of Literature By and About Negro Americans.* Stevens Point, Wisc.: Wisconsin State University, Wisconsin Council of Teachers of English, 1966. A comprehensive bibliography, without annotations, of literary work by Negroes.

Children's Services Division of the American Library Association. *Selected Lists of Children's Books and Recordings.* Washington, D.C.: Office of Economic Opportunity, 1966.

Crosby, Muriel. *Reading Ladders for Human Relations.* Washington, D.C.: American Council on Education, 1963. Available in paperback also. Books are chosen for five reading levels under six problem areas, Over 600 books are annotated.

Denby, Robert V. "Literature By and About Negroes for the Elementary Level." *Elementary English* 46 (1969): 909-13.

Glancy, Barbara. *Children's Interracial Fiction.* Washington, D.C.: American Federation of Teachers, 1969. An unselective annotated bibliography of interracial fiction published from 1951 through 1967, arranged alphabetically by author, reading levels, and interest ages. Also includes a reprint of author's article on uses of interracial fiction to heighten elementary students' awareness of current state of race relations.

Grambs, Jean. *Intergroup Education: Methods and Materials.* Englewood Cliffs, N.J.: Prentice-Hall, Inc., 1968. Discussions of kinds of materials and ways to use them for intergroup education with exhaustive bibliographies for each kind of material.

Interracial Books for Children. Quarterly published by The Council on Interracial Books for Children, Inc. New York: 9 E. 405th Street. Excellent articles by authors, publishers, illustrators in this field.

Jasik, Marilyn. "A Look at Black Faces in Children's Picture Books." *Young Children* 34 (October, 1968): 43-54. A review of the picture books published in 1966-67.

Joint Committee of the American Library Association. Children's Services Division and the African-American Institute. *Africa: An Annotated List of Printed Materials Suitable for Children.* New York: UNICEF, Information Center on Children's Culture, United States Committee on UNICEF, 1968. Annotated bibliography, especially useful because of the international scope of the selection committee.

Kircher, Clara J. *Behavior Patterns in Children's Books.* Washington, D.C.: Catholic University of America Press, 1966. Five hundred and seven annotations of books dealing with twenty-four behavior problem categories with information on characters' race provided.

Koblitz, Minnie W. *The Negro in Schoolroom Literature, Resource Materials for the Teacher of Kindergarten Through Sixth Grade.* New York: Center for Urban Education, 33 W. 42nd Street, 1966.

Morris, Effie Lee. "Blowing in the Wind." *Library Journal* 94 (March 11, 1969): 1298-1300. List of about one hundred books in human relations area.

National Association for the Advancement of Colored People. New York: NAACP, 1967. *Integrated School Books: A Descriptive Bibliography of 399 Pre-School and Elementary School Texts and Story Books.* Primarily devoted to multi-ethnic textbooks by subject area, a great many interracial trade books are also annotated for the reader.

Office of Adult Services, eds. *The Negro in the United States: A List of Significant Books,* 9th ed. rev. New York: The New York City Public Library, 1965. A periodically revised list of books considered of value by a committee of librarians of the New York Library System. Periodically updated. Also available are separate bibliographies of books on Africa.

Office of Education, Bureau of Research. *Bibliography of Materials By and About Negro Americans for Young Readers.* Atlanta, Ga.: Atlanta University, 1967.

Professional Rights and Responsibilities Committee. *A Bibliography of Multi-Ethnic Textbooks and Supplementary Materials.* Washington, D.C.: National Education Association, n.d. Brief listing of integrated texts, films, etc., by subject areas.

————. *An Index to Multi-Ethnic Teaching Materials and Teacher Resources.* Washington, D.C.: National Education Association, 1967. Supplement to *A Bibliography* . . . prepared after two additional years. Lists primarily other sources of information for teachers on multi-ethnic materials.

————. *The American Negro in Paperback.* Washington, D.C.: National Education Association, 1967. Annotated list of various books arranged by author with recommended reading levels. No attempt to be exhaustive.

Rollins, Charlemae. *We Build Together*. Champaign, Ill.: National Council of Teachers of English, 1967. Excellent bibliography of fiction and non-fiction—annotated under subject and literary types with recommended grade levels. Also included is an excellent historical review of children's interracial books. Approximately 300 titles included in this selective list.

Watt, Lois B. *Literature for Disadvantaged Children, A Bibliography*. Washington, D.C.: Office of Education, U.S. Department of Health, Education and Welfare, 1968. A lengthy collection of titles arranged under categories that seem arbitrary. A variety of topics with a small list devoted to black Americans often without reference to the fact that the book is interracial.

CHAPTER 4

"Dick and Jane" Go Slumming: Instructional Materials for the Inner-City Negro Child

Jean Dresden Grambs

introduction

A classroom without textbooks is as inconceivable—to most Americans—as a classroom without walls. There are some rumblings among teachers, curriculum specialists, and media producers suggesting that textbooks are not the most appropriate sources for learning, but incursions on the domain of the textbook are sporadic, experimental, expensive, and speculative. For some years to come, we would predict, the textbook will reign supreme as the organizing base for most elementary and secondary instructional activities.

The general role of the textbook in the evolution of American education was explored in chapter one. Textbooks, as a major source of instructional content, have particular importance when one considers the impact of such sources on the understanding of the black experience in America. In a later section of this volume (chapters five and seven), several studies are reported regarding the black-related content in texts for secondary school use. In this chapter, Jean D. Grambs is concerned

---

*An earlier version of this chapter appears in A. Henry Passow, ed., *Reaching the Disadvantaged Learner* (New York: Teachers College Press, 1970), titled "Instructional Materials for the Disadvantaged Child," pp. 167-182.

with what the elementary school child learns from textbooks about the black minority and the realities of inner-city life.

Not so very long ago, a number of compelling attacks were launched on the vapid world of the elementary school textbook: the one in the "grey-flannel cover" that prepared students to conform to the world of suburbia.[1] It was a world where everything was fun and games, where babies were born though no woman was ever pregnant, where the worst that could happen was that the dog fell into the backyard dishpan, and where, of course, everyone was white.[2] These books evaded the issue of the elimination of some six million Jews under Hitler and delicately handled the problem of the black in America by omitting any mention of his troublesome presence after the "War Between the States."[3] As far as texts for elementary school children were concerned, religion was a nice thing for everyone to acquire, provided that this was accomplished in a white-steepled "Christmas-card" church on a snowy New England hill, denomination unidentified.[4]

For similar reasons, the illustrations of elementary school readers and other elementary textbooks in social studies, science, spelling, and arithmetic were enlivened by white Anglo-Saxon children, their parents, and their pets. No dark-skinned person intruded upon these pages unless he was a foreigner or in his own foreign country. The few blacks who appeared in textbook illustrations, and then only in social studies books, were Pullman porters, distant figures picking cotton, or occasionally, George Washington Carver, Booker T. Washington, and in more recent books, maybe Marion Anderson, Ralph Bunche, or Jackie Robinson.

These now familiar criticisms of the school textbook had some minor impact upon textbook publishers. The more gross stereotypes disappeared after the textbook study of the American Council on Education.[5]

---

1. Albert Alexander, "The Grey Flannel Cover on the American History Textbook," *Social Education* 24 (January, 1960).
2. Abraham Tannenbaum, "Family Living in Textbook Town," *Progressive Education* 13 (March, 1954): 133-41; Jason Epstein, " 'Good Bunnies Always Obey'; Books for American Children," *Commentary* 32 (February, 1963): 112-22.
3. Lloyd Marcus, *The Treatment of Minorities in Secondary School Textbooks* (New York: Anti-Defamation League of B'nai B'rith, 1961).
4. Judah Harris, *The Treatment of Religion in Elementary School Social Studies Textbooks* (New York: Anti-Defamation League of B'nai B'rith, 1963).
5. Howard Wilson, *Intergroup Relations in Teaching Materials* (Washington, D.C.: American Council on Education, 1950).

Since then, another factor, which has had a very significant impact upon textbooks, has been added: Blacks are now serving on the textbook selection committees in major metropolitan areas, and most black children are now going to school in these areas. These facts regarding educational reality finally came home to textbook publishers in the early 1960's. Until this time, the critics were rather like Don Quixote breaking his lance against a windmill. However, despite some change, recent reports about textbooks still identify oversimplifications, distortions, and omissions.[6*]

Nevertheless, the picture has literally been "colored" in. Today's text, even in such neutral subjects as arithmetic, spelling, and science, has its share of so-called "integrated" pictures. A recent bibliography published by the National Education Association lists an extensive variety of "integrated" textbooks.[7]

the coming of the "integrated" textbook

The development of integrated textbooks is of some interest. The earliest major breakthrough appears to have come with the reading series prepared and published by the Follett Publishing Company for use in the Detroit schools. It has been reported that the original pictures for the series showed some typical city backgrounds, crowded streets, tenements, not very elegant interiors, and so forth. However, on the advice of Negro educators reviewing the books, these backgrounds were eliminated lest it appear that when blacks were in a picture they were to be seen only in slum surroundings.[8] As a result of this recommendation, the published books now show children playing on streets without houses or other background, standing inside rooms with no visible walls or furniture, and sitting on steps that lead nowhere. Except for the fact that some of the children have light brown faces and others have white faces, it's now simply integrated fun and games. It was noted in the hearings be-

6. Lerone Bennet, "Reading, 'Riting and Racism: The Negro in Textbooks," *Ebony,* March 1967, pp. 130-38; R. A. Billington, "Bias in History Textbooks," *Saturday Review,* January 15, 1966.

7. *An Index of Multi-Ethnic Textbooks and Teacher Resources* (Washington, D.C.: National Education Association, 1967).

8. City Schools Reading Program (New York: Follett Co., Publishers, 1966).

*For a complete bibliography of studies of textbook content see: Barbara Finkelstein, Loretta Golden, and Jean D. Grambs, "A Bibliography of Research and Commentary on Textbooks and Related Works," *Social Education* 33 (March, 1969): 311-336. A shorter and revised version of this bibliography also appears on page 177 of this book.

fore the House of Representatives Committee on Education that the Detroit readers seemed to be "painting white faces black."[9]

The innovation of the Detroit readers was so popular—or potentially so—that other major publishers amended revisions of elementary school textbooks so that they, too, could have a piece of the urban school market. An interesting thing happened: two social studies series came on the market almost simultaneously with parallel special editions designated by a star in one case, by a diamond in the other. An examination of thees volumes showed that the star or diamond indicated a book that had Negro faces in some pictures. Aside from this difference, the contents of both the books and the teacher's manuals were completely unchanged.[10] The publishers were undoubtedly trying to have the best of both possible worlds: secure sales in the unreconstructed Southern and lily-white suburban areas and entry into the urban systems with their multi-racial selection committees. Irritation with this procedure prompted several systems to protest, either by stating that only genuinely integrated materials would be acceptable,[11] or by promoting the writing of their own materials.[12]

The elementary child, long considered a delicate and sensitive creature, is now apt to find in his newest textbooks in almost all subjects scattered pictures of Negro children or adults. Because it does take time for textbooks to wear out, it is likely that most children for some years to come will not be so confronted. But the charge of all-white textbooks can no longer be made. Most of the major publishing firms within the last few years have announced that they will not produce nonintegrated materials for national distribution. However, "special" editions of standard textbooks continue to be published in order to meet the demands of such big-sale states as Texas, which still (in 1966) wanted all-white books.

It may surprise the average reader to realize that publishers have tailored their materials to meet varying regional eccentricities in a way

---

9. *Books for Schools and the Treatment of Minorities*, U.S., Congress, House Hearings before the Ad Hoc subcommittee on De Facto School Segregation of the Committee on Education and Labor, 89th Cong., 2d Sess., August 23-September 1, 1966.

10. Social Studies Series, Elementary Grades (Star Series) (New York: Follett Co., Publishers, 1965); Social Studies Series, Elementary Grades (Diamond Series) (Glenview, Ill.: Scott Foresman & Co., 1965).

11. Michigan Department of Public Instruction, *The Treatment of Minority Groups in Textbooks* (Lansing, Mich.; Michigan Department of Public Instruction, 1965).

12. New York City Board of Education, *Call Them Heroes* (Morristown, N.J.: Silver Burdett Co., 1965).

that appears to border on the fraudulent.[13] According to Jack Abromowitz, in a recent article in *Social Education,* the tailoring of materials "is, of course, a shady part of the publishing business and companies involved in the practice are unwilling to carry the full burden of blame. They tend to stress that they are only meeting the requirements of the districts they service, and there is probably a measure of justification in that claim."[14]

In order to determine the extent to which companies were continuing the publication of "star" editions, Abromowitz queried thirty-one leading publishers in 1968. Seven of the twenty-seven companies that replied stated that they had issued "star" editions of texts in preceding years, and two stated that they were still doing so. However, the practice was to be phased out as contracts for the purchase of such books were completed. The letters received by Abromowitz indicate that the publishers agreed generally that "star" editions were undesirable and that publishing policy would no longer support such practices. Most children, then, in the years to come will be exposed to "integrated" materials. Meanwhile, it is important to consider the effect upon children of being exposed to inadequate materials.

evaluating textbook impact

Implicit so far is that reading, whether in trade books or textbooks, does have an impact on children. Research supporting this contention is very limited. The classic study by Trager and Yarrow[15] is one of the few in which researchers explicitly attempted to see if the content of what was read to young children would really affect their out-of-class behavior. The study did, in fact, show this to be true. The children who were read *Little Black Sambo* proceeded to play-act the story in the school yard with black peers as the targets of derisive chants; the children who were read a specially developed story about a Negro boy, his dog and his friend, were interested in the way the story developed, and did not show any adverse changes in their playground behavior.

13. William W. Joyce, "Minority Groups in American Society: Imperatives for Educators," *Social Education* 33 (April, 1969): 429-33; Mark M. Krug, "Freedom and Racial Equality: A Study of 'Revised' High School History Texts," *School Review* 78 (March, 1970): 300.
14. Jack Abromowitz, "Textbooks and Negro History," *Social Education* 33 (March, 1969): 306-09.
15. Ruth Trager and Margaret Radke-Yarrow, *They Learn What They Live* (New York: Harper & Row, Publishers, 1942).

Few studies of text content show *how* the content makes a difference in children's responses. Everyone seems to assume that children do learn more from a reading textbook than just recognizing new words; some meaning is conveyed. And certainly the lessons of civic and national pride are closely guarded in the books that discuss American history and social life. Yet few researchers have actually told us much that is reliable about the impact of instructional materials on children. Most of what is stated is based on inference and logic. The study, described following, is one of many (and one of the best) which views with horror the assumed evil that biased instructional materials have on children.

In an intensive study of the impact of school experiences upon inner-city school children, Eleanor Burke Leacock found that there were serious distortions and omissions in the books used in the schools studied. Of twenty-three social studies texts, (circa 1961) used in three all-black schools, only one mentioned Africans as early settlers of the new America, though ironically the same text is quoted as saying, " 'they [the early settlers] all had much the same experience.' "[16] Dr. Leacock points out the vast difference between the life situations of the "Dick and Jane" books with that of the inner-city child:

> Instead of a house set in a lawn, studded with trees and bushes, the children lived in apartment houses or city projects. In the housing projects there was chained-off greenery; around the apartment houses there was no greenery but an occasional tree. In place of the neat and inevitable three-child family, three-quarters of the children [in the study schools] had three or more siblings, and one-third had uncles, aunts, grandparents, or boarders included in the household. Much has been written about the role of the mother as the sole parents in the Negro family, *yet this was not the main point of difference in this relatively stable working-class neighborhood* [italics in original]. Four out of every five children interviewed in the study were living with both their mothers and fathers.[17]

The books portrayed, however, life styles suitable only for suburban living; even the games played by the children in the "Dick and Jane" readers would be unfamiliar to the inner-city child. This lack of congruence with the lives of the inner-city child serves to "reinforce the distance from life, not only for black children, but for most working-class children as well."[18]

---

16. Eleanor B. Leacock, *Teaching and Learning in City Schools* (New York: Basic Books, Inc., 1969. pp. 76-77.)
17. *Ibid.*, pp. 78-79.
18. *Ibid.*, p. 79.

Dr. Leacock continues in her criticism of the instructional materials supplied:

> Thus the content of school readers can utterly devalue the experiences of Negro and working-class children by erasing them from the world; it poses the problem that in order to accept formal educational goals that involve mastering such material, they must devalue themselves. Further, this is often seen by teachers as the conscious intent of such materials. When asked about the failure of school texts to portray anything familiar to the children in the all-Negro low-income school, the second-grade teacher responded that the children's backgrounds were "so limited that there's very little that you can base a reader on." She felt the content of readers to be good, because "it enriches their experiences to read these things and talk about them. Maybe it will give them a few ideas on how they would like to live when they grow older."[19]

The teacher felt that it was desirable for these children to read about the " 'lovely toys, and mother is so sweet, and they have a dog and a cat, and go shopping.' " Yet, as the researcher comments, "these were children . . . who from grade to grade fell increasingly behind in their reading achievement."[20]

The final indictment of the instructional materials used in the schools is one with very significant implications for all:

> The denial of their very existence must impede school learning for Negro and working-class children, but what kind of learning is engendered in middle-class white children when it is coupled with extreme depersonalization? The pernicious and undermining effect on dark-skinned children of a history presented as shaped by white people alone and an environment in which only blond people exist has been pointed out. Less often is it suggested that the presentation of such an illusory world also creates problems for the healthy development of white children. One need but consider the near-psychotic reactions of white adults who are deeply committed to the myth of their superiority when it is shaken and remember the German Nazis and their insane attempt to preserve an illusory world. Here the valuing of one's individual self is even less assured than is suggested by psychologists for burdened Negro children in a white-dominated world.[21]

The depths of insensitivity to black children, and the stereotyped reactions of white children to both color and social class is amply documented by Alice Miel. Both elementary students and teachers were able to give the "right" answers regarding their own perceptions of minority groups. However, the research and interview data showed that, in fact,

---

19. *Ibid.*, p. 80.
20. *Ibid.*
21. *Ibid.*, p. 81.

black children were not welcomed in the school, and that children had stereotyped views of the behavior of black children. Teachers on the whole showed little awareness of the black students around them. The white children assigned poverty roles exclusively to black students and rejected the idea that whites could be poor.

The role of the school in this situation is indeed striking, since not only were the black children in the school ignored, except for negative reactions toward them, but the lack of perception regarding problems of interracial diferences and tensions only served to reinforce the stereotypes of both groups.[22] The Long Island community studied by Dr. Miel, one where "we have no problems with people of different races," is so typical of most American communities as to leave one dubious about the potential of the school to change interracial relations; in fact, the school's posture may only make things worse.

That text revision is continuing is at least a heartening sign of awareness on the part of one segment of the educational system. But are the revisions, and the new materials, adequate? A content analysis by Richard Waite of seven text series published in 1965 and 1966 showed that most of these series of first grade reading textbooks "have perpetuated the portrayal of children in a nonurban environment."[23] Only two series of the seven studied were significantly multi-ethnic, and nonrural in orientation. Dr. Waite concludes his study by commenting:

> First, what may appear to be a multi-ethnic first grade reading series may, upon closer inspection, contain few significant characters of ethnic background other than White Anglo-Saxon. Second, the inclusion of "other" ethnic groups in no way implies that the environmental setting of the stories is in any way different from that of the traditional, all-white suburban-rural series. However, in writing multi-ethnic series, *some*, [italics in original] authors may have a tendency to emphasize failure and/or need for help more than they do when writing traditional first grade reading books.[24]

Another recent intensive study of textbooks by James A. Banks revealed that interesting shifts in textbook writing for the elementary school child have taken place. The findings show distinct changes between 1964 and 1968 in six American history texts for use in grades four

---

22. Alice Miel, *The Shortchanged Children of Suburbia* (New York: Institute of Human Relations Press, 1967).
23. Richard R. Waite, "Further Attempts to Integrate and Urbanize First Grade Reading Textbooks: A Research Study," *Journal of Negro Education* 37 (Winter, 1968): 62-69.
24. *Ibid.*, p. 69.

to eight. By 1968, books were apt to include references to black achievements, and also to mention "racial violence, and conflict, peaceful resistence to discrimination, and deliberate acts of discrimination . . ."[25] However, Dr. Banks concludes that, although there have been some shifts in emphasis, the changes have not necessarily been adequate for today's educational needs. He states:

> While textbook authors often attempt to explain or rationalize racial discrimination, they more frequently discuss discrimination without either explaining it or condemning it. This finding supports that of other researchers who have suggested that textbook writers "avoid taking a moral stand . . ."
>
> The authors depicted the achievements of black Americans in literature, music, art, science, industry, sports, entertainment, education and in other fields more frequently than they referred to any other events which relate to the black man and race relations. For example, the physical and psychological deprivations of black Americans were rarely discussed. Thus, the achievements of individual black heroes were emphasized rather than the plight of the majority of black people in this country.[26]

Despite the impression that textbook writers may be perpetuating specific racial stereotypes in an obvious fashion, James Banks' study indicates that such stereotyping no longer occurs; a more subtle kind, noted above, is now the likely posture. Similarly, the facts of racial violence are muted, despite the pervasiveness of such occurrences in the years prior to the publication of the most recent books. Presumably, textbook authors are expected to provide a "nice" view of American history.[27]

avoiding the realities of life

A critical look at the current textbook reach for the urban market reveals, unfortunately, that life in the tenement and the slum is really pretty good and pretty much fun for all: Dick and Jane have just gone slumming. The mishaps are never devastating, the adults are almost invariably helpful, other children learn lessons of friendliness, and everyone lives happily ever after. In one set of readers for the urban child, he is even told that it was really a good thing that he failed second grade.[28]

---

25. James A. Banks, "A Content Analysis of the Black American in Textbooks," *Social Education* 33 (December, 1969): 954-57.
26. *Ibid.*, pp. 956-57.
27. See chapter five, "Educating for Social Stupidity."
28. Bank Street Readers, *My City* (New York: Macmillan Co., 1965), pp. 224-29.

A textbook for third grade discusses the problems of poverty and urban renewal in a few pages. One picture, showing a slum setting, has no people in it. A second picture, showing the happy aftereffects of renewal, depicts a group of integrated children playing in a new school yard. The text suggests that urban renewal is quite simple:

> Mayor Tucker and other city leaders set out to change the poor parts of St. Louis. They wanted to make their city a good place for all of its people to live.
> How could they make a better St. Louis? What could be done to help the poor parts of the city?
> Now many years ago, parts of St. Louis had become poor places to live in. These parts of the city were called *slums*. Slums are neighborhoods where people are crowded together in ugly, worn-out houses. People live in slums because they do not have enough money to live in better places. . . .
> Mayor Tucker and other leaders of St. Louis decided that the slums must be torn down. But before the slums could be torn down, new homes had to be found for the people of Mill Creek Valley. Some people moved into apartment buildings nearby. Others moved into apartment buildings and houses in many different parts of St. Louis . . .[29]

If only reality were as easy as this textbook describes! The true St. Louis story bears no resemblance to the above simplistic version. Why?

A textbook by Martha Munzer designed for upper grade or junior high readers is devoted entirely to the problems involved in environmental control. The book should gain a wide audience with the current enthusiasm for ecology. However, the interested student or teacher would find people only peripheral to the problems discussed in the book.[30] The reporting is accurate and well done; the pictures are carefully selected; the data impeccable. What is missing is people. No mention is made of the prejudice that wraps a white collar around the black inner-city where urban renewal is desperately required. No mention is made of the struggle of city residents to obtain decent and safe housing near to jobs and other amenities of life. Planned communities, such as Reston, Virginia, are pictured and described, but there are very few blacks in Reston. Reston is an urbane escape from the urban mess. This the text does not examine.

The role of citizen and youth action to assist reforestation, halt pollution, and aid in beautification is well portrayed by the author, but the controversial nature of citizen action programs is not touched upon.

29. V. Phillips Weaver, *People Use the Earth* (Morristown, N.J.: Silver Burdett Co., 1969).
30. Martha E. Munzer, *Planning Our Town* (New York: Alfred A. Knopf, Inc., 1964).

Though Martha Munzer's book is a good introduction for the upper-grade student of the problems of environmental control, it is regrettable that the author has avoided any of the politically controversial problems surrounding urban renewal and environmental conservation. For thousands of students in urban areas the reality of the power confrontations regarding who will have control over urban projects and planning is very close. When such material is omitted from textbooks, it is unlikely on the basis of our past observations, that teachers, on their own, will venture into such areas of controversy. Yet these are the students who will soon be participants in community decision-making, hopefully with reason rather than disorder. Unless the school provides education about these issues, the education the average inner-city citizen will receive will be from other media, and from leaders vying for a power base.

One volume, a significant departure from the usual text, explicitly directed to the black child, is *Black Pride,* by Janet Harris and Julius Hobson.[31] Designed as a textbook, the volume speaks directly to black children. The books ends with this look to the future:

> Another outgrowth of today's movement is the proud new self-image that black people are gaining. Black artists, writers, and actors are creating a new awareness of black culture. To young people today, the words "black is beautiful" are more than a slogan. And more and more agree with poet Langston Hughes, that their color is to be worn "Like a banner for the proud."[32]

To what extent this book will become used as a text cannot be known presently. That it was published by a large standard textbook house (McGraw-Hill) is, however, evidence that publishers are no longer as squeamish as they once were about commercial ventures into controversial areas. Research is desperately needed to indicate whether reading *Black Pride* does in fact have a significant impact on black children, and also and significantly, if it has an effect on white children.

poverty in textbook land

In elementary school textbooks, discussions of poverty are increasingly found in newer series. However, when poverty is apparent, it is only implied by using illustrations with city backgrounds. Even the tenements, though, are cleaned up. The problems associated with poverty,

---

31. Janet Harris and Julius Hobson, *Black Pride: A People's Struggle* (New York: McGraw-Hill Book Co., 1969).
32. *Ibid.,* p. 152.

too, are rarely mentioned, or, if discussed, are resolved with ease. In one textbook story, for instance, the family is too poor to have enough chairs for a family reunion. One member of the family works as a janitor at a school, and the school authorities let him have some discarded school chairs which he can proudly bring home, so everyone can sit down.[33] It is an unreal world in which a lack of chairs can be readily solved by a beneficent coincidence; true life is unfortunately less likely to produce such benefactors in the lives of most poor families.

In another text written primarily with an urban class in mind, there are many ethnic groups represented. The illustrations clearly show that there are black individuals in many key roles—including a black lady judge—and also the use of Spanish surnames provides an opportunity to make an inference about the roles that can be taken by persons with a Spanish-speaking background. However, neither race nor ethnic origin is explicitly mentioned, nor are problems of intergroup relations raised.[34] The fact that most of the stories take place in and around an inner-city slum area shows clearly the dilemma of the textbook writer when trying to deal realistically with poverty, within the context of the textbook view of life.

The quandry of the textbook writer and publisher is well illustrated by other aspects of this text. The stories have "happy" endings, but they also include problem episodes which have a touch of slum life reality. For instance, when the class visits the City Hall and has a session with Mr. Morales in the tax collector's office, one child recalls:

> Chino knew it was Emma Mae's mother who paid the rent.
> He also knew how hard Emma Mae's mother had worked to get enough money for food for her six children ever since Emma Mae's father had skipped out and left them two years ago.[35]

The teacher's edition, from which the above quote was taken, is annotated in red to indicate to the teacher points to be raised, words to discuss, and items to clarify. With the above statement, the annotation for the teacher is: "Who could take care of the needs of the family? (Parents)"

Previous annotations indicate that words such as "tenement," "sales tax," "whopped," "snickered" should be discussed. The rather interesting phrase, "skipped out" in the quote above is not circled, nor is there any in-

---

33. Virginia Brown, et al., *Who Cares: Skyline Series, Book C* "Not Enough Chairs," pp. 52-70. St. Louis: Webster Division, McGraw-Hill Book Co., 1965).
34. Jack McClellan, et al., *Citizens All*, teacher's edition (New York: Houghton-Mifflin, 1967).
35. *Ibid.*, p. 51.

dication at any point that a class discussion of this interesting fact should or could take place.

This text, unlike others reviewed, has some episodes—as in the instance cited—which do illumine the lives of inner-city children. The tone of the book is exemplified by the last story which revolves around the ceremony for new citizens. The problems of inner city life are resolved on the upbeat note of the promise implicit in the final story: we are all citizens, and everybody can live happily ever after.

A series with the interesting title of *The Human Values Series*[36] is composed of three volumes. Each volume has short episodes revolving around typical problems children may face. The problems are neatly resolved in each instance, whether it is cheating, stealing, lying, being left out, being a newcomer, and similar situations. Though clearly designated for promoting intergroup understanding through the use of black characters and people with ethnically identifiable names, in no place are the problems of interracial relations treated with reality. Poverty is touched on only in a manner to reassure children that things really are not so bad, that people who went to a one-room schoolhouse in the "olden days" were to be pitied, because we have it so much better in our big schools now. There is no denying that young people can use extensive analysis of the values we live by, but this series is far from providing insight into our contemporary value conflict.

In a recent handbook for teachers describing suggested social studies activities, the human relations aspects of the program are given four pages out of forty-eight. In those pages, the emphasis is upon sharing, being good citizens, and encouraging everyone to be friends with everyone else. A particularly fascinating activity is suggested: each child is to describe a member of his family tree in order to demonstrate "the complex makeup of American society" represented by the children in the classroom.[37] One wonders how the teacher will cope with black children who are likely to have non-Negroid parents or grandparents, or with the child who has no legitimate father. Have the authors and distributors of this pamphlet designed these materials to be used exclusively in all-white suburbia?

---

36. V. Clyde Arnspiger, et al., *The Human Values Series* (Austin, Texas: Steck-Vaughn Company, 1967). Titles in the series are: *Our Values; Values to Live By;* and *Values to Learn.*

37. Caleb W. Bucher, *Activities for Todays' Social Studies* (Dansville, N.Y.: F. A. Owen Publishing Co., 1965), p. 32.

who is responsible?

There may be a good reason why children's textbooks fall short of reality: with few exceptions, it appears that teachers and administrators do not want young children to read or talk about the existence that faces them each day. Testimony in the case of *Hobson vs. D.C. School Board, et al.*,[38] by a black principal of a school in one of the worst poverty-stricken areas of the District of Columbia, was to the effect that the principal could really see no need for such children to read about black children or about out-of-school reality. After several years of study and classroom experimentation, it seems clear that both white and black teachers, even those with the best motives in the world, feel uncomfortable or even incompetent in dealing with questions of race and cultural differences.[39]

The dilemma is obvious. Shame, guilt, and even fear propel the adult away from the child's unpleasant environment. Who really *likes* to face crumbling plaster, foul smells, brazen rats, crunchy cockroaches, sidewalks littered with paper and broken glass, the weaving drunk, the flashy pusher? Birds, bees, and butterflies are so much more "pleasant."

The answer typically given to the dilemma posed above is that children deserve to be allowed to be children, even if they live in the center of an environment in which few children can grow up decently. Just as adults escape into fantasy fiction or enjoy vicarious spying and lovemaking with Agent 007, so do these same adults prescribe, without question, escape literature for children.

One teacher, described by Francis Ianni, received great praise for the creativity of his children when one of them wrote a poem on going to the store with Mom, but the same teacher was in deep trouble when he sought to publish another bit of creative effort entitled 'The Junkies." Such a subject, the teacher-editor said, an eleven-year-old "just could not know anything about."[40]

It is of more than passing interest to note that Herbert Kohl, the teacher Dr. Ianni refers to, has, in his evocative book, *36 Children*, managed to reach an audience of interested parents, educators, and citizens

---

38. *Hobson vs. D.C. School Board,* et al.
39. Lincoln Filene Center for Citizenship and Public Affairs, Research Reports (occasional), 1965, 1966, 1967. See also, Marcia R. Coulin and Martin Haberman, "Supervising Teachers of the Disadvantaged," *Educational Leadership* 24 (February, 1967): 393-98.
40. Francis A. Ianni, "Cultivating the Arts of Poverty," *Saturday Review* 50 (June 17, 1967): 60-62ff.

who understand his vision of "open education" in which a child's creativity is let loose to help him understand his environment, and in so doing, to learn how to conquer it.[41] When these procedures are incorporated into textbooks or instructional materials, then perhaps we may be more sure of the impact of Kohl—and others, such as John Holt, Nat Hentoff, Johnathon Kozol, and George Dennison, who follow in the same tradition.[42] So far, few instructional materials have made a beginning in the direction outlined.

New developments in instructional materials suggest greater boldness on the part of publishers in directing children's attention to the problems of daily life. The Shaftel discussion picture series,[43] for instance, are designed to develop in children the ability to analyze the problems that confront them, and, through role-playing, to work out solutions which make sense to them. Some of the pictures show only all Negro characters. There is one in which a small child and his older sister are shown with a TV set. Another scene shows a small white boy standing on a kitchen stool; at his feet there is a box of spilled cereal, and his father is just entering the room. In still another picture, there is a struggle between a black and white boy for possession of a building block. The question one might raise is: does it matter if the children or adults are all black, all white, or in integrated situations? Where there are several children and it is obviously a school or play scene, the children are of many hues. The family-based pictures show only one race. Some of the conflict pictures are between members of different races; some are not. Discussion of the pictures as suggested by the Shaftels may or may not focus on racial differences, nor are problems of poverty in the foreground at any point. The universality of the problems, irrespective of race, becomes the significant message. One may wonder, however, if children will be able to make the transfer and the related generalization: that differences among us are, after all, only skin deep. Or, conversely, that skin color does make a difference, if one wants to make it so.

---

41. Herbert Kohl, *36 Children* (New York: New American Library, 1967).
42. John Holt, *The Underachieving School* (New York: Pitman Publishing Corp., 1969); Nat Hentoff, *Our Children Are Dying* (New York: Viking Press, 1968); George Dennison, *The Lives of Children* (New York: Random House, 1969); and Jonathan Kozol, *Death at an Early Age* (New York: Houghton Mifflin Co., 1967).
43. Fannie Shaftel and George Shaftel, *Words and Actions* (New York: Holt, Rinehart and Winston, Inc., 1967).

A similar set, developed by Raymond Muessig,[44] has an even broader scheme: his pictures embrace the world. Children from many cultures are depicted in situations which illustrate the major themes of social relatedness: i.e., interdependence, the need to be cared for, the need for safety, curiosity, generational differences. A careful reading of the teacher's manual does not reveal one instance in which special attention is to be paid to racial differences. One picture, for instance, showing a black and a white boy playing side by side, is presented to the teacher as depicting the concept of play as an activity one can undertake alone or with others. The fact that the boys are of different races is not mentioned. Where cultural differences are apparent in the picture, the child is labeled "Chinese" or "Arabic." Poverty is not mentioned, but the student is told of the variety of ways in which different people in different cultures work to obtain the necessities of life. However, pictures which clearly show subsistence level cultures are not discussed in terms of the abject poverty of these peoples.

The large folio pictures developed by the John Day Company[45] have somewhat greater potential for depicting realities of life, particularly in the set entitled Renewal Is . . . . Unlike the bland discussion of renewal in the V. Phillips Weaver text,[46] these pictures may convey to children the upheaval experienced by those who are "renewed." None of these pictures, however, deal with prejudice or poverty.

A good predictor of things to come is a very elaborate instructional kit, Early Childhood Discovery Materials, published by Macmillan.[47] The textbook in this instance has been replaced by a "package." The package consists of many teaching units: a large picture with many people in it; booklets with no words, few words, with more elaborate language skills; puzzle boards for developing concepts of sequence. Similar kits, which include records, filmstrips, and large pictures, have been produced by Scott, Foresman, and Company,[48] and other companies.[49]

44. Raymond Muessig, *Discussion Pictures for Beginning Social Studies* (New York: Harper & Row, Publishers, 1967).
45. *Urban Education Studies* (New York: John Day Co., 1965).
46. Weaver, *People Use the Earth*, op. cit.
47. *Early Childhood Discovery Series*, (New York: Macmillan Company, 1969).
48. Paul A. Hanna, et al., *Elementary Social Studies Series* (Chicago: Scott, Foresman and Co., rev. ed., 1969-1970).
49. *Primary Social Studies*: "Families and Their Needs," "Communities and Their Needs," (Morristown, N.J.: Silver Burdett Co., 1967).

If the Macmillan set is a prototype, and examination of the other sets suggests that it is, then one is still stuck with a "Dick and Jane" version of childhood. The sample set which Macmillan distributes includes a large picture of a city park. It is integrated: black families and white families, black children and white children; all ages, many occupations—policeman, ice cream seller, gardener, some black and some white. One sample book shows a struggle over a pail between a small black boy and a white boy. Is it merely coincidence, or something in the system: the white mother comes to the rescue, shows how both boys can play with the pail, and returns to read at her bench. No black mother appears. Another sample booklet is about a cat in a tree. (Each of these episodes is pictured in a large park picture.) In this instance, a white boy and girl call on a white park attendant for help. The cat is rescued.

Would that city parks were like this! The colors are pastel; the stories are interesting, without violence or "trouble," and all ends well. Although the medium has undergone some creative transfusions, the message is the same: all is well and happy only now in a "nice" integrated smiling world. A more exciting, and far less known approach to urban life is included in one of the Matchbox series.[50] The City Box, as it is called, includes a set of booklets about urban life. Many flat pictures about many aspects of city living are also included. There is a street plan of a city. The task of the class is to plan its own city, with blocks representing various kinds of industries, institutions, and homes. Students must think about safety, convenience, and services. The place of the black resident appears as one of many incidental aspects of city life in the pictures, and in the booklets. The task of the class is to "construct a city" in any way they may wish. Instructions suggest using the class to study its own school neighborhood as one starting point and then develop an ideal "city" from there. The task leads outward to many intriguing educational possibilities, rooted in everyday reality. On the basis of performance, it is likely that more schools will "buy Macmillan" than will "buy Matchbox." And it is not just money that makes the difference; The City Box is simply far more realistic (and thus potentially explosive) than the new "Dick and Jane."

---

50. *The Match Program* (Boston: American Science and Engineering, Inc., 1969). "Japanese Family," "City," "Greece." Another program which shows much promise for the direction of elementary social studies is that directed by Paul E. Brandwein, *The Social Studies Concepts and Values Series* (New York: Harcourt Brace Jovanovich, Inc., 1970).

An interesting approach to social understanding is presented in materials prepared by Ronald Lippitt, Robert Fox, and Lucille Schaible.[51] The intent of these materials is to help young people become "Scientists Who Ask Questions About People."[52] As a guide to developing a whole new concept of how social studies might be approached, via the active investigation by children of social phenomena, these materials seem to provide an excellent model. As one examines them, however, one notices again a subtle but pervasive evasion of the key problems of race, prejudice, and poverty, although there is ample space given to such a "difference" as food preference. Ethnic differences occur in a few places, specifically in references to an Italian boy who does not understand English very well, and to a girl who is also from a "different" background and misunderstands requests made of her so that students do not understand her behavior. An anecdote about "The Boy with Green Hair" indicates the irrelevance of such a physical characteristic in making decisions about ability or merit. There is a brief discourse on Eugene Hartley's use of the social distance scale (no mention is made of the one by Emory Bogardus), and then the authors gently suggest:

> One thing that Dr. Hartley's experiment showed was that people have unfriendly feelings about groups of people they have not had any contact with. They don't have any reason to have unfriendly feelings except that the groups are strangers. If someone dislikes all strangers, or even one kind of stranger— *like a person with a different skin color*—he tends to apply this dislike to all groups that seem different [italics added].[53]

It is not, as Dr. Hartley says, only the stranger whom we may dislike because of color; it may be our neighbor. What then? One can only wonder why such responsible social scientists as the authors are known to be have presented such a singularly limited view of what is known about the roots of social dislike.

The material is marred by omission, even from the glossary, of the words *prejudice* or *race*. These are not suitable terms, evidently, for budding social scientists to learn, though they are to be introduced to such complex and basic concepts as stereotyping, rank order, deviance, and multiple causation. One might add, too, that "social class" is among the

---

51. Ronald Lippitt, Robert Fox, and Lucille Schaible, Social Science Laboratory Units, Grades 4-6, (Chicago: Science Research Associates,   ).
52. *Ibid.*
53. *Ibid.*, Social Science Resource Book, p. 87.

missing social science concepts. Our "Dick and Jane" are still safe from confrontation with the disagreeable—the cutting edges of poverty, discrimination, prejudice and violence. Despite the virtues of the Lippitt, et al., materials in providing an imaginative and original guide for teachers and children in learning how to learn about social interaction, the blandness of content is pervasive. There are hurt feelings, there are misunderstandings, there are errors in perception and in judgment, but it all seems to take place among basically "model" middle class children.

summary

The "new Dick and Jane" are not really very new. Although they may now have black, Puerto Rican, or Mexican playmates and may now appear on city streets and—almost—near tenements, and although their adventures carry them far beyond the backyard and playing ball with Spot, the genre is still recognizable. The stories always end on an upbeat, there are no tears wept in anger or fear or despair; there are no pangs of hunger or vicious envy; the inventive nastiness of children is never even hinted at. That illness, death, divorce, and crime abound in the world of the city and the worlds of the suburb and the farm is a fact of human experience still noticeably absent from textbook life.

Newer materials, although not yet at the textbook level of utilization, are edging closer and closer toward reality. Some of the material shows what appear to be real children in real conflict with each other, with parents, and with other groups. Some material may suggest to children that there is more to human experience than meets the untrained eye. But by and large the values which pervade materials prepared for children in elementary school are still restricted by the bland code which critics of "Dick and Jane" have found so distressing.

CHAPTER 5

Educating for Social Stupidity: History, Government and Sociology Textbooks

Juel Janis

introduction

Jules Henry has commented that there is a kind of education that can be described as "education for social stupidity," by which he means that when schools simply confirm popular mythology rather than showing young people that society might be wrong or leading young people to inquire about social validity, schools serve to miseducate.

An examination of many widely-used secondary-school history and sociology textbooks suggests that Dr. Henry's observation cannot be taken either as hyperbole or as a simplistic generalization. The following chapter details aspects of history, government and sociology texts which justify Dr. Henry's remark.

In the first section of the chapter, "Old Bottles—New Wine: History Textbook Revisions in the Sixties," the "befores" and "afters" of fourteen history and government texts are considered, demonstrating the "accommodations" made in these books toward the black experience in America of the sixties.

In the second section of the chapter, ways are considered in which five sociology textbooks have shortchanged whites *and* blacks through a distorted presentation of what it is like to be an American—alive and functioning in the second half of the twentieth century.

old bottles—new wine: history textbook revisions in the sixties

Although most Americans view the practice of rewriting history to suit current ideology as a uniquely non-Western phenomenon, little attention has been paid to the adeptness with which American textbook writers have engaged in this practice. A careful examination of fourteen high school social studies texts written during the past decade reveals that in the coverage of topics such as slavery, the Reconstruction Era, and the Civil Rights movement, historical rewriting has been the rule rather than the exception.

But there is more at stake here than an ideal of historical truth. To the student unaware of a concern so esoteric as "historical truth" a textbook *is* history. And, because he regards it as such, his view of the past and the present is influenced by the positions espoused by textbook authors. Students exposed to the historical "facts" presented in the texts of the 1950's and the early 1960's learned a very different sort of history than those who learned their "facts" from texts written in the middle and late sixties.

A glimpse at the types of historical facts presented in the older texts as compared with the more recent texts is instructive. Typically, the older books present material which many historians have described as being both distorted and factually inaccurate.* An awareness of the failings of these older texts is of particular relevance for educators in school systems still using these texts.** For those schools using the newer ones, an awareness of the differences between these texts and the older ones can provide a timely lesson in historiography and also allow the student to examine some of the "historical truths" taught in this country only a few short years ago.

---

*There have been several studies which documented these historical inaccuracies: The American Council on Education's *Intergroup Relations in Teaching Materials* (Washington, D. C.: American Council on Education, 1949); Lloyd Marcus' *The Treatment of Minorities in Secondary School Textbooks* (New York: Anti-Defamation League of B'nai B'rith, 1961); Irving Sloan's *The Negro in Modern American History Textbooks* (n.p.: American Federation of Teachers, AFL-CIO, 1966); Kenneth Stampp, et al.'s *The Negro in American History Textbooks* (Sacramento: California State Department of Education, June, 1964); and *A Report on the Treatment of Minorities in American History Textbooks,* (published by the Michigan Department of Education, 1968).

**To cite but one example: In the Spring of 1968 ten out of eleven high schools in the District of Columbia were using social studies texts five years old or older, and almost a quarter of these schools were using texts which were ten to twelve years old.

In the early 1960's, high school students studying American history were typically presented with material which glossed over the hardships of slavery, ignored the positive gains achieved during the Reconstruction Era, included pictures of blacks depicted only as slaves, and omitted any discussion of the problems of discrimination encountered by blacks over the last half century. To be sure, none of the material in these texts is quite as blatant as one classic "work" problem found in an old confederate text: "If 5 white men can do as much work as 7 negroes [sic], how many days of 10 hours each will be required for 25 negroes [sic] to do a piece of work which 30 white men can do in 10 days of 9 hours each?"[1] Yet most of these texts include material significantly different from that found in texts written in the late 1960's.

The social ferment of the late 1950's and early 1960's did not begin to have its effect on publishers and textbook writers until the middle of the 1960's. By the end of the decade, as a result of studies on the treatment of minority groups in textbooks,[2] and assorted Congressional hearings,[3] and as a result of the pressure exerted by civil rights groups and black representatives on textbook selection committees, textbook authors had made significant revisions in their treatment of the history of the black man in America. While these changes are laudable since they more accurately reflected the findings of contemporary historians (although most of the changes represent the inclusion of material which had been known by American historians for over twenty-five years), it is unfortunate that these revisions were made not because textbook authors had gained new information on these subjects, but because of the changing political and social climate.

---

1. Hillel Black, *The American Schoolbook* (New York: William Morrow and Co., Inc., 1967), p. 87.
2. The American Council on Education, *Intergroup Relations in Teaching Materials* (Washington, D.C.: American Council on Education, 1949); Lloyd Marcus, *The Treatment of Minorities in Secondary School Textbooks* (New York: Anti-Defamation League of B'nai B'rith, 1961); Irving Sloan, *The Negro in Modern American History Textbooks* (n.p.: American Federation of Teachers, AFL-CIO, 1966); Kenneth Stampp, et al., *The Negro in American History Textbooks* (Sacramento: California State Department of Education, June, 1964); *A Report on the Treatment of Minorities in American History Textbooks* (published by the Michigan Department of Education, 1968).
3. *Books for Schools and the Treatment of Minorities,* U.S. Congress, House, Hearings before the Ad Hoc subcommittee on De Facto School Segregation of the Committee on Education and Labor, 89th Cong., 2d Sess., 1966.

textbook changes: a study of three widely used textbooks

The following examination of three of the most widely used American history textbooks highlights the differences between their 1963 and 1964 editions and those published in 1966 and 1967.

In Bragdon and McCutcheon's 1964 text, the authors note: "Once slaves had been put to work on American plantations they were seldom cruelly treated, since it was to the interest of the master to keep them healthy and contented. They had little protection, however, from the occasional vicious owner."[4] This paragraph was omitted from the 1967 edition. In its place, the authors substituted the following:

> The laws of the southern colonies declared the Negroes to be slaves for life . . . they even forbade masters to teach Negroes to read for fear that they might acquire dangerous ideas. Whereas in the Spanish colonies slaves were obliged to marry and the integrity of the family was protected, in the English plantation colonies slave marriages had no standing in law and children might be sold away from their mothers. Slaves could own no property and had slight legal protection against irresponsible or cruel masters. In brief, Negroes were treated as cattle. Their only protection was that they were such a valuable commodity that it was to the interest of the master to keep them reasonably healthy and reasonably provided with food, clothing, and shelter.[5]

Similar changes on this same subject can be seen in both Platt and Drummond's *Our Nation From Its Creation*,[6] and Todd and Curti's *The Rise of the American Nation*.[7] In both instances, textual material was added in the 1966 edition which provides a much broader understanding of slave life than that found in the 1964 edition. While the 1964 Todd and Curti text did not include any information on the "Middle Passage," the 1966 edition noted:

> Probably no other immigrants to America were ever so completely separated from their past. Driven at the crack of whips onto slave ships lying along the African coast, these desperate men, women, and children were forced to leave behind them all that they held dear in the land of their birth.[8]

---

4. Henry W. Bragdon and Samuel P. McCutcheon, *A History of a Free People* (New York: The Macmillan Co., 1964), pp. 19, 22.
5. Bragdon and McCutcheon, *A History of a Free People*, 1967, p. 20.
6. Nathaniel Platt and Muriel Joan Drummond, *Our Nation From Its Creation* (Englewood Cliffs, N.J.; Prentice-Hall, Inc., 1964, 1966).
7. Lewis Paul Todd and Merle Curti, *The Rise of the American Nation* (New York: Harcourt, Brace and World, Inc., 1964, 1966).
8. *Ibid.*, 1966 ed., p. 303.

Following this last paragraph is almost a page of discussion of the early African civilizations including observations about the "well-organized society" and "elaborate social life" which typified these societies.[9] Obviously, the student gains a very different perspective from the 1966 text than he would have from the earlier edition. Along these same lines, in the Todd and Curti text, the authors make the following comment in their 1964 edition regarding social groups in the early 1800's: "Except for the Negroes, energetic and ambitious men were continually moving from lower to higher economic groups."[10] Two years later, the authors state: "Except for the *slaves who had no opportunity to better their lot,* energetic and ambitious men were continually moving from lower to higher economic groups [italics added]."[11]

These kinds of changes are also found in the 1964 and 1966 editions of Platt and Drummond. While the earlier version did include material on the skilled work performed by slaves as well as an acknowledgement of the fact that "some" slaves were the descendents of ancestors from well-developed civilizations in Africa,[12] the 1966 edition added four additional paragraphs to this particular section including a detailed explanation of the slave codes of the Southern states. In addition, while both editions noted that many planters and some historians have asserted that, in spite of the codes, many slaves were treated fairly well, the later edition added the following observation: "But more and more historians today challenge this view. To justify their stand that slaves were not contented, they give as evidence the many runaway slaves, the slave suicides, the slave uprisings, and the fact that slave parents sometimes murdered their children to save them from a life of slavery."[13] And, while the 1966 text also described the active part played by blacks in the Underground Railway and in the abolitionist movement, the 1964 edition failed to include any of this information.

Substantive additions in the newer texts are accompanied by new illustrations. For example, while the 1958 Bragdon and McCutcheon text did not contain a single picture of a black, the 1967 version included nine. Furthermore, not only have the number of pictures changed, but the subject and context of the illustrations are materially different. One instance of this may be seen in a Currier and Ives lithograph of a southern plantation found in Todd and Curti's 1964 and 1966 texts. The 1964 edition in-

---

9. *Ibid.*
10. *Ibid.,* 1964 ed., p. 311.
11. *Ibid.,* 1966 ed., p. 303.
12. Platt and Drummond, *Our Nation From Its Creation,* 1964 ed., p. 315.
13. *Ibid.,* 1966 ed., pp. 314-15.

cludes a caption under this rather idyllic picture of slave life* which reads as follows: "In later years the famous lithographers, Currier and Ives, imagined this scene on a southern plantation."[14] The treatment of this lithograph is quite different in the 1966 edition. Here, the authors placed an actual photo of slaves, taken in 1862, on the same page as the lithograph, and the caption for both pictures states: "The rare photograph above shows slaves in 1862 as they actually looked . . . In later years the famous lithographers, Currier and Ives, imagined, *and perhaps idealized*, the cotton plantation below (italics added)."[15] Note the addition of the phrase "and perhaps idealized" included in the newer text.

While the preceding excerpts are all examples of errors of omission, another equally common and perhaps more serious error in terms of contributing to the charge of "historical inaccuracy" leveled at these earlier texts are errors of commission. The following selections from Bragdon and McCutcheon's *A History of a Free People* present an example of this type of error. These selections are particularly interesting when compared with a later treatment by the same authors.

On the subject of the Freedmen's Bureau, the 1964 edition stated:

> In addition to providing by law for Negro suffrage, the *Radicals sent agents* into the South to encourage the Negroes to vote. To care for the wants of former slaves, Congress in 1865 had set up the Freedmen's Bureau . . . *It was not difficult for agents of the Freedmen's Bureau to persuade the Negroes whom they fed and clothed to vote for the Republican party* [italics added].[16]

In this version the Freedmen's Bureau is viewed as a political tool of the Republican party. Compare this interpretation with the one offered in the 1967 edition, in which the Freedmen's Bureau is described as "providing permanent constitutional protection for the rights of Negroes, [whereby] Congress made a temporary effort to provide for their economic and educational needs."[17] Furthermore, in the later edition, following this last paragraph, the authors included examples of the services provided by the Freedmen's Bureau and omitted the last sentence of the paragraph used in the earlier edition. In the preceding example, note how "Radicals sent agents . . ." changed in the later edition to "Congress made a temporary effort . . ."

---

14. Todd and Curti, *The Rise of the American Nation,* 1964 ed., p. 310.
15. *Ibid.,* 1966 ed., p. 305.
16. Bragdon and McCutcheon, *A History of a Free People,* 1964 ed., p. 362.
17. *Ibid.,* 1967 ed., p. 369.

*One black man is lounging on a cotton bale, some are chatting with each other, and others are standing idly about in the cotton fields.

Bragdon and McCutcheon's treatment of both the carpetbag governments and the Reconstruction era reflect similar changes. While the 1964 edition stated: "The carpetbag governments were inefficient and corrupt,"[18] the 1967 edition modified this to read "*Many* of the carpetbag governments were corrupt (italics added)."[19] And, while the 1964 text stated, "No matter what can be said in their favor, . . . the carpetbag governments caused such resentment that they were often kept in power only with the protection of federal troops,"[20] the 1967 edition omitted this last sentence and, in accord with recent historical scholarship, noted instead: ". . . the carpetbag governments were not unique in being graft-ridden. Unfortunately, political corruption was characteristic of politics all over the United States in the period after the Civil War."[21]

Perhaps the most interesting observation which can be made on the preceding comparisons is that while all of these changes relate to subjects which are one hundred years old, and deal with material in which the more modern interpretations have been supported by historians for some time, the inclusion of these interpretations in high school history books has only occurred within the past few years.

In a recent, surprisingly candid article on the "Dilemmas of a Textbook Writer," Bragdon acknowledged that "It would be disingenuous of me to maintain that I am not influenced by certain unspoken barriers."[22] And, while he stated that he could not "remember offhand" any barriers which influenced him in writing A *History of a Free People,* he concludes by noting that "one cannot get away from the Confucian proverb that: 'The superior man knows what is right; the inferior man knows what will sell.' I'd be happier about A *History of a Free People* if it were not so obviously designed as an article of commerce."[23] It seems apparent from the preceding excerpts that A *History of a Free People* was "obviously designed as an article of commerce," and that it was quite specifically influenced by a recognition of "what will sell" rather than by "what is right."

The newer edition of the Bragdon and McCutcheon text presents a picture of slave life, the carpetbag governments, and the Reconstruction era which is clearly more in keeping with modern historical scholarship

---

18. *Ibid.,* 1964 ed., p. 363.
19. *Ibid.,* 1967 ed., p. 370.
20. *Ibid.,* 1964 ed., p. 363.
21. *Ibid.,* 1967 ed., p. 370.
22. Henry W. Bragdon, "Dilemmas of a Textbook Writer," *Social Education* 33 (March, 1969): 293.
23. *Ibid.,* p. 294.

on the subject.[24] This change of emphasis is also reflected in the material on contemporary civil rights problems. Here Bragdon and McCutcheon included several new pages of material omitted from the earlier editions including a discussion of topics such as "The Negroes in the North," "Truman and Civil Rights," "Jim Crowism," "The N.A.A.C.P.," and "The Negro Revolution." The Todd and Curti and the Platt and Drummond texts also have made similar changes in these areas.

Unfortunately, while these alterations represent the inclusion of new material on the history of the civil rights movement in the sixties, they are sometimes made in such a grudging manner as to give a biased overtone to all of the new material. An example can be found in the following remark by Platt and Drummond in the 1966 edition of *Our Nation From Its Creation* regarding criticism of the omission of the black man from American history texts: "Civil Rights advocates charge that there has been a kind of conspiracy throughout American history to hide the important role played by Negroes in helping to make the United States a great nation."[25] From this statement one might assume that this "charge" was merely an aberration or peculiarity of "Civil Rights advocates" which had no basis in actual fact. The somewhat righteous tone is amusing when one observes that only three pages later the authors reversed a position they themselves had taken in their 1964 text. In their analysis of the Supreme Court's position on enforcement of the 1954 Supreme Court school desegregation decision, the authors had noted in the 1964 edition: "The Court, however, felt that to insist upon immediate desegregation in the seventeen Southern states having segregated schools would be impractical. Therefore, in another decision the following year, it implied that desegregation *should be gradual* [italics added]."[26] Contrast this statement with the one in the 1966 text: "In another decision the following year, [after the 1954 decision] the Court stated that local communities should be required to 'make a prompt and reasonable start toward full compliance' and to act *'with all deliberate speed'* in putting the 1954 decision into effect [italics added]."[27] Note that in their 1964 edition the authors emphasize the Court's decision that "desegregation should be

24. Harold M. Hyman, ed., *The Radical Republicans and Reconstruction 1861-1970* (New York: The Bobbs Merrill Co., Inc., 1967); Mark M. Krug, "On Rewriting of the Story of Reconstruction in the U.S. History Textbooks," *Journal of Negro History* 46 (1961): 133-153.
25. Platt and Drummond, *Our Nation From Its Creation*, 1966 ed., p. 884.
26. *Ibid.*, 1964 ed., p. 889.
27. *Ibid.*, 1966 ed., p. 884.

gradual," while in their 1966 edition they indicate that the Court had in fact asked for "full compliance" with "all deliberate speed."

While the preceding material illustrates the kinds of significant alterations made by many textbook authors during the past few years, not all revisions are quite so dramatic. In fact some of the changes are often innocuous and hardly justify the publishers' reference to the newer text as a "revised" edition. An example can be seen in the following excerpt from the 1964 edition of Eibling, King and Harlow's *History of Our United States*.[28] Since a 1966 House hearing on the treatment of minorities in textbooks had produced evidence which indicated that the 1960 edition of this text presented the Reconstruction era in a totally unfavorable light,[29] the 1964 edition apparently attempted to offset this criticism by the ubiquitous insertion of the word "some" at every opportunity in its discussion of this period. The resulting effect would be comical if it were not truly sad:

> Besides the carpetbaggers and scalawags, the new legislatures had many Negroes. *Some* of these were educated freemen; *some* were ex-slaves who had never had an opportunity to read or to write or to study government. *Some* of the carpetbaggers and scalawags influenced their fellow legislators to spend state money unwisely, and in *some* cases fraudulently, piling up huge state debts. *Some* of the new state governments did pass good laws. In *some* of the Southern states the legislators voted to restore or to establish public school systems, to build hospitals, schools, roads, and railroads, and to found orphan asylums [italics added].[30]

Apparently, all of these qualifying "some's" were too much for the authors to swallow and in the very next sentence following the preceding paragraph, they are more direct in their assessment of these Reconstruction governments: "Southerners soon looked for a way to rid themselves of corrupt politicians. . . ."[31]

textbooks on government: the elusive truth

These changes in historical interpretation are not confined to history textbooks. In the case of government texts, typically the older editions failed to mention the fact that devices such as the grandfather clause, poll taxes, and literacy tests were established primarily to prevent the

28. Harold H. Eibling, Fred M. King, and James Harlow, *History of Our United States* (River Forest, Ill.: Laidlaw Bros., 1964).
29. *Books for Schools and . . ., op. cit.*, pp. 218-220.
30. Eibling, King, and Harlow, *History of Our United States*, p. 357.
31. *Ibid.*

black from voting. The Supreme Court school desegregation decision, as well as the recent Civil Rights Acts, are either omitted or dismissed in one or two sentences. Most of the earlier texts contain no pictures of blacks, and the few books which do, depict them as slum dwellers, welfare recipients, or unskilled laborers.

In Brown's and Peltier's *Government in Our Republic,* published in 1960, the authors make some of the following observations under the heading, "Some Problems of Civil Rights," in reference to the poll tax:

> If a poor Negro cannot pay a poll tax, he is in no different condition from a poor white who cannot pay it. If a Negro businessman loses customers by going to the polls, it cannot be said that a *state* has denied him his voting privilege.[32]

Contrast this approach with the 1967 edition of McClenaghan's *Magruder's American Government* which describes the poll tax as a device that was "a part of the concerted effort to disfranchise the Negro."[33] Obviously this latter explanation presents a more realistic interpretation of the poll tax than the former. It is interesting, though, to compare this latter explanation of the poll tax taken from *Magruder's* 1967 edition with the 1960 version of the same text. While the later edition describes the poll tax as *"part of a concerted effort to disfranchise the Negro,"* the 1960 version merely notes that the purpose of the poll tax was "to *discourage* voting by Negroes who could pass the education test . . . [italics added]."[34]

The context in which Brown and Peltier discuss "discrimination" makes it appear that discrimination is actually both a right and a privilege. The authors state:

> . . . if a private employer refuses to give Negroes (or Jews or Protestants or anyone else) equal opportunity for a job, it cannot be said that either a state or the federal government is denying anyone his right to a job. There is, as a matter of fact, no federal law requiring employers to hire anybody. . . .[35]

These authors devote exactly two sentences to the 1954 Supreme Court decision which is two sentences more than that contained in a 1956

---

32. Stuart Gerry Brown and Charles L. Peltier, *Government in Our Republic* (New York: The Macmillan Co., 1960), p. 400.
33. William A. McClenaghan, *Magruder's American Government* (Boston: Allyn and Bacon, Inc., 1967), p. 152.
34. *Ibid.,* 1960 ed., p. 435.
35. Brown and Peltier, *Government in Our Republic,* p. 400.

government text by Flick and Smith.[36] This latter text, in fact, has the distinction of making absolutely no references to blacks throughout the entire book.

The 1960 edition of *Magruder's* devotes two paragraphs to the 1954 Supreme Court decision and the author's view of this decision is easily discerned. After discussing the 1806 "separate-but-equal doctrine" and noting that this rule was later extended to the field of education, the author writes: "In the last several years, however, the Court has been *chipping away* at the separate-but-equal rule. In an historic 1954 decision, segregation was outlawed" (italics added).[37]

The 1967 edition interprets this decision in essentially the same way, but this time the phrase *chipping away* is placed in quotation marks, and the phrase "in the last several years" changes to a specific date: " . . . in 1938, the Supreme Court began to 'chip away' at the rule laid down by *Plessy v. Ferguson.*"[38]

Despite the fact that the 1967 edition spends several paragraphs discussing this decision and includes a three-paragraph quotation from the decision itself, the injection of a phrase such as "chip away" can only cloud the validity of the Court's decision when it is presented in this manner. Moreover, the pejorative use of "chip away" in this context serves to place the doctrine of "separate-but-equal" on a pedestal on which it should presumably stand, unmolested, immutable, in perpetuity.

While the 1960 edition of *Magruder's* contains only two pictures with blacks, the 1967 edition contains sixteen. However, further analysis of these sixteen pictures reveals that nine depict blacks performing some type of unskilled labor, as welfare recipients, lined up to vote with a white registrar, or as part of an audience in an illustration of propaganda techniques—the association in the latter case being that they are part of a group who are being "duped" by these techniques.

In reviewing the changes made between the 1960 and 1967 edition of *Magruder's*, although more material about blacks has been added, a few adjectives changed and two pictures of blacks extended to sixteen, the "tone" of the text remains essentially unchanged. Interestingly, this text is one of the most commonly used U.S. Government textbooks in the nation.

---

36. Oka Stanton Flick and Henry L. Smith, *Government in the United States* (River Forest, Ill.: Laidlaw Brothers, 1956).
37. McClenaghan, *Magruder's American Government*, 1960 ed., p. 401.
38. *Ibid.*, 1967 ed., p. 119.

Bruntz and Bremmer's *American Government*[39] published in 1965 is a revision of Bruntz's 1963 text, *Understanding Our Government*.[40] The changes made in the 1965 edition are equally as radical as those already noted. The following are but a few of the differences between the 1963 and the 1965 editions of this text:

On Suffrage

1963

"The Fifteenth Amendment . . . provides that no state shall deny the right to vote to anyone because of race, color or previous condition of servitude."[41]

1965 The preceding sentence from the 1963 edition is now followed by this notation:

"In spite of this clear bar against racial discrimination in suffrage, Negroes in some states and localities must overcome almost impossible obstacles to become registered to vote."[42]

On Literacy

1963

"The purpose of this [voting requirement] is to keep the ignorant from voting."[43]

1965 The preceding sentence is omitted. Instead the authors have substituted this explanation:

"The literacy test can be defended as a legitimate device to sort out potential voters who are uninformed . . . Yet very often these tests have been used to disqualify Negroes. In some cases, trivial errors by whites pass unnoticed, while similar errors keep Negroes from qualifying."[44]

On Registration

Both texts define "registration" similarly. Compare, however, the conclusion of the 1963 edition with that made by the 1965 edition:

---

39. George G. Bruntz and John Bremer, *American Government* (New York: Ginn and Co., 1965).
40. George G. Bruntz, *Understanding Our Government* (Boston: Ginn and Co., 1963).
41. *Ibid.*, p. 26.
42. Bruntz and Bremer, *American Government*, p. 69.
43. Bruntz, *Understanding Our Government*, p. 27.
44. Bruntz and Bremer, *American Government*, p. 70.

1963
"Registration, therefore, safeguards against illegal voting."[45]
1965 The preceding sentence is omitted. In its place is the following paragraph:
". . . voter registrars have used their office effectively to disenfranchise Negroes. Other devices used to block Negro registration include the closing of the registration office when Negroes appear, requiring Negroes to see the registrar personally instead of having the business handled by a lower clerk, and permitting the registrar to exclude applicants who in his judgment are lacking in 'good moral character.' "[46]

It is apparent then, from all of the preceding examples, that the social studies textbooks written in the 1950's and early 1960's presented students with a dramatically different set of facts than those included in textbooks written in the late 1960's. The newer texts included many of the less palatable facts about the hardships of slave life, thereby giving students a better understanding of the physical and psychological meaning of slavery as an institution. Discussions of the Reconstruction era were revised to reflect the most recent findings of modern American historians on this subject. The "amoral optimism" found in the earlier texts, which implied that discrimination was not really a problem in this country, was modified to include an admission that there indeed was much still to be done in this area. And, recent gains in civil rights were given a much more comprehensive treatment.

Obviously, textbook authors and publishers are influenced by their environment. What is disconcerting is the fact that many authors and publishers of social studies texts remained insensitive to the changes in their social environment for so long a time. And, while "historical truth" is, after all, an elusive thing where (as one historian recently noted) "one man's truth is another man's bias,"[47] it seems that the pattern for the history textbook writers of the early 1960's was to include only those "truths" which offended as few buyers as possible.

It is difficult to speculate about the potential damage created as a result of the distortions contained in many of these textbooks—in particular, what effect they might have on the reinforcement of prejudicial attitudes and beliefs. There is no clear answer, since to date there appears

---

45. Bruntz, *Understanding Our Government*, p. 28.
46. Bruntz and Bremer, *American Government*, p. 72.
47. Ray Allen Billington, *The Historian's Contribution to Anglo-American Misunderstanding* (New York: Hobbs, Dorman, and Co., 1966), p. 102.

to have been no empirical study of the psychological effects of using this type of material. For whites, however, it seems clear that such material would infect them with the virus of racism, while to the black man it would seem to say: "You don't count! Who you are, what you have been, and who you will become, is not a part of American history. White America is not concerned with you."

sunday sociology

Within the past few years, while history books have been seriously criticized for having performed a "cultural lobotomy" by obscuring and distorting the role of the black in American history texts, little attention has been paid to the fact that sociology texts are probably even *more* culpable in their failure to deal straightforwardly with the problems of discrimination and prejudice as they affect the black.

In 1964, six University of California historians cited a number of substantive points regarding black history which are now used as evaluative criteria in the selection of American history texts in the State of California.[48] Some of the issues cited by these historians are equally appropriate to consider in the evaluation of sociology texts. In particular, these historians raised a point which is often ignored in the evaluation of social studies texts: namely, the importance of what they called "tone." By tone, the historians were referring to a presentation which in its "blandness and amoral optimism" implicitly denies the obvious deprivations suffered by Negroes,[49] or which does not describe realistically the gains made as a result of the civil rights movement, but instead presents them as "an ode to the inevitable justice and progress of the democratic system."[50] And they noted that the "tone of a textbook is almost as important as anything it has to say."[51]

The following examination of several widely used high school sociology textbooks illustrates the way in which soft words are used to conceal hard truths and also helps to explain why so many of today's citizens lack the proper sociological background for understanding the racial crisis which this nation is currently undergoing.

As recently as the spring of 1968, over three-quarters of the high school students in Washington, D.C. were using a text by Cole and

---

48. Stampp, et al., *The Negro in American History Textbooks.*
49. *Ibid.*
50. *Ibid.,* p. 6.
51. *Ibid.,* p. 2.

Montgomery entitled *High School Sociology.*[52] Like many urban school systems, Washington has a student body which is predominantly black. Imagine the response of these students to a text which discusses discrimination and prejudice and uses the American Indian as the sole example of a group which has suffered from prejudice in this country.

In these examples of "the more common ways in which individuals show their prejudices"[53] Cole and Montgomery discuss:

Denial of privileges: ". . . For a long time the Indians of some states were denied voting privileges which non-Indians had demanded earlier. . . ."

Segregation: ". . . The system of segregation of Indians on reservations grew out of prejudices even though many whites held that reservations were necessary for the protection of the Indians. . . ."[54]

Justification for prejudice, as in this last phrase quoted, appears frequently and is typical of this text. Obviously, the criticism of the preceding passages is not a denial of the very real fact that the Indians in America have been subjected to a "denial of privileges" and "segregation." Rather, the criticism is primarily directed at the authors' failure to acknowledge that other minority group members have also experienced these forms of prejudice in this country.

In this same book, the authors illustrate "discriminatory practices" as a form of prejudicial behavior with this example: An individual, they say, "may not be elected to another group because he is an industrialist. . . . A man may be opposed for office because of his occupation. . . . An entire group of interests may be legislated against to satisfy the whims of another prejudiced group. . . ."[55] In this instance, to use an industrialist who is excluded from a particular group as an illustration of "discriminatory practices" is perhaps one of the clearest examples of "blandness" imaginable. The following passages continue in the same tone:

Aggression and conflict: ". . . In Hitler's Germany the Jews had their property taken and *some* were put to death . . ."[italics added].

---

52. Juel M. Janis, "Black Schools—White Books: A Review of U.S. History Government, and Sociology Textbooks in the District of Columbia" (unpublished manuscript, University of Maryland, College Park, Spring, 1968).

53. William E. Cole and Charles S. Montgomery, *High School Sociology* (Boston: Allyn and Bacon, Inc., 1964), pp. 318-19.

54. *Ibid.*

55. *Ibid.*

Use of symbols of inferiority: ". . . In Hitler's Germany people were required . . . to wear certain garb . . . indicating they were Jews. The use of the back door or the back seat in public transportation is a fast-disappearing symbol of segregation and prejudice imposed by a *dominant* group on a *minority* one [italics added]."[56]

These two passages merit scrutiny for several reasons: First, it is difficult to understand how the authors are able to use the word "some" as a substitute for the six million Jews exterminated in Hitler's Germany. Second, it is the closest reference these authors make to discrimination against Negroes in the United States; third, since segregated seating in public transportation no longer existed when this text was published (1964), the reference is factually incorrect; and fourth, in its use of the terms *dominant* vs. *minority*, the authors create an improper dichotomy —the more correct usage being, of course, *majority* vs. *minority*.

The only direct references to blacks in the Cole and Montgomery text—other than a one-sentence mention of the N.A.A.C.P. at the conclusion of a chapter on minority groups—are found in a discussion of life expectancy and illiteracy rates. In the case of the former, the text includes a chart comparing the life expectancy of blacks and whites during the first half of the twentieth century.[57] These statistics do reflect the gross differences which actually exist between these two groups, but because there is no explanation given for this phenomenon, the student is left to conclude that the differences are due to innate causes rather than environmental conditions.

The authors' approach to illiteracy is, however, not quite so subtle. After pointing out that in "1952, ten out of every one hundred non-white persons were illiterate, as compared with two out of every one hundred white persons,"[58] they then add: "The armed forces look with suspicion upon the person who has less than five years of schooling. . . ."[59] This statement is followed by a quote from the U.S. Office of Education which states that: "Illiteracy reduces national wealth. Results in social and cultural lags. Weakens national security . . . [and] Endangers democracy."[60] Since the authors give no explanation for the differences in illiteracy rates, the student might erroneously conclude that the higher

---

56. *Ibid.*
57. *Ibid.*, pp. 193-94.
58. *Ibid.*, p. 250.
59. *Ibid.*
60. *Ibid.*

rates of non-white illiteracy are either the result of genetic differences or represent a self-imposed condition.

Social Living, by Landis,[61] parallels the Cole and Montgomery text in many ways. In a discussion of group prejudice, the author notes that "every now and then we encounter evidences of group prejudices" such as the "white against the Negro," the "Christian against the Jew," the "native-born opposed to foreign-born, and vice versa." He continues: "such *irritations* indicate that we have not yet fully attained the democratic ideas of mutual respect and equality of opportunity [italics added]."[62] Again we find an interesting choice of words to describe a serious social problem. One wonders whether "irritation" is actually the most appropriate word to use to describe the types of "group prejudices" practiced by the "white against the Negro" in America?

Landis' *Sociology*[63]—a revised edition of *Social Living*—emphasizes a belief in the fluidity of social classes in America. In this text, the author notes that it is the school system which may be "counted upon as the most important device by which all may rise."[64] What a cruelly ironic effect this statement must have on those students who are immobilized in a segregated school system—(which is itself the result of a rigidly segregated residential pattern)—and who know that they are not receiving the kind of education by which they too may rise.

Perhaps nowhere is the author's "all-white" bias so well illustrated as in the following comment: "Historically, it has been true that to be born with light skin color has meant high status. . . . Even in countries where the white race was much in the minority, white skin color meant high status."[65] The egocentric subjectivity inherent in this last statement is particularly inappropriate in a sociology text. One is tempted to ask: "In whose history? The Far East's? The Middle East's? Africa's before the eighteenth century?"

In contrast to the Cole and Montgomery text, Landis' *Sociology* does present a brief discussion of different problems faced by blacks in areas such as housing, jobs, schools, and voting. This section concludes on the following note:

> The *extreme* groups are impatient with "tokenism" and "gradualism."
> . . . In 1963 their crusades erupted in dramatic suddenness in protest

61. Paul H. Landis, *Social Living* (Boston: Ginn and Co., 1961).
62. *Ibid.,* p. 313.
63. Paul H. Landis, *Sociology* (Boston: Ginn and Co., 1964).
64. *Ibid.,* p. 141.
65. *Ibid.,* p. 97.

marches . . . boycotts, and picketing. *Extremist* organizations among both Negroes and whites gained memberships.

The resulting violence and unrest shocked the more conservative leaders of both races. They saw the progress made through the moderate approach being threatened by the spread of racial hostility [italics added].[66]

This paragraph undoubtedly expresses a commonly held opinion of the civil rights movement, but to the student it appears as a fact, not an opinion.

Landis concludes the chapter on minority groups by discussing what students can "do as persons about prejudice and discrimination."[67] Among the list of suggestions is: "If you are a member of an unpopular minority, appraise your own personality and behavior."[68] Adorno, Frenkel-Brunswik, Levinson, and Sanford in their classic study of *The Authoritarian Personality* (1950) presented conclusive evidence to indicate that the causes of prejudice do not lie, as Landis suggests, in the "personality and behavior" of those who are discriminated against, but rather in the personality of those who discriminate.[69] In offering such a recommendation, this text helps to perpetuate a notion which was authoritatively discredited almost two decades earlier. Thus, Landis' admonition is not only an example of bad sociology, it is poor psychology as well.

Koller and Couse's *Modern Sociology*[70] is similar in both tone and overall approach to the Cole and Montgomery and the Landis texts insofar as all of these authors avoid a straightforward discussion of social problems. Topics such as "social conflict" and "social mobility" are presented without mentioning blacks. In the Koeller and Couse text, the student is told that India is an example of a society with a "class system" while an "open-class" system prevails in the United States.[71] And, in a paragraph on residential segregation, the student is told that it is in South Africa where one may find an example of this form of discrimination.

---

66. *Ibid.*, p. 400.
67. Landis, *Sociology*, p. 401.
68. *Ibid.*
69. T. W. Adorno, Else Frenkel-Brunswick, D. J. Levinson, and R. N. Sanford, *The Authoritarian Personality* (New York: Harper & Row, Publishers, 1950).
70. Marvin R. Koller and Harold C. Couse, *Modern Sociology* (New York: Holt, Rinehart & Winston, Inc., 1965).
71. *Ibid.*, p. 156.

it can be done

Surely, these texts lend support to those critics who have charged the schools with presenting an irrelevant, antiseptic, and artificial curriculum.[72] Consequently, it is refreshing to find a textbook that is not only free of such flaws but which also demonstrates that high school sociology textbooks can deal effectively with such subjects as segregation and prejudice. Gavian and Rienow's *Our Changing Social Order* is a good example of such a textbook.[73]

While the authors of the previously discussed texts practiced a kind of "Sunday sociology" in which the Negro was sermonized about in a special chapter on "Minority Groups," Gavian and Rienow include the problems faced by black Americans as an integral part of their presentation. Contrast their strong comments on prejudice with those made by the others:

> The *exploitation* and mistreatment of the members of the minority group are justified by saying that the minority group is too ignorant, too dishonest, or too lazy to handle equality were it accorded them. An example of this can be found in the economic exploitation of the Negro in our country. In many areas Negroes are allowed to work only in positions of unskilled labor; they are denied opportunity to advance to higher positions; and they are paid substandard wages for their work.[74]

Gavian and Rienow deal with such pertinent topics as the psychological effects of discrimination on minority groups; they document the obstacles encountered by the rural poor in obtaining an education, and they include an entire chapter on urban housing problems. Furthermore, they do not avoid unpleasant facts, pointing out for example that despite recent legislation forbidding racial discrimination in federal housing, "when a Negro tries to rent or purchase a home in a better section of town he is sometimes blocked by the refusal of whites to accept him as a neighbor."[75] In contrast with the other sociology texts, the newer editions of this book includes a number of pictures of blacks. It is the only text that includes pictures of blacks illustrative of "a family" *qua* family and not as examples of "famous" blacks or "problems of minority

---

72. Mario D. Fantini and Gerald Weinstein, *The Disadvantaged; Challenge to Education* (New York: Harper & Row, Publishers, 1968).
73. Ruth Wood Gavian and Robert Rienow, *Our Changing Social Order* (Boston: D. C. Heath, 1964).
74. *Ibid.*, p. 239.
75. *Ibid.*, p. 242.

groups." This is significant because it is precisely the inclusion of such a picture which does more to acknowledge pluralism as a fact and not as a slogan than three additional pages of trite sermonizing.

With the exception of the Gavian and Rienow text the most commonly used sociology textbooks effectively ignore any reference to discussions of social conflict in this country. Jules Henry calls this kind of teaching "education for social stupidity"[76] because a student is only given material which confirms popular social mythology. As a result of such an approach, many history and government texts perpetuate "sentimentalities about agrarian, rural, entrepreneurial America," and portray city government as a "kind of Cub Scout Den presided over by a scoutmaster";[77] sociology texts do not deal with the hard evidence of racial, economic and social disadvantage which form a real part of this nation's social structure. Evasion of controversial issues is often defended on the grounds that children should be sheltered. Fielder, on the other hand, suggests teachers, not children, wish to be sheltered.[78]

An examination of textbooks in history, government and sociology is disturbing for many reasons, not the least of which is the knowledge that so few schools (especially those in urban areas) have the money to purchase the more recent texts and will, thus, continue to use the older ones. The possibility for healing our educational wounds through better teachers, more enlightened community pressure, and locally designed instructional materials does exist. But what also exists is the reality that most teachers must continue to use older textbooks.

In the past year it has not been uncommon to hear many social studies teachers defend their use of these older texts by insisting that they could not afford to get rid of these older books because they represented too big an investment. This statement highlights an interesting contemporary paradox: the phenomenon of an economic system which has resulted in unparalleled prosperity now challenged by radicals who wish to destroy this system, juxtaposed with the unwillingness of the established institutions to make even so minimal a response to this threat as, say, the purchase of new textbooks. It is not unreasonable to suggest that we might consider what kind of an investment the continued use of obsolete textbooks really represents in order to gain a clearer picture of precisely what we can or cannot afford.

---

76. Jules Henry, "Education for Social Stupidity," *The New York Review of Books* (May 9, 1968).
77. William R. Fielder, "Two Styles of Schools Talk About Values," *Social Education* 31 (1967): 36.
78. *Ibid.*

CHAPTER 6

Their Own Thing: A Review of Seven Black History Guides Produced by School Systems

Juel Janis

introduction

The following chapter examines samples of educational materials on black history written and published by local school systems. These guides merit attention for several reasons. First, they indicate that teachers and students in different school systems are exposed to a number of widely divergent ideas on what constitutes black history. Materials discussed here reveal two basically different attitudes toward the compilation of black history guides. One approach assumes that black history should be presented in terms of black heroes and black contributions. The other stresses the need to deal with heroes and contributions, along with the social and psychological aspects of black-white relations in American history.

Obviously, the Negro history supplements used by a particular school system play an important role in determining how students and teachers will perceive the subject matter. Second, an examination of these booklets clearly demonstrates that some school systems are better qualified than others to prepare a quality product. Some booklets are plagued with historical distortions, grammatical errors, and the omission of many pertinent facts. Others are historically accurate, well-written, and provide the student with a straightforward analysis of the issues involved. Third, these booklets highlight a significant difference in attitude of educators toward the treatment of controversial issues, some approaching these issues directly, others avoiding them altogether.

Preparing a local publication is not a simple matter. Despite the apparent advantage of not being handicapped by commercial considerations (i.e., the need to write in order to appeal to the widest possible audience), the quality of these guides is influenced markedly by the adequacy of financial resources, sufficient time and skill for scholarly research and writing, the availability of resource materials, the assistance of qualified professional consultants, the political and philosophical persuasion of local pressure groups, and the attitudes of the local school hierarchy.

The debate over the merits of locally prepared materials is particularly relevant at this time. If the increasing demand throughout the nation for local control becomes reality, it is possible that large amounts of educational curricula will be written by teachers and neighborhood parents. The following chapter attempts to provide the reader with insight into what happens when school systems "do their own thing."

In the mad scramble to respond to the continuing accusation of racism in American history texts, many school systems have decided to "do their own thing." Doing one's own thing these days may mean many things; in this particular context it means producing supplementary materials on black history. The notion is that such an undertaking will correct the errors and omissions of the older history texts.

The pattern is clear: several teachers, supervisors, and administrators form a committee to write a black history supplement which is subsequently published by the school system with titles such as *The Negro in American Life, Contributions of the Negro,* or *The Negro in American History,* etc. The booklet is used either by teachers as a teaching guide or by students as a supplementary text. The liberals who have urged the school system to "do something" are pacified; the militants proclaim their victory; and the school system is off the hook. But "doing something" and "getting off the hook" can often be only short-term palliatives. Sometimes merely "doing something" is not enough.

One educational commentator some years ago marveled at the masochistic tendencies of those educators who spent long hours faithfully counting the number of pages on which blacks were not mentioned. Masochistic or not, these efforts resulted in significant revisions in many of the most widely used U.S. History and Government textbooks.[1] So far,

1. Juel M. Janis, "Old Bottles—New Wine: Textbook Revisions in the Sixties," *Teachers College Record* 72 (December, 1970): 289-301.

the same critical eye has not been directed towards the new black history booklets. This is unfortunate, since an examination of five such booklets published by educators in the District of Columbia, Milwaukee, New York City, Madison, and the State of Kentucky reveals substantial differences in the quality of these publications. Teachers and administrators who intend to write a booklet of this kind for their own school system or who plan to use one already available should be aware of these differences if they wish to benefit from the insights contained in some of these booklets and avoid perpetuating the inaccuracies and distortions found in others.

The guides analyzed here were selected for detailed presentations since they illustrate the range of quality to be found in school-produced material, as well as the varied forms such material may take. Additional titles of similar guides may be found under the appropriate heading in the annual compilation of curriculum materials published by the Association for Supervision and Curriculum Development, National Educational Association, Washington, D. C.

While reading the following report it should be remembered that a number of these guides have been revised or are in the process of revision. As experience mounts in the teaching of black history, and understandings are extended, more adequate materials will be forthcoming. As commercial publishers recognize the vitality of the interest in black history, also, the pressure for school-produced materials may wane, even though—as other chapters in this book demonstrate—such commercial materials may not be as adequate as the times demand.

Obviously, the black history booklet used by a particular school system plays an important role in determining how students and teachers view this subject. Most of these booklets reveal two basically different attitudes toward the compilation of a black history guide. One approach assumes that black history should be presented primarily in terms of black heroes and black contributions. The other stresses the need to deal with heroes and contributions as well as with the social and psychological aspects of black-white relations in American history.

district of columbia

Typical of the first approach is the District of Columbia's *The Negro in American History*[2] written in 1964. Designed primarily to supplement

---

2. *The Negro in American History: A Curriculum Resource Bulletin for Secondary Schools* (Washington, D.C.: Public Schools of the District of Columbia, 1964).

the standard texts already in use, it was intended to function as "an integral part of the definitive course in American History required of all high school students in the eleventh grade."[3] Therefore, its chronological arrangement corresponds with the typical progression of material covered in most American history courses.

Although its stated objective was "to substitute facts for distortions and false assumptions"[4] and to develop an appreciation of "the role, achievements, and significant contributions of Negro Americans . . .,"[5] it fails on both counts. In their zealous efforts to correct the errors of many "all-white" texts, the authors have only provided the student with information that is factually inaccurate, a style that is at best paternalistic, and a tone that is misleadingly optimistic.

Ironically, these shortcomings seem to have grown inadvertently out of their own objectives. For the authors, in their attempt to glorify black Americans, fail to consider the realities of what it has meant to be black in a white America. The resulting distortions are obvious when one compares excerpts from this booklet with discussions of similar material from one of the newer American history texts and with the brief but incisive presentation found in the Kerner Commission's Report on Civil Disorders.

The D. C. booklet's description of the role and status of the black during the Revolutionary War, for example, clearly illustrates how glorification can result in distortion. The reader of this booklet is told that:

> . . . the history of the Negro soldier must be viewed as part of the history of the American soldier in the Revolution. So thoroughly were Negroes integrated in colonial and Continental military units that it is usually difficult to identify a soldier as to race. Moreover, since most Negroes of the period were unlettered and thus generally inarticulate, few records have come to us from their hand. One *clue* to racial identity, however, is the use of the prefix "black" before a name or the use of only a single name for an individual [italics added].[6]

However, the reader of the Kerner Commission Report is told that:

> Negroes were at first barred from serving in the Revolutionary Army, recruiting officers having been ordered . . . to enlist no "stroller, Negro or vagabond." Yet Negroes were already actively involved in the struggle for independence.[7]

---

3. *Ibid.*, p. 1.
4. *Ibid.*, p. 3.
5. *Ibid.*, p. 5.
6. *Ibid.*, p. 17.
7. Report of the National Advisory Commission on Civil Disorders, Washington, D.C., March 1, 1968, p. 96.

These accounts obviously reflect two entirely different approaches to this subject. Although, in a later paragraph in the D.C. guide, the reader is told that the official policy of both colonial and Continental officials called for the rejection of Negro soldiers, its introductory statement, which stresses how "thoroughly integrated" into the Revolutionary Armies blacks were, tends to give the student a false understanding of the events of this period.

Parenthetically, one wonders about the use of the term "integrated" in this passage from the D.C. bulletin. With the word *black* perpetually attached to his name and with only a first name for identification it seems unlikely that the black soldier was as *integrated* as the authors would like to believe. Also, judging from the tone of the earlier reference, the authors are apparently unaware of the demeaning implications of identifying individuals by only a single name. This passage also illustrates the tendency of this booklet to praise one example of a black *contribution* to America while at the same time allowing some derogatory or paternalistic material to creep into the text (i.e., the reference to "unlettered" and "generally inarticulate" blacks).

A discussion of the black in nineteenth century America contains similar defects. Again, the emphasis is primarily upon achievements and contributions. For example, the authors state: "Throughout the period 1820-1877, the Negro's desire for freedom and equality produced Negroes of stature and resulted in contributions or achievements by Negroes which strengthened the democratic way of life."[8] In contrast, the Kerner Commission Report described these years as a period of "frustration, disillusionment, anger and fantasy"[9] for the black man in protest against the place American society assigned to him: "'I was free,' Harriet Tubman said, 'but there was no one to welcome me in the land of freedom. I was a stranger in a strange land.'"[10]

In comparing these two passages, it is apparent that the determinedly optimistic tone maintained by the authors of the D. C. booklet gives the students a very restricted interpretation of these years. And, while optimism as an outlook in a history text may not be objectionable per se, when it results in a presentation that is historically distorted and inaccurate, it is indefensible.

An insistence on discussing primarily those facts which may be viewed as inspiring is similarly reflected in the way the authors of the D.C. booklet discuss Lincoln's attitude toward blacks: They state:

---

8. *The Negro in American History* . . ., p. 33.
9. Report of the National Advisory Commission . . ., p. 98.
10. *Ibid.*

He was undoubtedly opposed to slavery which he considered wrong . . .
But, he could not be brought to denounce the whole class of slave owners . . . Moreover, his easy and gracious association with specific Negroes
indicates his lack of concern over such an issue as social equality. Lincoln
frequently invited and met with Negro leaders at the White House . . .[11]

While the attempt to present Lincoln as a man unconcerned "over
such an issue as social equality" is understandable, it is inexcusable in the
light of historical fact. Actually, he had "said repeatedly, in public and
private, that he was a firm believer in white supremacy."[12] In a speech
in 1858, Lincoln also said:

I will say then that I am not, nor ever have been in favor of bringing
about in any way the social and political equality of the white and black
races—that I am not or ever have been in favor of making voters or jurors
of Negroes, nor of qualifying them to hold office, nor to intermarry with
white people; and I will say in addition to this that there is a physical difference between the white and black races which I believe will forbid
the two races living together on terms of social and political equality.[13]

One of the supposed values to be gained by slighting the painful aspects of black history and stressing black achievements is to give black
students a pride in their heritage which should hopefully contribute to
an enhanced self-image, and overcome the negative self-concept which
unfortunately characterizes so many black children.[14] Thus, it is ironic
that the D. C. booklet, in its emphasis on heroes and achievements, has,
in its description of Booker T. Washington, created a picture of him
which is actually far less enhancing to a black child's self-concept than
another description of Washington offered in a current American history
text. The D.C. booklet states:

With the seemingly impossible task of changing a penniless, slavery-stunted people into a compact mass of agricultural or mechanical technicians,

11. *The Negro in American History* . . ., p. 41.
12. Lerone Bennett Jr., "Was Abe Lincoln a White Supremacist?" *Ebony*,
February 1968, p. 36.
13. Charles E. Silberman, *Crisis in Black and White* (New York: Random
House, 1964), pp. 92-93.
14. Mary Ellen Goodman, *Race Awareness in Young Children* (Cambridge,
Mass.: Addison-Wesley Press, Inc., 1952); Kenneth Clark and M. F.
Clark, "Racial Identification and Preference in Negro Children," *Read-
ings in Social Psychology,* edited by T. M. Newcomb and E. L. Hartley
(New York: Holt, Rinehart & Winston, Inc., 1947); David Ausubel and
Pearl Ausubel, "Ego Development Among Segregated Negro Children,"
in *Education in Depressed Areas,* edited by A. Henry Passow (New York:
Teachers College Press, 1963); William C. Kvaraceus, et al., *Negro Self-
Concept* (New York: McGraw-Hill Book Co., 1965).

Booker T. Washington, like Columbus who discovered the West while seeking the East, plunged courageously into the undertaking.[15]

Whereas, Wade, Wilder, and Wade note:

> In 1895 Booker T. Washington delivered a speech . . . in Atlanta. It was the first time that a Negro had spoken to a large mixed audience in the south. Everyone waited to hear what he would say about the Negro's separate status. "In all things that are purely social," Washington said, "we can be as separate as the fingers, yet one as the hand in all things essential to mutual progress." Perhaps this was the only position a responsible Negro leader could take in 1895. But a few restless, well-educated Negroes resented Washington's "Atlanta Compromise." In the early 1900's they would spearhead a movement to win not only equal economic opportunities for Negroes but equal social and political rights as well.[16]

From the first account the student reads of a "penniless, slavery-stunted people" who were changed "into a compact mass of agricultural or mechanical technicians" by a leader who had to plunge "courageously" into this "seemingly impossible task"—hardly a description that can enhance his self-concept. From the second account, the student is told that, given the conditions of that period, Washington's speech was perhaps a necessity. For many well-educated Negroes of that time, however, true equality meant not only economic equality but social and political equality as well.

Reviewing the preceding examples from the D.C. booklet, it is apparent that the authors' very admirable goal of substituting "facts for distortions and false assumptions" is not attained. And, as one critic recently noted, although the blacks have been ignored or lied about in American history in the past, this does not mean that it is now necessary to "tell other historical lies to repair the damage. Distortion of one sort does not make defensible other kinds of distortions."[17]

milwaukee

The Negro in American Life,[18] written in 1967 by school personnel in Milwaukee, is similar in format to the District of Columbia's publica-

---

15. *The Negro in American History* . . ., p. 126.
16. Richard C. Wade, Howard B. Wilder, and Louise B. Wade, *A History of the United States* (Boston: Houghton Mifflin Co., 1966), p. 398.
17. Jean D. Grambs, *Harvard Educational Review* 39 (Summer 1968):605-611.
18. *The Negro in American Life* (Milwaukee: Public Schools of Milwaukee, 1967).

tion. Its organization is chronological. Eleven units cover material from the early colonial period to the present. Unlike the D.C. booklet, this guide was not written as a supplementary text for students, but as a parallel to the eleventh grade teacher's guide on U.S. history.

Its more realistic treatment of many of the facts of black life in America marks it as superior to the D.C. publication. Paternalism is recognized and the paternalistic attitudes which characterized many of the abolitionist organizations are acknowledged. A good description of the negative effect of slavery on family structure is coupled with the observation that Southern blacks encountered hostility even in northern environments. However, it still perpetuates the mythology of Lincoln as a "kind and considerate person" whose "relationships with Negroes extended from official to private and unofficial action."[19] And, it describes school desegregation as a fait accompli following President Eisenhower's decision to order federal troops into Little Rock.

Moreover, the overly optimistic tone of the D.C. booklet is present here too. Almost without exception every chapter ends on an unfailingly cheerful note. This optimism has resulted in the formation of factually inaccurate conclusions which are similar to those in the D.C. publication. For example, in an attempt to illustrate the importance of the particular accomplishments of outstanding black men in American history, the authors have adopted a position which appears to assert that these accomplishments helped to change white prejudicial attitudes and beliefs in relation to blacks. Specifically, the reader is told that because of the talents of Benjamin Banneker "*more Americans came to realize* that, given the latitude to develop their skills, Negroes were gifted and capable of intellectual productivity [italics added]."[20] Frederick Douglass is said to have "*proved to many*, that, given a chance, the freed slave could excel,"[21] and, in reviewing the accomplishments of black musicians, scientists, educators, etc., the authors state that the achievements of these individuals "*made the thinking public realize* that Negroes were endowed with the same talents as other humans [italics added]."[22] In each of these examples, it is possible to draw the conclusion that the racial discrimination experienced by blacks in this country is the result of a lack of opportunity to display their skills and talents. Therefore, if and when black men are given the opportunity to demonstrate their abilities white Americans will "come to realize" that Negroes "are endowed with the

19. *Ibid.*, p. 36.
20. *Ibid.*, p. 17.
21. *Ibid.*, p. 29.
22. *Ibid.*, p. 68.

same talents as other humans." As with so many things there is a grain of truth here. Obviously, the successful accomplishments of any minority group member tends to reduce the opportunity for stereotyping of the majority. Yet, to suggest that these accomplishments significantly reduce prejudice not only fails to deal with the social and psychological factors responsible for racial prejudice, but also ignores its irrational aspects.

Perhaps this booklet's most glaring weakness is its inclusion of material which, in the lingo of *Time* magazine, can only be labeled as "non-facts," that is, facts which are three-parts fluff and one-part substance. For example, in a supposed attempt to stress the high level of civilization attained by the early African societies the reader is told: "The social institutions we find in contemporary America existed in the way of life accepted by the citizens of these [African] nations. Although they took different forms, the people of these societies had family life, government, religion, the arts, and economic systems."[23] One wonders how these basic characteristics differ from those of any society? Perhaps these facts do provide a modicum of information for the teacher who lacks any anthropological background, but it does not provide him with any understanding or appreciation of the level of development of these African societies —the very information, in fact, that the authors intended to convey. At best this booklet is superficial and certainly does little to help a teacher understand black history.

detroit

The Struggle for Freedom and Rights; Basic Facts About the Negro in American History,[24] originally published in 1963 by the Detroit Board of Education, is not comparable to the D.C. booklet or the Milwaukee publication because it was written expressly for eighth grade students. Though one might expect, because of its lower grade level, that its presentation would be even blander than the other two, this is not the case. In this booklet, black history is not presented only as a story of heroes. The material it offers deals quite straightforwardly with many of the unpleasant aspects of the black experience in America. Over a third of this booklet is devoted to the history of slavery. The authors point out its ancient origins, note that it did not always represent the domination of one

23. *Ibid.*, p. 2.
24. *The Struggle for Freedom and Rights* (Detroit: Detroit Public Schools, 1967).

race over another, and deal with the moral issues it raises. The misery of the slaves in America is treated in some detail, and there are numerous examples cited of slave rebellions and attempted escapes. While the Milwaukee booklet stressed the protests against slavery by the early colonists, the abolitionists, and some political leaders, the Detroit publication bluntly acknowledges the fact that slavery continued despite these protests because so many "people were so busy going about their daily business that they really paid little attention to it."[25]

Unfortunately, this otherwise fine book is weakened by its overly brief treatment of the period from the Supreme Court school desegregation decision in 1954 to the present. There is a brief reference to the Civil Rights movement under Martin Luther King's leadership, but there is no reference to such timely issues as black power and black militancy. Furthermore, other than a brief footnote defining such terms as *discrimination, prejudice, segregation,* and *integration,* there is no direct attempt to deal with these problems. This publication, like the D.C. and the Milwaukee booklet concerns itself only with a purely historical presentation, foregoing any opportunity of exploring racial issues.

Disregarding for the moment the specific failings of the D.C. and the Milwaukee booklets, one might well question the legitimacy of any approach to black history that deals only with "heroes" and "contributions." Larry Cuban recently considered this question, delineating two types of history—Black History and Negro History. Black History, he posited, was written for the express purpose of instilling racial pride, stressing "only the hero, only the victory" and as such was purely propaganda.[26] Negro History, on the other hand, offers a more balanced view of the American past and present, and thereby corrects the distortions and fills in the "enormous gaps of information about people of color in this nation. Restraint and balance mark this approach. . . ."[27] If one accepts Cuban's distinction, then his conclusion that Black History, designed to improve black self-concept and to instill racial pride, belongs in a parochial education and not in the classroom, seems obvious. But Negro History, dealing with both successes and with the social and psychological explanations for failure, is most appropriately taught in the public schools.

---

25. *Ibid.,* p. 21.
26. Larry Cuban, "Black History, Negro History, and White Folk," *Saturday Review,* September 21, 1968, p. 64.
27. *Ibid.*

guides for teachers: two in new york city

Still another way to classify these black history guides is to separate them into those that are limited to a purely historical approach and those which also include lesson plans, suggested readings, and other curriculum activities. *The Negro in American History*, issued in 1964 by the New York City Board of Education, as well as the D.C., Milwaukee, and Detroit publications, are examples of booklets which offer only an historical presentation.[28] On the other hand, *Lesson Plans on African-American History*, issued in the fall of 1969 by the United Federation of Teachers in New York City, combines an historical presentation with sections on music, poetry, and biography, each with a separate lesson plan.[29]

Two black history guides in New York City might seem superfluous. Thus, one might assume that the difference in format between the two books resulted from the U.F.T.'s attempt to supplement the Board of Education's publication. While the assumption may be valid, unfortunately the material in the U.F.T. book on the whole is so inferior to the Board of Education book that the use of these two books as a complement to one another is infeasible.

Irving Cohen, a New York City high school social studies teacher, wrote the Board of Education book with the help of John Hope Franklin, who served as a special consultant for this project. Early drafts of this manuscript were reviewed by such scholars as Aaron Brown, Oscar Handlin, Benjamin Quarles, and Charles H. Wesley. The book was published as a result of proposals made by an *ad hoc* committee of teachers and supervisors charged with the responsibility of assessing curricular material dealing with minority groups. According to the New York City U.F.T. President Albert Shanker, the United Federation of Teachers book was the culmination of over a year's work by a union committee composed of more than a dozen black and white teachers.[30] The frontispiece of this booklet notes that it was "compiled, written and edited by New York City teachers."

These books differ considerably in both format and in content. The Board of Education book which begins with a chapter on "Slavery in the Old World" and ends with a chapter on "The Quest for Equality: 1945-

---

28. *The Negro in American History* (New York City: Board of Education, 1964).
29. *Lesson Plans on African-American History* (New York City: United Federation of Teachers, AFL-CIO, 1969).
30. "U.F.T. Issues in Negro History," *The New York Times*, p. 47, October 21, 1969.

1964," offers a chronological, continuous narrative account of black history. More than a third of this guide deals with the history of the black man in the twentieth century, and covers such topics as "The Negro and the New Deal Program," "Unions and Employment," and "Civil Rights During the Roosevelt Era." The last chapter presents an excellent summary of problems blacks have faced in such areas as housing, employment, travel, voting rights, and education—issues barely touched upon in the U.F.T. publication.

Brief historical and biographical reports, each with its own "Lesson Plan," are presented in segmented fashion in the U.F.T. book. Its chronological presentation extends only through the Reconstruction Era, and the last third of the book contains primarily a number of biographical sketches, a few pages on the Niagara Movement and the N.A.A.C.P., and a rather long section on migrant workers. In spite of its length (204 pages as compared to the Board of Education's 150 pages), this book lacks both the depth and the breadth of the Board of Education publication. Too often it offers information that is either redundant or only remotely associated with black history—for example, two paragraphs are devoted to a description of the geographical location of Africa and an entire page is devoted to the life of the anthropologist Louis Leakey. Because much of the material in this book is presented in shotgun fashion, the effect is impressionistic, much like a Fellini film or a Joyce novel, with free-floating imagery and sparks of challenging ideas but with no apparent effort to coordinate these pieces at the editorial level. For example, in the section on the Reconstruction Era, a page of background material is followed by a poem that is a page and a half long. This in turn is followed by five pages of *"Work Songs of the Black People,"* and the section concludes with a six-page list of "Myth's" and "Truth's" on the Reconstruction Era.

On the other hand, the Board of Education book is well-organized and presents considerable material that is barely mentioned in any of the other guides. In particular, a fascinating chapter on "The Latin American Experience" provides an interesting foil for a discussion of slavery in the United States. Perhaps the most noteworthy quality of the Board of Education book is its acknowledgment of differences in historical interpretation. Frequently, rather than offer only one explanation for a particular event, the author notes: "Some historians stress," "Others point out that," "Others place the blame on," and "Still others stress. . . ."[31]

31. *The Negro in American History* (New York City: Board of Education, 1964), pp. 51-52.

Both booklets were intended solely for teacher use; but the authors of these two publications seem to hold differing views of the intellectual capacity of New York City school teachers. Compare, for example, the following comments on Paul Laurence Dunbar from the U.F.T. book with those included in the Board of Education publication:

United Federation of Teachers

Paul Laurence Dunbar was born in Dayton, Ohio, June 27, 1872. His mother and father came from Kentucky where they had been slaves.

Paul was a most unusual little boy because he wrote his first poem when he was seven. He got his love for poetry from his mother who used to read to him. She also liked him to read to her.

Paul worked at many jobs but did not enjoy any as much as when he was writing poetry.

Most of his poetry is about the simple folkways of black people but he also wrote books and serious poetry.

He never got the fame he deserved when he was alive, but all of us will remember once we say and read his poetry.[32]

Board of Education

Paul Laurence Dunbar ranks as the best known poet of the period. . . . Dunbar wrote classic English verse but is best known for his dialect poems. Described by William Dean Howells as the first Negro poet "to feel the Negro life esthetically and express it lyrically," Dunbar attempted to portray rural Negroes as real human beings. While Dunbar has been criticized for romanticizing rural Negro life (he never had any first-hand contact with slavery or with the deep South), the sociologist E. Franklin Frazier nevertheless described his verse as "a repository of the colorful and poetic language of the Negro folk." Dunbar was only thirty-four years old when he died in 1906, but he had already won tremendous popular acclaim and a secure place in the history of American literature.[33]

Prose styles aside for the moment, it is interesting to note the differences in interpretation regarding Dunbar's "fame." The U.F.T. book claims that Dunbar "never got the fame he deserved when he was alive." The Board of Education guide states that at the time of his death "he had already won tremendous popular acclaim." How much "fame he deserved" is, of course, relative. Yet, a check with a standard history of American literature points out that William Dean Howells, one of the most important men in American letters in the late nineteenth century,

---

32. *Lesson Plans on African-American History . . .*, p. 161.
33. *The Negro in American History* (New York City: Board of Education, 1964), p. 88.

had written an introduction for Dunbar's *Lyrics of Lowly Life,* published in 1896.[34] This alone is an indication of the positive critical recognition Dunbar received early in his writing career, and would seem to support the interpretation offered in the Board of Education book.

Stylistic differences in these selections are striking. Neither selection is atypical. The simplistic, one and two sentence paragraphs illustrate the way in which much of the material is presented in the U.F.T. book.

For the most part all of the newly published black history guides were written for the purpose of correcting the errors of earlier materials which either ignored this subject or tended to perpetuate past misconceptions. Rather than destroying past misconceptions, the paucity of data in the U.F.T. book somehow seems to create almost the opposite effect. Consider, for example, the unit designed to "develop respect for African civilization and culture" consisting of a two page account by a slave trader of his visit to a West African tribe. In describing this tribe his assertion that he *"never saw a man or woman bask lazily in the sun"* is underlined. A significant part of the story concerns the slave trader's leaving a chest of goods in the village. When he returns he finds the chest "nearly full of the merchandise [he] had placed in it." One of the "Points to Emphasize" in the Lesson Plan accompanying this account suggests that the "children compare their own previous conceptions of Africa with what the slave trader found."[35] The slave trader's description of the industry and honesty of these people is intended to refute negative stereotypes children may have regarding African life.

Such an approach is questionable. Placing so strong an emphasis on such points as "industry" and "honesty" tends psychologically to lend credibility to the stereotype. Furthermore, the use of a single document to "develop respect for African civilization and culture" seems to be a particularly poor teaching technique, since it expects a student to generalize on the basis of such scant data. And, to expect that this one "document will" (as this book claims) *"do much to help correct* [the] false picture" and the "very negative view" children as well as adults have "toward the culture and civilization of Africa" is certainly unreasonable (italics added).[36]

While both publications acknowledge the inadequacies of present texts in dealing with the African heritage, the Board of Education publi-

---

34. Robert E. Spiller, et al., *Literary History of the United States* (New York: The Macmillan Co., 1965), p. 854.
35. *Lesson Plans on African-American History . . .*, pp. 25-27.
36. *Ibid.*, p. 25.

cation delves into some of the reasons for these inadequacies, citing not only the "bias and bigotry existing within the halls of academe," but also the problems faced by historians who explore Africa's past.[37] Specifically, it notes that the historian

> must, for example, work with primary source materials other than writings . . . He must, . . . define the "Africa" with which he means to deal . . . he must consider that the African Negro shared his continent with the Semitic tribes and the Hamitic peoples of the north and that biological and cultural fusion . . . took place throughout Africa from the earliest times.[38]

These observations are followed by an eight page discussion of three West African kingdoms and an analysis of African culture traditions including a summary of different marriage patterns, religious practices, music, and languages. The chapter concludes with a comment on the "public and scholarly controversy concerning the transmission and preservation of African culture in the New World . . ."[39]

In a foreword to the U.F.T. book, the reader is told that the opinions expressed "are those of the individual writers and are not necessarily the opinions of all writers . . ." Surely, the editors' desire to "recognize the right of dissent and freedom of opinion" among the contributors to this book is commendable; nonetheless, a modicum of editorial supervision would have been welcomed if for no other reason than to give the reader a more balanced presentation than is offered here. The editors' interpretation of the "right to dissent and freedom of opinion" seems to be used as the rationale for absolving them of all editorial responsibility for providing a more balanced picture of the philosophic responses black Americans have made to life in America.

Specifically, a very good section on Black Nationalist Movements (including concise biographical sketches of Marcus Garvey and Malcolm X followed by many provocative questions) and a particularly hard-hitting ten page section on the plight of the migrant worker are separated by an Uncle Tom-ish story whose moral seems to be that "house servants" shouldn't complain about their work. (One of the objectives of this story is to allow teachers to "stress the importance of every job no matter how menial"[40]—a valid objective certainly, but one which is ill-served by this

---

37. *The Negro in American History*, p. 11.
38. *Ibid.*, p. 12.
39. *Ibid.*, p. 18.
40. *Lesson Plans on African-American History . . .*, p. 188.

particular story.) However, between the militancy of the Marcus Garvey-Malcolm X, and migrant workers pieces, and the submissive tone of the house servant story, the philosophy of Martin Luther King is strangely absent. Actually this appears to be the result of an editorial oversight, since the table of contents lists: "Church Leaders: Dr. Martin Luther King and Others."* In fact, in this section the only reference to Dr. King is a suggestion in the lesson plan that teachers assign a report on his life. Only two other brief allusions to Dr. King appear in the entire book.

Other inexplicable omissions in the U.F.T. book, which also result in an inadequate presentation of black history, occur in a chapter entitled "Short Biographical Sketches." The rationale for the selection of names included in this chapter is obscure. In many cases relatively unknown figures are listed while more notable ones are omitted. Only Ralph Bunche and Thurgood Marshall are included in the list of "*Statesmen and Politicians*"; Robert Weaver, Edward Brooke, Adam Clayton Powell Jr., and Carl Rowan are not discussed. Comparatively little-known authors such as Charles Johnson, Alain Locke, and J. A. Rogers are cited under "*Writers*," (along with more famous authors such as James Baldwin and LeRoi Jones), but no mention is made of Ralph Ellison, Richard Wright or Lorraine Hansberry, nor are there any references here to outstanding black athletes, entertainers, or musicians.

In an era when mentioning editorial or typographical errors is considered "carping," such details are introduced at one's peril. Nevertheless, a closer look at this section reveals numerous errors which not only are indicative of the sloppy editing found throughout this book, but also adversely affect the reader's ability to utilize the information presented. For example, almost a quarter of the names listed here do not note either the dates of birth or death. In other cases, a name is followed by a birth date without a death date even when it is highly unlikely that this individual is still alive—"(1806-   )" or "(1844-   )." And, while some sketches quote from specific sources, often these quotes include only an incomplete reference such as "(*Eyewitness*—Katz)."

Such criticisms aside for the moment, the selections dealing with music and poetry in the U.F.T. book are perhaps the most effective contribution of this particular guide, providing the teacher with material not offered in any of the other guides. Numerous poems and songs (with

---

*A similar oversight may be found in the introductory statement which notes that the conclusion of the book provides "background information on *White Racism* based on the . . . U.S. Advisory Committee of Civil Disorders" report. In fact no such material is included.

music) are included throughout the text accompanied by pertinent questions to help teachers analyze this material with their students. But even here most of the material and the assignments following it are appropriate primarily for elementary pupils and are generally unsuitable for junior and senior high school students.

madison, wisconsin

In light of the exceptional excellence of the Board of Education guide as well as the failings of the U.F.T. book, it is impractical to attempt to use these two books to consider the merits of a lesson plan approach to black history as opposed to a purely historical approach. However, *The Negro in the Social Studies Curriculum*,[41] published by the Madison, Wisconsin school system, and *Contributions of the Negro*,[42] published by Kentucky's State Department of Education, provide more appropriate material for judging a "Lesson Plan" presentation, since both of these publications combine discussions of black history with suggestions for integrating this material into the school curriculum.

Both of these booklets fall into the category of Negro History and reflect a philosophy which asserts that it is impossible to have black history without white history, or white history without black history, since the history of the black man in America is, according to this position, clearly woven into the fabric of American history. Thus, to suggest that "black history" is a thing apart is misleading. Kenneth Clark has summarized his argument succinctly:

> An inescapable reality is the fact that the American Negro is inextricably American . . . He is America. His destiny is one with the destiny of America. His culture is the culture of Americans. His vices and virtues are the vices and virtues of Americans. His dilemmas are essentially the dilemmas of Americans.[43]

From this second point of view, the whole notion of "contributions" or "heroes" is contrived and artificial, and mentioning "black heroes" and "black contributions" without discussing the effect of slavery and the his-

---

41. *The Negro in the Social Studies Curriculum* (Madison: Public Schools of Madison, 1968).
42. *Contributions of the Negro* (Frankfort, Kentucky: Department of Education, 1968).
43. Kenneth Clark, *Dark Ghetto* (New York: Harper & Row, Publishers, 1965), p. 219.

tory of racism represents a presentation that is equally as distorted as the material found in most "all-white" texts.

The Madison booklet, published in 1968, is a 105-page guide for teachers. It is divided into five "instructional episodes": Kindergarten through third grade; grade 5; grades 8-9; grade 11; and grade 12. Unlike some of the other publications it includes both a bibliography to use in conjunction with the guide and a list of resource materials. Also included are proposals for class discussions, role-playing activities, field trips, research projects, etc. No heroes here, no sharp separation of white and black history. In fact, the authors' notation that black history should not be presented as a separate episode and "taught as a self-contained unit of work at a given grade level" only to then be "put back with complacency"[44] is a direct refutation of such a separation.

In the Madison booklet the willingness of its authors to deal with the reality of the past as it relates to the present results in assignments which ask a student not only to study civil rights legislation but to consider a question such as: What is "the difference between a law being passed and a law being enforced?"[45] Here there is an attempt to deal with historical facts as such as well as with the social, political and psychological implications of these facts.

Unfortunately, the five instructional episodes in this booklet are not all of the same caliber. Apparently, this material was prepared by several authors, and some quite obviously approached the assignment with greater competence than others. In particular, the material suggested for children in the early primary grades is unrealistic and inadequately developed. For example, to give children an understanding of minority group membership, it is suggested that children be grouped according to hair color, height, shirt colors, etc. Although this latter technique has been used well with older white children (in experimental studies where these grouping assignments were accompanied by discriminatory practices on the part of the teacher against certain groups), it is difficult to see how this assignment, as it is presented here, serves any purpose other than to illustrate grouping differences according to visible characteristics. Certainly, this assignment does not offer a white child an insight into the actual feeling of slum life, nor does it offer him the *meaning* of minority group membership. It is of course possible to challenge the validity of attempting to give very young children an understanding of pov-

---

44. *The Negro in the Social Studies Curriculum . . .,* p. ii.
45. *Ibid.,* p. 28.

erty and discrimination, since these are obviously difficult experiences to convey. Yet, the authors of this section have posed problems for this age group which are actually even more challenging. In one section, teachers are advised that if in the current events period a child brings in a newspaper article which relates to problems of racial conflict, then the child, after some classroom discussion, should be asked "what can we do to help or alleviate this situation?"[46] This is a tough question for urban planners, let alone first and second grade children, and the very asking of such a question tends to hide its complexity and may even give a child the illusion that he is somehow capable of successfully addressing himself to a problem of this type.

The presentation of material for students at the fifth grade level is markedly uneven. Teachers are instructed, for example, to ask their students to prepare an essay "on thoughts of a black as he compares his native land with new homeland (sic),"[47] or to write a play "on a Negro family that came to America during the Revolutionary War."[48] There is an air of fantasy to both of these assignments. In the first instance, this booklet does not include background references for the student or the teacher to use as a guide to answer this question. The student's essay must be based solely on his own ideas about life in Africa as opposed to life in colonial America. In the second instance, asking a student to write a play on a black family during the Revolutionary War effectively obscures from the student the historical facts regarding the effect of slavery on black family life.

Despite these examples, this fifth grade unit includes much data that is particularly relevant for students in Wisconsin. There is a question and answer section which reports the black population figures for Wisconsin, the types of jobs blacks hold in the state, and the unemployment and school dropout figures for blacks in Wisconsin. Furthermore, the booklet includes the results of a survey which reported how blacks felt about the discrimination they experienced in housing and in employment in Wisconsin. There are also data on the number of blacks at the University of Wisconsin from Madison (three) and the number of black teachers in the Madison Public School System in 1968-1969 (fourteen). In place of vague allusions to the effects of discrimination, students are given specific facts; and in place of optimistic claims regarding employment oppor-

46. *Ibid.*, p. 9.
47. *Ibid.*, p. 22.
48. *Ibid.*, p. 23.

tunities in the state, students are told exactly how many jobs such as teaching are actually filled by blacks in one of Wisconsin's largest cities.

Units written for eighth and ninth grade students present material that is equally pertinent. According to the authors, one objective of this unit is to allow students to develop a greater understanding of life in America's urban ghettoes. Hence, students are asked to first read a series of articles on the history of ghettoes in America and then to respond to such discussion questions as "What were the ghetto conditions like in 1900? What are they like today? Have conditions changed?"[49] Ideologically, this assignment reflects the authors' belief that schools can and should serve as forums for the discussion of contemporary social problems. Even more illustrative of this belief is a teaching strategy such as the following: Debate the resolution: "the American Negro civil rights movement should adopt violent means to achieve those civil rights which are guaranteed to all Americans."[50] After the blandness of so many social studies curriculum guides, it is encouraging to see that this material was endorsed by Madison's Superintendent of Schools, and is now, hopefully, being used in Madison's schools.

Units written for the eleventh and twelfth grades are equally as challenging. Reading material from the Kerner Commission Report and *Transaction* magazine is assigned to eleventh grade students. Furthermore, students at these grade levels are expected to examine the subtle differences between Northern and Southern approaches to race relations, and they are expected to be able to evaluate the significance of the rise of the black power movement in Northern cities.

Twelfth grade students are asked to consider the psychological appeal of the black power movement within a context which emphasizes the importance of this movement in stopping the social pathology of the ghetto. An implicit assumption of this unit is that students must confront the civil rights issue not as "a *static* question" but rather as "a continually *evolving*" process.[51] Tough questions such as "How can society best satisfy the changing needs of the black American without breakdown in our social order?"[52] are typical of the questions posed for students at this grade level. Critics who charge the curriculum with being "remote" and "artificial"[53] might find the material in this booklet quite surprising.

---

49. *Ibid.*, p. 70.
50. *Ibid.*, p. 76.
51. *Ibid.*, p. 96.
52. *Ibid.*, pp. 96-97.
53. Marion D. Fantani and Gerald Weinstein, *The Disadvantaged; Challenge to Education* (New York: Harper & Row, Publishers, 1968).

kentucky

Contributions of the Negro to American Life and Culture, published in 1968 by the Kentucky Department of Education, is similar in tone to the Madison booklet. It is well-documented, sensitively written, and deals with controversial issues in a direct manner. Not only does it include a carefully researched set of facts, but it also attempts to deal with the social and psychological implications of these facts. This booklet was written primarily for teachers, administrators, and curriculum supervisors and is based on the belief that it is imperative for schools to make a "frank examination and critical evaluation of the psychological, historical, and cultural bases for the prejudices which operate against the minority groups in our midst."[54] Accordingly, the reader is told that this booklet was written in order to encourage a "much greater effort on the part of Kentucky school people to narrow the broad chasm which exists between the democratic ideal of equality to which we pay lip service and the cold reality of prejudice which continues to be evidenced in our actions."[55]

This study is divided into three interrelated areas of inquiry: "(1) the Negro's historical and contemporaneous status; (2) the contribution of the Negro to American life; and (3) the dimensions of prejudice that have made it increasingly difficult for the Negro to assume the place in the American mainstream that he is constitutionally guaranteed and to which he is further entitled by all the unwritten laws of humanity."[56] This last section in particular presents a clear explanation of racial differences, discusses the effect of class and racial differences on social advancement, and describes the numerous manifestations of prejudicial behavior in our society.

After years of exposure to the cliches of the sociology texts,[57] the material in this booklet is refreshing. In place of the notion that "every man can rise regardless of his class," one finds the observation that "In many areas of American life, skin color is still the major determinant of the job and, consequently, the way of life."[58] In place of the belief that constant contact between races will reduce racial prejudice, the authors note that contact *per se* may not be sufficient and that it may, in fact, "simply reinforce existing stereotypes and thereby increase prejudice."[59] This book-

---

54. *Contributions of the Negro . . .,* p. 1.
55. *Ibid.,* p. 3.
56. *Ibid.,* p. 2.
57. Janis, "Old Bottles—New Wine:Textbook Revisions in the Sixties."
58. *Contributions of the Negro . . .,* p. 21.
59. *Ibid.,* p. 18.

let offers evidence which contradicts the popular belief that educated
people "tend to be less prejudiced than those [who are] less well educated," suggesting that:

> "There is little evidence that school consistently causes stereotypes to be
> rejected, or that the educated are less prejudiced or discrimination mind-
> ed in their personal lives. On many issues, the educated show as much
> prejudice as the less educated, and on some issues, they show more."[60]

Current notions equating adjustment and prejudice are also challenged. The authors point out that "the well-adjusted person can be expected to exhibit about the same amount of prejudice as his parents and
his subculture, for what is normal behavior in these [cultures] is his behavior."[61] Accordingly, they note that if an individual "seriously questions the prejudices of the group, he threatens his comfortable niche, his
status, in the group."[62]

Unlike the authors of so many books on intergroup education who
suggest that the use of their books will lead the way to "future brotherhood" and "inter-racial harmony," the authors of the Kentucky booklet
stress the fact that the use of their publication represents only a "mere
beginning" toward the alleviation of prejudice. They state that if the
overall atmosphere of the school experience remains the same, then the
addition of new units and the inclusion of new concepts will not make a
significant difference.[63]

These authors fully acknowledge the difficult problems posed for
teachers and administrators who wish to challenge the social atmosphere
of a school in "a community which jealously guards its prejudices and
biases,"[64] and yet that assert their belief that the role of the school in today's society involves more than the passing on of a cultural heritage—it
also involves a commitment to positive social change. They state their
position with unusual candor:

> . . . if tomorrow's society is to be better than today's—if indeed any rem-
> nant of our society is to survive—then changes must be wrought now
> through education rather than later through greater violence. The school
> must take into account the unique nature of the community it serves, but,
> if it merits the name of "school," it must willingly accept its role as a pow-
> erful agent for social change.[65]

---

60. *Ibid.*, p. 16.
61. *Ibid.*, p. 17.
62. *Ibid.*
63. *Ibid.*
64. *Ibid.*, p. 18.
65. *Ibid.*

In order to implement their philosophy, the authors have outlined specific activities for school personnel to use which will help them to act as agents of social change. In place of the innocuous suggestions so often found in booklets of this type (observe a Negro history week, visit different churches, learn some new spirituals), administrators are advised to engage in such activities as the following: "Consciously plan and conduct public relations programs which will win community support; provide compensatory programs to reduce the learning gap between the affluent and disadvantaged students; and provide guides for extracurricular activities which will insure fair admission practices."[66] Members of the counseling staff are advised that it is necessary to "interpret test data in light of the out-of-school experience of the individual student," to study and develop expertise in counseling students of minority groups," and to "select and administer tests to measure intergroup skills and attitudes."[67] Teachers are advised to "work sincerely and consciously toward the elimination of prejudices and stereotypes which [they] may hold," to "develop expertise in socio-drama and group dynamics," and to "utilize every opportunity to sensitize students to the feelings of others."[68]

One chapter in this booklet deals with methods teachers can use in different subject areas to incorporate material on intergroup education into their own specialties. For example, mathematics teachers are advised to give their pupils data collection assignments relating to the income, occupational, and educational levels of various ethnic and racial groups in America. Science teachers are asked to have their students "Explain how stereotyping is the antithesis of science"; and music teachers are to allow their students to "Explore the relationship of the arts to oppression."[69] The implication of assignments such as these is clear: the elimination of prejudice is the responsibility of everyone in the school system and is not, as so many of the materials on intergroup education appear to suggest, limited to merely a few administrators and social studies teachers.

summary

Clearly, the differences in quality and attitude in these booklets are considerable. Not surprisingly, the inadequacies of some of them seem

---

66. *Ibid.*, p. 33.
67. *Ibid.*, pp. 33-34.
68. *Ibid.*, p. 33.
69. *Ibid.*, p. 41.

to reflect the same inadequacies one finds in many history texts. The errors of commission and omission are all there—unpalatable facts are avoided, palatable facts are stressed, and the result is an unnecessarily biased and distorted historical presentation. However, because these black history publications are relatively new, it is difficult to determine the extent to which they are used in school systems other than the ones for which they were written. Mrs. Kay W. Lumley, Supervising Director of the Reading Clinic in the District of Columbia, in testifying before the House Committee on Education and Labor in 1966, stated that the District of Columbia's booklet was employed not only in the local schools as "basic text material to supplement the classroom textbooks," but in other school districts as well.[70] The pamphlet *Guidelines for Textbook Selection: the Treatment of Minorities,* issued in 1969 by the Pennsylvania Department of Education,[71] lists the D.C. booklet in its selection of approved texts. Thus, it seems likely that this booklet with all of its shortcomings, is being used in cities other than the District of Columbia.

Interestingly, following publication of the D.C. booklet Mrs. Lumley was asked in a Congressional hearing on *Books for Schools and the Treatment of Minorities* if the District of Columbia had "sought or received evaluation from other historians with respect to the accuracy or completeness of the material"[72] used in the D.C. booklet. She replied:

> I don't know if you would call them historians, only other curriculum departments. I understood your question and answer by saying they were using it, which meant they thought it was authentic. I can't say whether it is or isn't. . . . It has history material which the District Department of Public Schools in the District of Columbia feels is appropriate. . . .[73]

Her response highlights one of the major problems that school administrators face when they attempt to compile their own guides on such a subject as black history. The District of Columbia's booklet illustrates the way a local publication can fail to provide students and teachers with sound resource material. However, the high quality of the Madison and Kentucky booklets suggests that some school districts are capable not on-

70. *Books for Schools and the Treatment of Minorities.* Hearings before the Ad Hoc Subcommittee on De Facto School Segregation of the Committee on Education and Labor, House of Representatives 89th Congress, 2nd sess. (Washington, D.C.: U.S. Government Printing Office, 1966), p. 169.
71. *Guidelines for Textbook Selection: The Treatment of Minorities* (Harrisburg, Penn.: Pennsylvania Department of Public Instruction, 1969).
72. *Books for Schools and . . .,* p. 183.
73. *Ibid.*

ly of writing their own black history booklets but of addressing problems which are unique to their own areas.

Accordingly, there are no hard and fast rules on the compilation of black history booklets. Rather, what is needed is a willingness on the part of educators to examine all of the present material with a critical eye before adopting an already published booklet or writing one of their own. Given the mood of the times, however, now that the catchword is "black is beautiful," many educators may be reluctant to criticize the new crop of black history booklets for fear of being misunderstood. This is unfortunate, since criticism is precisely what these black history booklets so desperately need at the present time.

Once teachers and administrators begin to examine the existing booklets critically, they will gain the experience necessary to establish specific guidelines on their own. Lacking such a critical review the continued use of second-rate booklets by school systems—no matter how well-intentioned—will produce a negative effect on teachers and students alike, negative because every single poorly written black history booklet that is approved and published by a school system says quite clearly to its white and black readers: "Why make a first rate effort for what we believe is only a second class subject?" But, if this is not what is intended, then there must be a concerted effort by teachers and administrators to publish material that is academically outstanding. Only in this way can they make credible their oft-asserted claim about the importance of black history.

CHAPTER 7

My Brother's Keeper: A View of Blacks in Secondary-School Literature Anthologies

John C. Carr

introduction

Just as secondary-school social studies textbooks have either distorted the image of blacks in their presentation of history, the operation of government, and the way in which people live together, so have literature anthologies extended the narrow and prejudiced view of the black experience in the United States.

In the following chapter, John C. Carr considers the ways in which blacks are represented and presented in three "traditional" hard-cover anthologies and in three "new" soft-cover collections.

The differences between the oldest of the traditional series and the newest of the paper anthologies is both illuminating and disheartening, encouraging and frightening.

While social studies texts concern themselves largely with men as social beings striving to live and thrive in their environment, literature anthologies should offer a view of men's souls: their aspirations, their dreams, their fantasies, their expression of how it feels to be alive and thriving—or failing—in this "the greatest of all possible worlds." For the reason that literature and social studies complement one another in their impact on our reactions to people and ideas, and because the anthology is the most used literature resource in schools, it is necessary to examine what those textbooks suggest about the black image in the United States —past and present.

Art for art's sake versus art for social purpose is a subject of long-standing debate, argued everywhere from Aristotle's Greece to Mao's China. Given the diversity of men's minds, a resolution of the debate is not probable, as Aristotle knew and Chairman Mao and his "cultural guardians" have come to recognize.

Proponents of literature study for young people who would confine that study to literature for its own sake simply do not know the realities of contemporary schools or the nature of the adolescent in the latter part of the twentieth century. Proponents of literature study who would use it simply to extend the social sciences, or convert it to a guidance function, violate its very nature. Surely, given the growing complexity of human relationships in a technologically-oriented world and the consequent greater need for individuals to develop a personal sense of esthetics, there must be some middle ground which will allow teachers and young people some direction and confidence in developing a value system that sees the relevance of literature as a two-sided coin: "Telling it like it is and might be" and "telling it beautifully."

The prestigious National Council of Teachers of English determined almost thirty years ago that literature instruction should "develop a keen sense of permanent social values" and that literary study should not be regarded as a "storehouse unrelated to the problems with which the world grapples today."[1] If students are asked to believe that literature is a mirror of life, it is reasonable to expect that they will be exposed to examples of it which will enable them to see the variety of all human experience it reflects. Until recently, secondary-school literature anthologies in the United States not only failed to achieve the NCTE's objective regarding social values, but also failed to show in their mirrors of life the multi-cultural and multi-ethnic society in which Americans live.

Just as social studies textbooks began to alter their stereotyped presentations of blacks by the middle of the sixties, so did literature anthologies. To compare the standard secondary-school literature collections of the late fifties and early sixties with the new paperback anthologies is to recognize that, quite literally, a whole new world has been discovered (or, more properly, uncovered).

1. Basic Aims Committee of the National Council of Teachers of English, "Basic Aims for English Instruction in American Schools," *The English Journal* 31 (January, 1942): 45. See also Herbert J. Muller, *The Uses of English* (New York: Holt, Rinehart & Winston, Inc., 1967), pp. 77-94.

The tradition of the textbook as the principle source of instructional material in secondary schools is so ingrained that the power of those books in influencing development is incalculable. And yet it is only in the last several years that young Americans, black or white, have had the opportunities to realize through literature texts that blacks have been literary artists as well as protagonists of literature—and in the process to further realize that black, like white, *is sometimes* beautiful.

In a study of thirty-seven anthology volumes, Dodds found that twenty of them did not have a single selection either by or about Negroes.[2] In another study, Sterling examined thirty-eight volumes, finding that twenty-seven of them "contained no material at all by or about American Negroes."[3] The volumes studied by Dodds and Sterling do not entirely overlap one another, just as the thirty-five volumes examined in this chapter do not entirely overlap those combined studies. Since anthologies are the most common literature resources used by secondary-school students,[4] the evidence accumulated by Dodds and Sterling, and reinforced here, is staggering and incontrovertible: most young people have been—are—exposed to a bland, white, Anglo-Saxon, Protestant view of literature.

While it is unfortunate, it is also accurate to observe that, in general, literature anthologies

> . . . imply a most dangerous falsehood: that over ten percent of [American] citizens do not exist.
> The people and problems that are front page news in almost every daily newspaper are completely left out of most English curricula. Textbooks are still subtly, but definitely, slanted toward white people's achievements, either by completely omitting any reference to Negroes or by presenting the few Negroes that are mentioned as caricatures or stereotypes.[5]

The exclusion or minimizing of blacks in literature anthologies is a double-edged sword: it makes possible the slow and devastating erosion

2. Barbara Dodds, *Negro Literature for High School Students* (Champaign, Ill.: National Council of Teachers of English, 1968), p. 3.
3. Dorothy Sterling, "What's Black and White and Read All Over?" *The English Journal* 57 (November, 1968): 818.
4. James R. Squire and Roger R. Applebee, *High School English Instruction Today: The National Study of High School English Programs* (New York: Appleton-Century-Crafts, 1968), p. 48. See also Fred I. Godshalk, *A Survey of the Teaching of English in Secondary Schools* (Princeton, N.J.: Educational Testing Service, 1969), pp. 16-28.
5. Dodds, *Negro Literature for High School Students*, p. 3.

of self-image for black students, and it also makes possible a sure and limiting restriction on social and artistic depth for those in the majority. The consequences are awesome for a world in trauma.

the role of anthologies

Young people can be helped to develop a system of social values through literature by helping them to enlarge their own lives by better comprehension of others, by allowing them the chance to understand life among people of other cultures, by encouraging them to discern the truth and beauty of the past, and by exposing them to artistic quality. The extent to which anthologies themselves can serve in these capacities is debatable. The emphasis on brief material, the truncating of longer works, the stereotyped "classic" materials presented, the tradition of not offending regional, political, religious, and social groups tends to create a "don't-rock-the-boat" atmosphere. Frequently, the use of anthologies raises the question of whether anything is achieved except providing every student with a copy of materials which may be more difficult to obtain otherwise. (That all students are required to read the same materials and that they are required to read much of the material presented in most current anthologies is another—and alarming—subject.)

One hopes that the better anthologists realize the limitations of their collections, that they expect—even encourage—that the collections be supplemented. For too many students, though, anthologies represent the only material read. In other cases, supplementary simply means "more of the same."

It is certainly true that all literature does not "deal primarily with man as a social animal but with particular men as unique and many-faceted beings."[6] However, anthologies have long been organized around basic socializing themes: self-discovery, family and peer relationships, integrity and patriotism.[7] Although much literature is concerned with man's uniqueness, literature anthologies seem to say by their arrangement, "You are not alone. Look how we are all alike!" Until the recent past, however, literature anthologies, through their omissions and distor-

---

6. James J. Lynch and Bertrand Evans, *High School English Textbooks: A Critical Examination* (Boston: Little, Brown and Company, 1963), pp. 154-55.
7. As Lynch and Evans suggest in their 1963 study, most literature anthologies are "overorganized." One often has the feeling that selections have been forced to fit a preconceived category.

tions, have said to black students: "You are alone. You are not like us at all!"

In studies by Lorang,[8] duCharms and Moeler,[9] and Child,[10] it has been shown that human values and behavior are effected by the literature one reads. Further evidence that individuals (and groups) are conscious of the value potentials of their reading and study is documented by recent and continuing demands that black history and literature be given their places in the curriculum. (Indeed, the history of literary censorship suggests that people have always believed that "reading maketh the full man.")

Aside from teacher direction, the chances a student has for developing values relating to blacks and whites through reading anthologies is directly related to his opportunity to see each reading experience in a context which clearly indicates that all people are appropriate subjects for artistic expression and are equally capable of making artistic comment.

Specifically, the ways in which anthologies create these opportunities are through choice of literary selections, use of illustrations, and editorial comment.

When literary selections are exclusively concerned with whites, as traditionally they have been, the reader begins to understand (if only through osmosis) that what is valued is a morality, a life style, and a view of beauty that is highly specialized and restrictive. The strong possibility exists that blacks come to see their own values undermined and undervalued. In light of the literature anthologies that have been used so long in the United States, is it not significant to consider their contributions to the present, violent repudiation of the image of "right, white, and good" that has been foisted upon black students.

In the six anthology series considered in this chapter, illustrations are an immediate index to the perceptions held by their editors regarding blacks in literature. When a black student progresses through an entire illustrated volume of American literary selections and nowhere finds

8. M. Corde Lorang, Sr., *Burning Ice: The Moral and Emotional Effects of Reading* (New York: Charles Scribner's Sons, 1968).
9. R. duCharms and G. H. Moeler, "Values Expressed in American Children's Readers," *Journal of Abnormal and Social Psychology* 64 (1962): 136-42.
10. Irvin L. Child, et al., "Children's Textbooks and Personality Development: An Exploration in the Social Psychology of Education," *Psychological Monographs* 60 (1946): 1-53.

either a photograph or a drawing of a Negro, what is he to conclude? When blacks are encountered in poses of ignorance, possessing "quaint, odd charm," or engaged only in violence, what more insidious conclusions may he draw? What is the magnitude of the sin of omission when photographs appear of white authors but not of the few blacks represented in a volume?

Next only to the teacher's responsibility in helping students to make inferences, to see relationships, and to draw conclusions is that of the editorial commentary of anthologies. The raising of significant questions, the raising of provocative considerations, the supplying of enlightening background, as well as suggestions of possible interpretation are essential. If no considerations are raised, directly or indirectly, which involve black and interracial relationships, young people may well conclude that literature has no relevance to these issues; they may, thereby, fail to discover that much literature has not only beauty but wisdom to offer those in search of answers to perplexing human questions.

An examination of the extent to which six anthology series allow students opportunities to find social relevance as well as beauty reveals enormous variance ranging from "token integration" to a truly interracial view of mankind.

In the order of their advancing success in presenting an interracial view of life the series are:

Ginn Literature Series,[11] (least successful);

Themes and Writers Series;[12]

Mainstream Series;[13]

America Reads Series;[14]

---

11. Ginn and Company, New York: *Introduction to Literature, The Study of Literature, Understanding Literature, Types of Literature, American Literature, English Literature* (all 1964), Edward S. Gordon, senior editor.
12. Webster Division, McGraw-Hill Book Company, New York: *Focus, Perceptions* (both 1969), *Insights, Encounters, American Literature, Western Literature* (all 1967), G. Robert Carlsen, general editor.
13. Charles E. Merrill Company, New York: *Courage Under Fire, Against the Odds* (both 1967), *They Were First, People Like You, In New Directions* (all three 1968), Charles G. Spiegler, editor.
14. Scott, Foresman and Company, Fair Lawn, N.J.: *Projection Through Literature, Counterpoint in Literature* (both 1967), *Outlooks Through Literature, Exploring Life Through Literature, The United States in Literature, England in Literature* (all four 1968).

Impact Series;[15]
Crossroads Series;[16] (most successful).
An examination of the first and last of these suggests that they are intended for young people living in totally different times and places—despite the fact that both are products of the sixties.

how not to do it

The Ginn Series seems best typified by the remark of a young teacher, who, after attempting to utilize three books of the set, observed, "The editors seem to be under the delusion that the last revolution in this country was the American Revolution. They don't seem to know that times and people have changed."

The Negro is dispatched with "Go Down, Moses" (and the observation that "the American Dream was movingly expressed in many Negro spirituals"), one poem each by Samuel Allen and Gwendolyn Brooks and an essay by James Baldwin, "The Creative Dilemma." For the uninitiated, Mr. Baldwin is identified only as one who ". . . grew up in *the Harlem section* of New York City" (italics added).[17]

Editorial comment in the Ginn Series does nothing to foster social understandings. The questions and commentary which accompany Samuel Allen's "To Satch" do not suggest that either Allen or Satchel Paige are black. The questions are typified by "Comment on the poet's use of colloquial language," "What impression of Satch does the poem give you?"[18] No mention is made of the discrimination which Paige met as one of the pioneers who desegregated American sports. A depth of understanding and appreciation is surely lost for the poem in the failure to suggest that Allen is writing in admiration of another black man who has triumphed in a hostile environment.

Following James Baldwin's essay in the American literature volume,[19] there are several questions which deal with Baldwin's ideas about

---

15. Holt, Rinehart & Winston, Inc., New York: *I've Got a Name, At Your Own Risk, Cities, Larger Than Life* (all 1968), Charlotte K. Brooks, general editor.
16. Noble and Noble, Publishers, Inc., New York, N.Y.: *Playing It Cool, Breaking Loose, Tomorrow Won't Wait, Love's Blues, In Others' Eyes* (all 1969), *Me, Myself and I, He Who Dares, Dreamers of the Dream* (all 1970).
17. *American Literature*, p. 771.
18. *Ibid.*, p. 686.
19. *Ibid.*, pp. 771-75.

the artist and society, but there is no suggestion of what Baldwin, in other places, has documented as the particular problems of the black artist. Such a suggestion is not possible in the questions, of course, because nowhere have we been told that Baldwin is black.

Supporting the generally mediocre, white, middle-class view of life that the text offers, the nondescript illustrations of the whole series further underscore a failure to see that the world is also inhabited by blacks.

The slick packaging of the *Themes and Writers* series deceives the eye. It takes a while to turn attention away from the pretty pictures (and for the most part that is what they are—reproductions of "romantic" and "neoclassic" paintings) to the staid, generally old-fashioned contents of the books themselves. Purporting to be humanities-oriented, the anthologies are, in fact, little more than traditional collections spruced up with "Galleries" of art work whose themes are essentially the same as the accompanying literature.

While society is recognized as more diverse in this series than it is in the Ginn books (and the literary selections better), the overall effect, especially in the ninth to twelfth grade volumes, is nonetheless limiting. Langston Hughes, Countee Cullen, Paul Laurence Dunbar, and Gwendolyn Brooks are the black Negro writers briefly included in these volumes. Harper Lee's *To Kill a Mockingbird* is excerpted; "Gallery" and individual illustrations show a handful of Negroes ("patients" and "helpers" of Albert Schweitzer, "Ruby Green Singing," "Ira Aldridge as Othello," and something vaguely seen and equally vaguely titled "Minority #1" and a photograph of "Helen Keller in Africa"). In the illustrations which accompany the beginning of a section called "The Human Condition" (in the last volume of the series),[20] portraits of five significant writers are shown, none of them black.

Curiously enough, the editors of *Themes and Writers* offer three divisions (again in the last volume) which seem ideally suited to presentation of minority views: "Critics of Society," "Conflict of Wills" and "Protests." Some of what we get is interesting enough (*Antigone*, Wilfred Owen, Gandhi, Alan Paton, Zola), but nowhere do we find criticism, conflict, or protest which American students can relate to immediately—and about which they have much knowledge and feeling. It is of more than passing interest that not one black is represented in these sections despite the fact that we find the observation, "Today's greatest conflicts are not with the elements, but between men and nations and within individual hearts and minds."[21]

20. *Western Literature*, p. 314.
21. *Ibid.*, p. 107.

The seventh and eighth grade anthologies (which bear a 1969 copyright) have a somewhat more interracial tone. In the seventh grade collection the reader finds selections by Gwendolyn Brooks (both poems and a story), Richard Wright, Langston Hughes (a poem and a biographical piece about Harriet Tubman). The illustrations of this volume show several blacks: Frederick Douglass, Jessie Owens, escaping slaves in a reproduction of a painting entitled "Canada Bound," details from four murals by Aaron Douglas (accompanied by the comment, "A history of the black man in America is a story of life against the odds"),[22] several black figures in a painting entitled "Billboards," two photos of Harriet Tubman, and a picture of black natives in a Winslow Homer painting "Watson and the Shark."

The eighth grade volume has fewer inclusions of blacks but still offers a more interracial view than the last four in the *Themes and Writers* series. Included are verses by Langston Hughes and Dubose Heyward and a "digested" version of *The Lilies of the Field.* In the latter there are five photographs of Sidney Poitier in scenes from the film, although he is not identified by name. A few photographs in the Gallery sections depict blacks.

The editors of the *Themes and Writers* series do not find it possible to present significant social problems or questions with the selections they include by blacks, simply because the subjects of black-written works are "safe" and preclude the introduction of such material.

The *Mainstream* series is one of a growing number of recent paperback anthologies designed for use with "underprivileged" students in urban settings. The series of five books is advertised as "designed for students whose experience and backgrounds have kept them out of the social and educational mainstream." While the series' intention is admirable, its success in blending social values and literature is less than felicitous. While black authors and characters are prominent in the series, what the reader frequently faces is undistinguished writing that depicts little more than an awareness of the fact that most people share the same personal struggles. The individual book titles (*Courage Under Fire, Against the Odds, They Were First, People Like You, In New Directions*) suggest the personal flavor of the selections included and at the same time seem to act as come-ons to the "underprivileged."

Primary emphasis is on self-awareness and self-image among blacks, Spanish-speaking Americans and indeterminate whites. The better selections are most often by Negroes: Lorraine Hansberry (an excerpt from *A Raisin in the Sun*), Gordon Parks, Langston Hughes and James

---

22. *Focus,* p. 334.

Baldwin. Among the works included are those which promote under-standing of those struggling for self-awareness, people being depicted as being "like us." Selections of high interest and relevance are those by Sammy Davis, Jr., Floyd Patterson, and Lillian Smith.

The volume *They Were First* contains the most relevant and inter-esting selections of the entire series, particularly in the longest section "In the Fight for Human Rights and Dignity." Jackie Robinson, Mary McLeod Bethune and Martin Luther King are clearly heroes in this vol-ume along with Susan B. Anthony, Abraham Lincoln and John F. Kenne-dy.

The illustrations in these short anthologies portray ordinary scenes in which blacks play an equal role with other ethnic groups. The books are intended to attract readers through the absence of questions and ac-tivities following the selections. (This is also true of the *Impact* and *Crossroads* series.) The stories and verses are briefly preceded by an in-troductory statement intended to supply motivation for reading as well as whatever background is necessary for comprehension. This seems an especially attractive feature for a series designed to attract "reluctant" or "disadvantaged" readers. However, the danger exists in all the paperback anthologies that the student operating on his own will not be led to con-sider anything more about the selections than what he is able to raise out of his own resources.

Ultimately, though, the *Mainstream* series emerges as cautious and somewhat paternalistic. The editors obviously do not intend to present selections which indicate social unrest, dissatisfaction, or protest. Read-ers are not led to foster doubts or pose questions beyond the "I am the Captain of my soul" rhetoric. A more positive contribution might have been made to value formation if some better material had been substitut-ed for the many insipid and artificial stories deodorized of the qualities which make group differences unique and vital. The formation of literary values would certainly profit.

Most successful of the three hardback anthologies considered here are the *America Reads* collections which incisively capture a sense of the individual functioning in a multi-racial and multi-cultural world.

In the first four books of the series, there is an admirable range of black authors including Richard Wright, Gwendolyn Brooks, Samuel Allen, Langston Hughes and Gordon Parks, as well as authors and stor-ies representing many other Western and non-Western cultures. Only in this particular hardbound series does a Negro (Harriet Tubman) emerge in heroic proportions. This series is also the only one of the six examined which finds George Washington Carver suitable as a biographical sub-ject.

The *United States in Literature* volume in the *America Reads Series* curiously fails to mantain the social awareness of the preceding volumes; nevertheless it offers works by James Weldon Johnson, Countee Cullen and Gwendolyn Brooks as well as a selection of Negro spirituals. The collection also contains two excellent and straightforward verses by Robert Hayden: "Runagate Runagate," which deals with the escape of Negro slaves via the Underground Railroad, and "Frederick Douglass," which offers a moving tribute to the black leader. This volume is notable, also, for presenting the Southern view of the Civil War (an excerpt from Freeman's *Robert E. Lee,* verses by Confederate poets, and "Robert E. Lee" from Benet's *John Brown's Body*).

An inadequacy of the series, with the exception of the Hayden poems, is its failure to pose questions which might provoke thinking about minority problems. The questions raised for Langston Hughes' "Dreams" is typical. Instead of raising the question "What kind of dreams do you think the poet is talking about?,"[23] more direct, socially significant questions might well have centered around the theme of the poem ("hold fast to dreams") and survival aspects for blacks. Gordon Parks' "Music in My Head"[24] has an accompanying "portfolio" of Parks' photographs which offers another example of restricted thinking. The text comments, "Beginning as a fashion photographer, he soon became more interested in picturing the poverty stricken areas of his own and other countries," but in only one of the five photographs is there an indication of Parks' concern with poverty.

Perhaps most disappointing of all is the handling of Countee Cullen's "Any Human to Another."[25] While the editorial commentary provides background on Cullen's life, and while the poem cries out for an interpretation that includes the black-white experience, no indication of such interpretations is made. John Donne's "No man is an island" observation is quoted and students are encouraged to "relate the ideas expressed by John Donne to the theme . . .," but that is all. A marvelous opportunity for ethnic and cultural understanding is ignored.

Illustrations in all six volumes of this series are excellent. The drawings involve the imagination; the photographs are relevant and the photographic portraits of authors, not very helpful in most series, are enlightening because the reader is confronted with the reality of artists who are sometimes also black.

---

23. *Counterpoint in Literature*, p. 272.
24. *Ibid.*, pp. 340-43.
25. *The United States in Literature*, p. 589.

some promising trends: two series

The *Impact* collections are attractive from the standpoint of graphic design and, thus, instantly inviting. Through an abundant use of black and white photographs and drawings, the books convey an immediate sense of the ethnic dignity and social participation of blacks in American society. While the *Impact* series occasionally suffers some of the same sentimental inadequacies as the *Mainstream* books, the selections present a better melding of literature and social awareness. Dick Gregory is prominent among the Negro authors who appear only here and in the *Crossroads* series.

Particularly interesting selections are Richard Wright's "The Fight" and Peter Quinn's "Challenged" which reveal a black and white view of survival in the city; an excerpt from James Baldwin's *Go Tell It on the Mountain;* and the lyrics for Joe Darion's popular song "The Impossible Dream."

While the use of "pictorial essays," "Peanuts" comic strips and magazine-technique layout consumes space which might be given to more prose and poetry, these devices are so attractive and relevant that they undoubtedly involve "reluctant readers" in selections they would ordinarily ignore—and in themselves raise many possibilities for discussion and writing related to literature.

Another attractive aspect of the series, as with the *Mainstream* and *Crossroads* books, is the fact that stories and poems carry no questions or activities with them. Throughout there is a prevailing sense of involvement, pleasure and enjoyment.

The *Crossroads* series, only eight volumes of which were published at the time of this writing, is even more effective than the *Impact* series because of its better literary selections and because its graphic design more honestly and interestingly depicts blacks in the United States.

The series is projected to include many additional volumes, recordings, a student activity book, a classroom library of selected paperback books, as well as teachers' manuals for the entire series. Its potential for student involvement in the questions of both literature and social purpose far outweighs that of any of the other five anthology series.

The emphasis of the books is on "being with it." The selections are particularly excitement- and adventure-oriented and the photographs and drawings futher that intention, as well as make comment on their own.

Titles of the books are themselves interesting: *Playing It Cool; Tomorrow Won't Wait; Love's Blues; Breaking Loose; Me, Myself and I; He Who Dares; Dreamers of Dreams; In Others' Eyes.* Selections are usually brief and provocative. Authors included are Dick Gregory, Martin

Luther King, Gwendolyn Brooks, Claude Brown, Langston Hughes (sixteen selections), William Melvin Kelley, Paul Laurence Dunbar, Countee Cullen, Gordon Parks, and a host of other lesser known black writers, one a high school student.

The black selections range widely: *Nigger* (Gregory), *Manchild in the Promised Land* (Brown), "We Real Cool" (Brooks), "Ballad of the Landlord" (Hughes), and "Gratitude: A Nupe Folk Tale," which ends, interestingly enough, "There comes a time for every man when he is treated as he has treated others."

Other especially interesting selections are Jimmy Breslin's "Selma Leaders," Kelley's "Connie," Jimmie Sherman's verse "Negro History," Martin J. Hamer's "The Mountain," and Kelley's "Cry For Me."

The outstanding graphics and layout of the series clearly depicts an interracial society. Some stunning photographs include one of a black man passing under a church sign stating "Love Thy Neighbor," another of a black man exiting from a "Whites only" restroom, a black protester wearing a sign saying "I *am* a man," black Olympics athletes giving the black power salute, a store front on which hangs a sign reading "Negro stay out," and numerous photographs realistically showing blacks in all walks of life. Relationships between the written selections and the illustrations are carefully conceived and the possibility for discussion and writing are vast.

In some cases, *Crossroads* blends photographs of blacks with materials written about whites, suggesting, thereby, that the experience depicted in the selection is a universal one; this is especially well done with "Graves" by Carl Sandburg (one of the graves depicted being that of Martin Luther King), and "A Mystery of Heroism" by Stephen Crane. Also of note are the photographs accompanying Hughes' conversational verse "Madam and the Rent Man," showing both characters of the poem as black.

A special mature and humane quality pervades the *Crossroads* series. Nowhere else can one find anthology editors willing to end a volume depicting (through selections and illustrations) blacks struggling for survival by using Dorothy Parker's tart verse on the futility of suicide ("Résumé"), the last line of which is "You might as well live."

No where else can one find a literature anthology making such an honest and qualitative effort to depict an interracial society while at the same time reserving enough sense of humor to print a photograph of a white boy eating a watermelon.

The *Mainstream, Impact* and *Crossroads* series are all attractive because of their compact sizes; they have avoided the overstuffed appearance of typical anthologies and are easy to handle. The *Impact* and *Crossroads* volumes have a pronounced magazine appearance which teachers who have used them report is especially attractive to "reluctant readers."

A shortcoming in all the paperback series, however, is that they present chapters (or adaptations of chapters) from full-length works without indicating in the anthology proper that the selections are excerpted from longer works or that the works have been altered. When a student reads one of these selections, he has no immediate evidence that he has not experienced the whole or real thing.

Considering their specialized goals and their intention of capturing "reluctant readers," both series may be more successful than anthologies with "loftier" goals and more stilted approaches. While all three are designed primarily for city schools, their use would do much to enlighten what Miel and Kiester call "the shortchanged children of suburbia"[26] as well as rural youngsters.

are anthologies the answer?

Except for the uniqueness of *Impact* and *Crossroads* which enable them to successfully project a black image in literature, one is left with many questions about anthology editors and their sense of literature as an expression of and about blacks. Why are such black spokesmen as Eldridge Cleaver and Malcolm X omitted? Why is Martin Luther King, Jr. represented in only two of the thirty-five volumes examined, and Ralph Ellison only in one? How is it that James Baldwin, Richard Wright and Claude McKay, and W. E. B. DuBois are all but ignored? Why is there not more publication of Lorraine Hansberry's *A Raisin in the Sun?* Where is *Uncle Tom's Cabin?* Where is Carson McCuller's *The Member of the Wedding* and Edward Albee's *The Death of Bessie Smith?* Where are the black playwrights LeRoi Jones and Ossie Davis?

Are the limitations and omissions of anthologies the result of ignorance, fear, malice? On whose part: editors and publishers, school systems and teachers? All? Wherever the fault does lie, there is at least one sure place where the fault may begin to be corrected—with teachers themselves. The secondary-school teacher has emerged in the last decade as an individual prepared to defend his right to earn a decent living and to protect his working conditions. It is time for him to leave his cocoon

---

26. Alice Miel and Edwin Kiester, Jr., *The Shortchanged Children of Suburbia* (New York: Institute of Human Relations Press, 1967).

entirely, establishing his professional competency and asserting his right to academic freedom. English teachers might well make their own beginning by reconsidering the approach to literature teaching. Are anthologies capable of meeting the needs of the new breed of American youth? If they are, then what changes are necessary in them to do the job? And in what ways must teachers learn to use them to complete advantage?

Evans and Walker have pointed out that ". . . seldom does a teacher disregard the grouping he finds in anthologies in favor of his own . . . there is no doubt that the types of organization a teacher finds in the anthology he is given to teach is the most significant factor in determining how the course will be organized."[27] To this add that teachers have not so far shown any great effort to supplement anthologies with other literature materials.[28] One concludes that what is happening in literature study is dependent on the anthologies available.

Editors and publishers of literature anthologies prepare materials for something other than entirely altruistic reasons. There *is* money involved. Evans and Walker indicate that as "Teachers order books, . . . they influence what publishers make available for them to order."[29] As long as teachers accept and use anthologies which are ineffective, so long, also, will those books continue to be published. Textbooks *are* commodities. We do not hestitate to reject inferior products in other areas of our living; why should we not be considerably more discriminating in such a penultimately significant area as learning materials?

summary

August Strindberg observed that those who encounter a work of art must be collaborators with the artist by remolding art out of their own experience. If secondary-school students are to become artistic collaborators, they must learn to mesh their social perceptions with their artistic understandings so that the experience of life and art are deeper and richer.

------

27. William H. Evans and Jerry L. Walker, *New Trends in the Teaching of English in Secondary Schools* (Chicago: Rand McNally & Co., 1966), p. 44.

28. See Squire and Applebee, *High School English Instruction Today . . .;* also see Godshalk, *A Survey of the Teaching of English in Secondary Schools.*

29. Evans and Walker, *New Trends in the Teaching of English in Secondary Schools,* p. 44.

If students have a limited experience which allows limited collaboration, it is the responsibility of those who teach—either through the act itself or by assembling materials for teaching—to confront students with those social realities which enable them to see life as it is and has to be lived within the confinements of our ethnic and cultural structures. Collaboration demands mutual understanding as well as participation and a sense of artistic integrity. Collaboration cannot occur when participants are encouraged to be ignorant, condescending, provincial, cautious, reactionary, or racist.

Literature anthologies which purport to offer a view of life and literature that is in any way accurate must present evidence that blacks as well as whites have lived, struggled and survived and are still alive and grappling with the immense problems of the twentieth century.

CHAPTER 8

Developing Racial Tolerance with Literature on the Black Inner-City

James A. Banks

introduction

One of the basic assumptions made in this book is that reading *does* make a difference. As has been noted earlier, the research to support this assumption has somehow eluded educators, perhaps because it is taken for granted. Certainly the criticism of texts and other materials by interested groups rests on a firm conviction that the written word influences the reader. In this chapter, James A. Banks argues that the aware and sensitive teacher can and should use literature to increase the understanding of children. Because of the endemic racism of American society, both white and black, some intervention by the schools seems necessary. The tool nearest at hand, and in many ways one of the most effective, is imaginative literature. Through literature a child may identify with the struggles and problems of children not like himself, and gain an insight into feelings and attitudes different from his own. Research does show that mere physical desegregation of children may do little to change the racist attitudes inculcated in the home. Through literature, therefore, children may move in another way toward explicit concern with others.

When white suburban children read that forty-seven blacks lost their lives in the explosive Detroit riot of 1967, and that an unarmed black teenager was gunned down by a white policeman in the Algiers Motel amidst that disturbance, their emotions are not likely to be deeply aroused because such cold statistics and incredible incidents seem remote from their lives and experiences. It is only when we are well acquainted with an individual or people that we suffer intensely when they are hurt or harmed. In literature, children can read about individuals from different cultures and subcultures, come to know them as human beings, develop intense feelings for them, and experience agony when they are exploited or mistreated.

Young readers are saddened when Lonnie is murdered by a white racist and David Williams is attacked by a white mob in *Whose Town?*. They react strongly to these incidents because author Lorenzo Graham builds his characters so successfully that children feel that Lonnie and David are their pals. When Lonnie is killed, children lose a cherished and delightful friend. They are enraged when David is beaten, because no sensitive child wants to see his pal beaten mercilessly, especially when he has done nothing to warrant attack. Some children conclude that limp and starving Zeke, a black ghetto child vividly and sympathetically portrayed in *The Jazz Man*, dies at the end of the story and weep because Zeke captures young children's hearts. Henry in *Durango Street*, Jethro and Fess in *The Soul Brothers and Sister Lou*, and Jimmy in *Dead End School* are other memorable characters of the black ghetto who evoke deep feelings and concern in young readers.

Given the immense racial crisis which pervades the nation, it is imperative that we help "culturally sheltered" children to develop positive attitudes toward persons who are different from themselves racially and culturally. An acquaintance with different cultures and groups *can* contribute to the development of the kind of tolerance so desperately needed in our highly polarized society. Since most American children live in tightly segregated communities, they have little opportunity to interact and to become acquainted with people of different races and groups.

Literature can help bridge the gap by acquainting children with people who belong to other racial and ethnic groups. However, like actual social contact, familiarity with other groups through literature *can* help develop racial understanding and tolerance, but *may* also reinforce stereotypes and misconceptions. A child who reads *The Jazz Man* may feel intensely negative toward Zeke's parents because they desert him, and conclude that all black parents in the inner-city are irresponsible and heartless. If inappropriate teaching strategies are utilized, literature will enhance rather than mitigate the development of racial bias.

To use such a book as *The Jazz Man* effectively in social studies, the teacher *must* help children see how characters such as Zeke's parents are the victims of harsh and painful discrimination. Zeke's father is unable to find a meaningful and challenging job; his mother deserts the family when she becomes disillusioned with her husband's working situation. Father turns to drinking when his wife leaves because he feels that he has failed as a man. He physically escapes from Zeke's life. With carefully structured questions, and by leading the children to factual informational sources on the black inner-city, the teacher can help children develop empathy and concern for both Zeke and his parents. The teacher could ask the children questions based on why Zeke's father can't find a good job, and why his mother buys groceries daily, and why the family lives in a dilapidated apartment. After carefully researching these kinds of questions, the student will discover that the real villain in the story is neither of Zeke's parents, but a society which discriminates against poor and black people. The teacher could ask the children to think of actions which could be taken by the larger society to eliminate the kinds of problems encountered by Zeke's family. They should also be encouraged to predict possible consequences of the actions they propose.

Other aspects of black ghetto life portrayed in children's literature might reinforce stereotypes without careful and effective teacher guidance. Most of the families depicted in children's novels lack a father, the home is crowded, mother works as a domestic and is the dominant family member, formal education is not often encouraged, and the family attends a storefront church. It is extremely important that the teacher help the child understand *why* these conditions frequently *do* exist in the black ghetto. However, it is imperative that children become aware of the extent of these conditions in the inner-city. For example, while nearly one-fourth of the black families in America are headed by females, a highly significant three-fourths are headed by men.[1] Recent educational literature suggests that most black parents *do* want their children to attain a formal education, but that they are often unaware of ways to actualize their aspirations.[2] If maximum benefits are to accrue from the utilization of realistic fiction in the social studies, the teacher must encourage students to ascertain the extent to which "realities" portrayed in literature can be generalized to the actual world in which they live.

---

1. James A. Banks, "A Profile of the Black American: Implications For Teaching," *College Composition and Communication* 19 (December, 1969): pp. 288-296. See also Andrew Billingsley, *Black Families in White America* (Englewood Cliffs, N.J.: Prentice-Hall, Inc., 1968).
2. Robert L. Green, ed., *Racial Crisis in American Education* (Chicago: Follett Educational Corporation, 1969).

When children read about riots in *Northtown*, they should make a survey of the cities in which riots have actually occurred, and determine the degree to which Mr. Graham's description of racial violence and conflict reflects factual information.

Children will be unable to fully understand and appreciate the American black experience unless they are acutely aware of the devastating effects of slavery on both the black man and his master. The legacy of slavery is still manifested in the black inner-city. Literature can help children gain insights into American slavery. In her beautiful yet poignant biography, *Amos Fortune: Free Man*, Elizabeth Yates vividly describes how Amos Fortune, an African prince enslaved in America, emerges from an overwhelmingly dehumanizing experience "humanized" and perhaps more human because of it. At times children may find this book excruciating beyond tolerance, but perhaps it is this grim kind of realism which helps us attain deeper insights and empathy. The stark realism which permeates this book would be difficult to portray in a social studies textbook.

Julius Lester's *To Be a Slave* is a highly selected and edited collection of documents dictated by former slaves which includes helpful editorial comments. The former slaves' vivid descriptions of suicides, merciless beatings, and the huts in which they lived will evoke intense emotions and reactions. This description of the scars inflicted upon an escaped slave will give children some feeling of what it was like to be a slave:

> My friend desired me to look at his back, which was seamed and ridged with scars of the whip and hickory, from the pole of his neck to the lower extremity of his spine. The natural color of his skin had disappeared and was succeeded by a streaked and speckled appearance of dusky white and pale flesh color, scarcely any of the original black remaining.[3]

At the turn of the century, most black Americans lived in the Southern states which had made up the Confederacy. Shortly afterwards, they began an exodus to Northern cities to escape the poverty, violence, and discrimination which they experienced in the South. The jobs which opened up in Northern cities during World War I and the prevalence of lynchings and other violent acts in the South were cogent factors which pushed the black man northward. Blacks poured into Northern cities again during World War II when jobs were prevalent in defense industries.[4] *South Town, North Town,* and *Whose Town?* by Lorenz Graham

3. Julius Lester, *To Be a Slave* (New York: The Dial Press, Inc., 1969), p. 124.
4. James A. Banks, *March Toward Freedom: A History of Black Americans* (Palo Alto: Fearon Publishers, 1970).

will acquaint children with the problems faced by a typical black Southern family, and how the Williams' attempted to solve them by migrating North. *South Town* is a poignant, gripping, yet realistic story about the family's painful experiences with racism in a Southern community. The book is replete with examples of harsh, overt, and unrelenting incidents of bigotry. The book is extremely powerful because the characters are completely believable.

In *North Town*, the Williams' discover, like many other Southern black migrants, that the North is no promised land. Their small house is in a slum, David no longer has a room of his own, and he gets into trouble with the police because he lives in a "bad" neighborhood. The family gradually discovers that prejudice "Northern style" is more covert and subtle but no less insidious than Southern racism. The adjustments which David and his family must make in North Town and the disillusionments which they experience epitomize the problems encountered by the black Southern migrant in the Northern city. The reader will sympathize with David's awkward attempts to adjust to a racially-mixed school which is covertly racist, and admire his courage as he leads the family through a major catastrophe. While most children's books on the black inner-city portray a fatherless home, this one depicts a closely-knit family whose greatest strength and power lies in a strong, loving, and understanding father. For this reason, it should be given special emphasis.

In the third and most outstanding book in his trilogy, *Whose Town?*, Graham effectively and poignantly describes the black revolt of the 1960's as manifested in fictional Northtown—which could be Newark, Detroit, Chicago or any other American city in which riots have occurred. In candid detail, he relates how the racial tension in Northtown results in brutal and unprovoked attacks against blacks, killings, and finally a riot when a small black boy is drowned by a white mob at a public pool. The author makes it clear that the pool incident merely triggered the riot, but that it had deeper causes. Gross unemployment, constant indignities and insults, stark poverty and slum housing, and white racism, which permeated the city, were the root causes. The teacher could ask the children to compare this description of the riot in Northtown to newspaper accounts of outbreaks in cities such as Los Angeles, New York, Detroit, and Chicago in the 1960's:

> Gradually the crowd fell back. The people began moving toward the east side. They left behind a block of stores and business places about half of which had been smashed open and several of which had been burned. Merchandise was strewn in the street. Some of it was carried away by looters. David could not tell how many had been arrested. Some who had

been hurt were carried off in ambulances and police cars. Others whose heads were bruised and whose faces were bloody were helped away by friends.[5]

Other harsh social realities are revealed in this seminal and gripping novel. The white man who kills Lonnie in cold blood is freed because of what the jury dubs "justifiable homicide." Children could compare this slaying with the Detroit Algiers Motel incident, as described in John Hersey's moving report, *Algiers Motel Incident: Three Killings in Detroit* (New York: Alfred A. Knopf, Inc., 1968). When David is attacked by a white mob, he, rather than the attackers, is jailed and humiliated. Mr. Williams' perpetual unemployment disrupts the family, forces Mrs. Williams to work as a domestic, emasculates him, and turns him into a bitter and disillusioned man. The strength and power which he evidences in the earlier novels is dissipated. Children can study factual informational sources on the inner-city to validate the reality of Mr. Williams' experiences. This novel vividly illuminates the powerlessness and alienation of the black community, and indicates how the black migrant's dream of finding a heaven on earth in Northern cities was almost completely shattered in the 1960's. *Whose Town?* is destined to become a classic in children's literature. In it, Mr. Graham attains the acme of his literary career.

One of the characteristic groups in the inner-city is the gang. Novels whose setting is the black ghetto can help children understand why boys sometimes join gangs, the needs they satisfy, and how a gang can be transformed into a constructive group when gang members are encouraged and helped to satisfy their group needs in more legitimate ways. Frank Bonham studied a number of gangs in Los Angeles and embodied what he learned in *Durango Street,* an interesting story about Rufus Henry and the Moors. When he is released from a camp for delinquent boys, Rufus and his sister are attacked by the Gassers, a local gang. After his attack, Rufus realizes that he must violate his parole and join a rival gang if he is to survive in his neighborhood. Young readers will sympathize with Rufus as he longs for a father, and will share his triumphs as he leads the Moors to street victories and finally into more constructive pursuits. In using this book, the teacher could ask the children to think of ways Rufus might have solved his problems without joining the Moors. They may conclude that he had few other alternatives.

Kristin Hunter's powerful novel, *The Soul Brothers and Sister Lou,* is a story about 14-year-old Louretta Hawkins, and her friends the

---

5. Lorenz Graham, *Whose Town?* (New York: Thomas Y. Crowell Company, 1969), p. 194.

Hawks, a Southside gang. A strong person, Lou persuades the Hawks to use their group efforts constructively. However, their attempts to pursue legitimate activities are continually frustrated by the local police, who perpetually harass them and brutally kill Jethro. The author skillfully and effectively handles police brutality and other violent acts which take place on the "rough" Southside. When reading this book, the class could study the causes of police brutality in the black ghetto and use factual sources to study actual cases. This book will also help the reader attain many insights into black family life in the inner-city. *The Soul Brothers and Sister Lou* has many strong characters and memorable incidents which will help the child develop empathy for ghetto residents. Fierce but brilliant Fess, talented and lonesome Blind Tom, shy and sensitive Calvin, and Lou, who searches relentlessly for her black identity, will deeply impress the reader.

Poetry by black American writers can be used in the social studies to help children develop empathy and understanding of the black experience and life in the inner-city. Most black poets express their feelings, emotions, and aspirations in their poetry. They have been preoccupied with themes dealing with oppression, freedom, and the meaning of blackness in America. In "Montage of a Dream Deferred," Langston Hughes asks what happens to a deferred dream and implies that it explodes. When studying race riots, this poem would be especially appropriate. The teacher could ask the children what dreams of black people have been deferred, and in what ways have they exploded. Claude McKay's anguished and evocative poem, "If We Must Die," can also stimulate a discussion on race riots. McKay penned this poem when riots broke out in our cities in 1919.

An infinite number of beautiful, poignant, and revealing poems are available for use to teach children the facts of ghetto life. *Bronzeville Boys and Girls* by Pulitzer Prize-winning poet Gwendolyn Brooks is a collection of poems about children in the inner-city. This book includes happy, sad, as well as thoughtful reflections by urban children which reveal their feelings and emotions. *On City Streets*, edited by Nancy Larrick, is a collection of poems about the inner-city which urban children helped to select. The book includes captivating photographs which enhance the appeal of the poems. Stephen M. Joseph's *The Me Nobody Knows: Children's Voices from the Ghetto* includes poetry and prose written by children who live in the inner-city. In their accounts they reveal their fears, aspirations, and a limited, but eventful world.

American Negro Poetry by Arna Bontemps, *I Am the Darker Brother: An Anthology of Modern Poems by Negro Americans* by Arnold

Adoff, and *The Poetry of the Negro* by Langston Hughes and Arna Bontemps are excellent and comprehensive anthologies of black poetry. Poetry can evoke interest and help children gain deep insights into the moods and feelings of black inner-city residents.

Our very existence may ultimately depend upon our creative abilities to solve our urgent racial problems. The flames that burned in Watts, the blood that ran in Detroit, and the willingness of black leaders to chance assassination by taking strong stands on social issues indicate that the black American is willing to pay almost any price to secure those rights which he believes are his by birthright. The reactions by the white community to the black man's new militancy have been strong and intense. A "law and order" cult has emerged to stem the tide of the black revolt.[6] Since our major social problems grow from the negative attitudes which whites have toward blacks,[7] we must modify the racial attitudes of whites if we are to create the democratic society that we verbally extol. When used effectively, literature can help white children in our sheltered suburban areas to develop racial tolerance and a commitment to the eradication of social injustice.

Children's Books Cited

Arnold Adoff, *I Am the Darker Brother: An Anthology of Modern Poems by Negro Americans* (New York: The Macmillan Company, 1968). Illustrated by Benny Andrews.

Frank Bonham *Durango Street* (New York: E. P. Dutton and Company, Inc., 1965).

Arna Bontemps, ed., *American Negro Poetry* (New York: Hill and Wang, 1963).

Gwendolyn Brooks, *Bronzeville Boys and Girls* (New York: Harper & Row, Publishers, 1965). Illustrated by John Kaufmann.

Natalie Savage Carlson, *The Empty Schoolhouse* (New York: Harper & Row, Publishers, 1965). Illustrated by John Kaufmann.

Robert Coles, *Dead End School* (Boston: Little, Brown and Company, 1968). Illustrated by Norman Rockwell.

Lorenz Graham, *North Town* (New York: Thomas Y. Crowell Company, 1965).

——. *South Town* (Chicago: Follett Publishing Company, 1958).

——. *Whose Town?* (New York: Thomas Y. Crowell Company, 1969).

---

6. James A. Banks, "Racial Prejudice and the Black Self-Concept," in James A. Banks and Jean D. Grambs, *Black Self-Concept* (New York: McGraw-Hill Book Company, in press).
7. *Report of the National Advisory Commission on Civil Disorders* (New York: Bantam Books, 1968).

Langston Hughes and Arna Bontemps, eds., *The Poetry of the Negro 1746-1949* (Garden City: Doubleday and Company, 1949).

Kristin Hunter, *The Soul Brothers and Sister Lou* (New York: Charles Scribner's Sons, 1969).

Stephen M. Joseph, ed., *The Me Nobody Knows: Children's Voices from the Ghetto* (New York: Avon Books, 1969).

Nancy Larrick, ed., *On City Streets* (New York: Bantam Books, 1964). Illustrated with photographs.

Julius Lester, *To Be a Slave* (New York: The Dial Press, Inc., 1968). Illustrated by Tom Feelings.

Mary Hays Weik, *The Jazz Man* (New York: Atheneum, 1967). Illustrated by Ann Grifalconi with woodcuts.

Elizabeth Yates, *Amos Fortune: Free Man* (New York: Dutton and Company, Inc., 1950). Illustrated by Nora Unwin.

CHAPTER 9

Black Image:
Strategies for Change

James A. Banks

In this final chapter, James A. Banks pulls together the several themes that have emerged from the analyses of texts, trade books, and other instructional material. As a black educator, he is particularly well aware of how schools have, by and large, failed to confront and thus to help diminish the racism which pervades American society. As he indicates, educators ultimately have no one to blame but themselves if instructional material is biased, prejudicial, and inadequate.

One salient and depressing conclusion can be derived from the chapters in this book: the image of the black American in teaching materials reinforces the negative and confused racial attitudes which children bring to school. The glorification of white and the degrading of black in textbooks perpeuates an ethnocentric chauvinism among white students and further deflates the black child's low self-concept. Education should liberate man, help him to make sound decisions, and enable him to shape a positive identity. However, in a society where institutionalized myths

---

*This chapter is based on a longer paper, "The Need for Positive Racial Attitudes in Textbooks," in *Racial Crisis in American Education,* edited by Robert L. Green, pp. 167-185. (Chicago: Follett Publishing Company, 1969). Used with permission of the publisher.

and lies are perpetuated, men's minds are not liberated but imprisoned. Men are frightened, unable to distinguish lies from truth, the real from the unreal, and confront an identity crisis.

White racism and the myths about Blacks which emerged to justify it have created a *crisis* in this nation which has been candidly documented by the National Advisory Commission on Civil Disorders[1] and the U. S. Commission on Civil Rights.[2] Racism creates illusions and inhibits thinking; a society populated by people who cannot think must perish. The public school must do all it can to save ours. Racism in textbooks must be eliminated.

Many recent attempts to portray the cultural diversity of American life, as several of the chapters suggest, have been expedient, superficial, and ineffective gestures made by publishers responding to the demands of educators who, in turn, have been coerced to take action by enlightened community pressure groups. Often these attempts have been little more than coloring all-white faces *brown*. Coloring white characters brown, or perpetuating a sterile middle class image of the black American, will not meet the criteria of objective treatment of the black man because such images are inconsistent with reality. The American child should be exposed to *all* types and classes of blacks, with illustrations depicting the diversity of Negroid racial traits. Overemphasis on one type or the creation of an ideal type will not suffice.

Professional educators are responsible for the omissions and distortions in the treatment of the black American in textbooks. To contend that publishers are responsible would be analogous to arguing that cigarette manufacturers are responsible for the alarming number of cancer victims in America. Textbook publishers create and distribute materials which are *demanded* and *purchased* by their customers. Whether we condone their policy or not, most publishers are more committed to increasing sales than to ethical principles. Their interest is in producing materials that will be purchased by their customers.

Lip service has frequently been given to the objective and realistic treatment of blacks in textbooks. But if such verbalizations were sincere, massive, constructive action would have been taken, beginning with the simple refusal to purchase books that distort the image of the black

---

1. *Report of the National Advisory Commission on Civil Disorders* (New York: Bantam Books, 1969).
2. The U. S. Commission on Civil Rights, *Racism in America and How to Combat It* (Washington. D.C.: U. S. Government Printing Office, 1970).

man. However, books which distort blacks must inevitably perpetuate myths about whites.

Only myths and distortions which are *approved* by educators and the larger society are tolerated in schoolbooks. If a textbook stated that George Washington and Lincoln were racists, it would be on the blacklist of every large school district before the ink was dry. Yet educators have continued to purchase thousands of books that present the image of the contented slave whose emancipation was forced upon him by benevolent Lincoln. How many school children know that only under pressure, and reluctantly, did Washington permit blacks to join his forces and even then at less wages than white soldiers-in-arms?

When educators attempt to shift the responsibility for the treatment of blacks in textbooks to publishers, they are rationalizing their contentment with the stereotypic and distorted image of the black American. Educators purchase teaching materials which are distorted because such materials are consistent with their own attitudes, expectations and social perceptions. Writes Smith, ". . . whites . . . lack the social perception to penetrate the mass of white racism that permeates the American school but is almost imperceptible to them."[3] Educators have looked for a scapegoat to blame; textbook publishers, who rarely have been apostles in race relations, have been convenient and vulnerable targets.

The pivotal strategy for changing the image of blacks in textbooks is to modify the racial attitudes and dispositions of professional educators. Teachers, like other Americans, bring negative racial attitudes to school and later to college. Their college experience apparently has little effect on their racial feelings and perceptions. A number of studies have illuminated the negative attitudes which teachers manifest toward black and other poor children. In a study conducted by Clark, white teachers in black schools told white student interviewers that blacks were innately inferior and could not be expected to learn as much or as readily as whites. They suggested that black schools should be custodial rather than educational institutions.[4] Gottlieb found that white teachers are more likely to describe black children negatively than black teachers. White teachers most frequently described black children as talkative,

3. Donald H. Smith, "The Black Revolution and Education," *Racial Crisis in American Education,* edited by Robert L. Green, p. 63. (Chicago: Follett Publishing Company, 1969).

4. Kenneth B. Clark, "Clash of Cultures in the Classroom," *Integrated Education* 1 (August, 1963): 10.

lazy, fun-loving and happy more often than they described them as cooperative, energetic or ambitious.[5] Teachers who sit on selection committees will continue to adopt racist textbooks until their own perceptions and attitudes are changed.

While research has indicated that curricular experiences can modify children's racial attitudes, it is less certain that such experiences can significantly affect the attitudes of adults. However, in spite of the limitations of our knowledge in this area, the urgent need for change makes it imperative that we attempt to modify the racial attitudes of teachers, administrators, and supervisors with appropriate curricular experiences. Courses in cultural anthropology, sociology, social psychology, and history—with emphasis on the role of minority groups in American life—may effect constructive changes. Certainly, we must help teachers and other educators who sit on textbook adoption committees to examine their own racial attitudes.[6]

Concomitant with training teachers, school districts could commission classroom teachers to write textbooks and offer them for publication. Under the Great Cities project, the Detroit Board of Education initiated such a plan. They insisted upon final approval of the content and illustrations in the texts, and the publisher granted the school board these privileges.

School districts could cooperate by assigning writers to such projects. Each participating district would have a voice in the selection of content and would also agree to adopt the finished texts. Under such a plan, school districts would have appropriate control of content without having the responsibility for the technical aspects of book production, such as printing, artwork, sales, and distribution. This plan would also be advantageous to publishers since they would be *assured* that their books would be adopted. But the review of school-produced materials by Janis (chapter six) shows that when free of commercial pressures, school systems must be extremely diligent or their product will be no better than the usual text or trade book.

Classroom teachers should be encouraged to do much more writing. They should be given time during the year or paid during the summer months to write creative and challenging materials for children. A reward system for writing, such as extra compensation or promotion, could be

---

5. David Gottlieb, "Teaching and Students: The Views of Negro and White Teachers," *Sociology of Education* 27 (Summer, 1964): 345-353.

6. Howard S. Becker, "Career Patterns of Public School Teachers," *Journal of Sociology* 57 (March, 1952): 470-477.

established. However, the "publish or perish" edict that exists in our leading colleges and universities must not be emulated. Effective teachers who do not wish to write should not be expected to write. But many teachers are potential authors. Publishers take advantage of this fact and solicit authors and editors in our public schools.

Because teachers may lack the academic background needed for writing in some disciplines, they could work with experts at local universities or academic experts could conduct workshops so that groups of teachers would benefit from their knowledge.

School districts produce many excellent text materials inexpensively without the cooperation of textbook publishers. The Winnetka Public Schools in Illinois have produced excellent textbooks in social studies and mathematics for local use. These texts have an additional asset in that they are designed specifically to meet the unique needs of the children in the community. Classroom teachers are provided time and extra compensation for writing. The texts are printed on quality paper with black and white pictures, utilizing a relatively inexpensive printing process such as multilith.

There is little empirical evidence that the colored pictures and ostentatious paraphernalia in today's commercially-produced textbooks contribute to learning. This author suspects that many of these "aids" actually distract the students from essential learning tasks. A school district should not be reluctant to plan a text because elaborate pictures and charts cannot be included.

Another strategy for changing textbooks is for school systems to utilize boycotts to demand accurate, quality text materials. When Harper & Row produced a science series that did not include pictures of minority groups, the Newark school system attacked the publisher for using "strereotyped middle class" illustrations.[7] Within a short time, Harper & Row issued an "Intercultural Edition" that included pictures of minority groups. However, the publisher continued to sell its all-white edition to school districts that requested them.

The Detroit Board of Education, responding to pressure from civil rights groups, initiated an effective boycott. When the N.A.A.C.P. complained that Laidlaw's *Our United States: Bulwark of Freedom* presented a stereotyped and inaccurate view of slavery, the Detroit Board concluded that the criticism was justified. At first the Board released a

---

7. Hillel Black, *The American Schoolbook* (New York: William Morrow, 1967), pp. 30-32.

supplement which corrected the flaws, but they later withdrew the book from use at the N.A.A.C.P.'s request.[8] The publisher revised the book with great speed. These incidents illustrate the tremendous influence and control that school systems can exercise.

Any school that wishes to initiate a comprehensive program in intergroup relations must formulate a policy for dealing with pressure groups in the community. If civil rights pressure groups had not demanded reforms in Detroit, perhaps the students would still be reading texts that are insulting to black students. Indeed, much educational reform emanates from without rather than from within educational circles. For example, the emergence of public universities to serve the masses was not initiated by educators; it was a response by educators to society's demand for large numbers of trained individuals to fill positions created by technology and industry.

The schools should be sensitive to the demands of community pressure groups and consider the validity of their ideas. The community should have the right to determine the goals of education for its children; however, the school should insist on its right to determine the means to achieve those ends. Among the major goals which our society has set for the schools is the development of democratic citizens capable of making rational decisions through reflective and critical thinking and citizens who have a basic respect for the integrity of individuals of all races and creeds. Since a major goal of American education is the development of democratic citizens, the school should consider the demands of each pressure group in terms of whether such demands, if implemented, would contribute to a democratic society.

Educators themselves must formulate educational policies which are consistent with our democratic heritage. If the schools instigate policies which are a breach of our democratic ethos, community groups have a right to demand change. But as long as educators are performing their duties with the best interests of all children in mind, they have a right to determine the means to educational goals—because of their professional status and because they are the ones who are ultimately responsible for the education of the children in the community.

Thus, the schools should always consider the demands of community pressure groups and respond to them in terms of their consistency with the basic aims of public education. If the demands of pressure groups are consistent with our democratic legacy, then the school should implement changes that reflect those demands. However, if the demands are incon-

8. *Ibid.*, pp. 108-114.

sistent with a democratic education, then the school must stubbornly resist them. Too often educators have been too sheep-like in dealing with pressure groups whose demands violate our democratic creed.[9] Educators frequently have used unreasonable demands as an excuse to relieve them of their professional responsibility, to justify their apathy and educational neglect, and to rationalize their contentment with questionable educational policies.

Every community wants the school to assume the responsibility for developing democratic and patriotic citizens. In order to accomplish this momentous and elusive goal, the school must help children develop racial attitudes that are consistent with a democratic ideology. The school must help children become aware of racial problems and sound approaches to solving them if we are to perpetuate a democratic society. Each generation must make its contribution. Democracy is not merely an inherited legacy; it is a process which must be perpetuated deliberately if it is to remain viable.

Racism in textbooks must be eliminated, and this fact must be communicated clearly to the community. Hunt and Metcalf contend that the community frequently reacts negatively when the school deals with controversial issues, such as race relations or communism, because the community is not sufficiently aware of the educational goals which educators seek by teaching such issues.[10] The problem is largely one of communication. The school has a responsibility to inform the community of the goals that it seeks when it deals with race and other controversial topics.

Blacks should write school books and other teaching materials dealing with life in their cultures and environment. In chapter four, Professor Grambs argues convincingly that few current textbooks describe the black ghetto realistically. Almost all currently available teaching materials were written by white authors and edited by white editors. *It is difficult if not impossible for a white writer to describe what it means to be black in white America.* White writers do not write convincingly about the black ghetto because most of them are unfamiliar with it; people who have lived in the black ghetto should write books about life in it. Tom Feelings, the gifted young illustrator of *To Be A Slave*, insightfully noted, "Truly meaningful writing about the black experience must come, of course, from those who have lived and know it—black people. That's

9. Ermon O. Hogan, "Blacktalk: Kvaraceus and the Nonbooks," (Letter), *Phi Delta Kappan* 49 (1968): 416-417.
10. Maurice P. Hunt and Lawrence E. Metcalf, *Teaching High School Social Studies* (New York: Harper & Row, Publishers, 1965), pp. 449-450.

what *authenticity* is about. Anything else, possibly of merit, is *synthetic.*[11] Chicanos, Puerto Ricans and American Indians should also write books about life in the United States as they have experienced it.

Textbook and tradebook houses should aggressively recruit young minority group writers. The Council on Interracial Books for Children exists primarily to help ethnic minority writers and illustrators find publishing outlets. The Council has given visibility to such talented writers as Kristin Hunter, author of *The Soul Brothers and Sister Lou,* and to John Steptoe, young author of *Stevie.* The Council's annual Awards encourage minority group writers to produce original manuscripts. *The Soul Brothers and Sister Lou* was a Council Award recipient. Publishers and educators should work with organizations such as the Council and The Institute of the Black World in Atlanta to solicit and publish works by minority group writers.

With an immense challenge before them, educators cannot afford to seek scapegoats, such as textbook publishers or community pressure groups, for the racism that exists in our textbooks. They must confront the fact that the image of blacks in textbooks accurately reflects educators' perceptions and attitudes toward blacks. Seeking rationalizations will not help solve the problem. Educators must face the dilemma, attempt to clarify and modify their racial attitudes, and take constructive action to ameliorate the situation. Only then can progress be made in building positive racial attitudes that are consistent with our professed national ethos. In facing this immense challenge, educators also have a tremendous oportunity to prove their professional leadership. If they fail to act *now*, they may find themselves trying to justify their existence to the communities that they allegedly serve. Acting now is *imperative.* Time is running out.

---

11. Tom Feelings, "White Authors and Lack of Authenticity," *Interracial Books for Children* 4 (Spring, 1970): 2.

Annotated Bibliography of Integrated and Black Books for Children

Barbara J. Glancy

annotated bibliography

The following bibliography of integrated and black books was compiled by Barbara Glancy after examining over 700 volumes published between 1951 and 1970. Individuals interested in book selection for readers between the ages of four and sixteen (plus) will find in the list ". . . many books which depict Negroes who are human beings with all the greatness and strengths and all the foibles and weaknesses of mankind."[1]

Earlier studies of books which were about or included black characters revealed that—with little exception—Negroes were presented in stereotyped fashion. Characters were inevitably janitors, maids, slaves, sharecroppers, or stevedores. In studies by Morris, Baker, Preer, and Rollins[2] a "negative stereotype" was discovered as typical in books depicting

---

1. Charlemae Rollins, ed., *We Build Together* (Champaign. Ill.: National Council of Teachers of English, 1967), p. xi.
2. Effie Lee Morris, "A Mid-Century Survey of the Presentation of the American Negro in Literature for Children Published Between 1900 and 1950." (Unpublished Master's thesis, Western Reserve University, Cleveland, Ohio, 1956):107-108; Augusta Baker, *Books About Negro Life for Children* (New York: The New York Public Library, 1963):5-6; Betty Banner Preer, "Guidance in Democratic Living Through Juvenile Fiction," *Wilson Library Bulletin* 22 (May, 1948):679; Rollins, *op. cit.*, p. 5.

blacks. In those books, Negroes were shown as having low social status, as not striving for social, educational, or financial betterment, as speaking dialect, as being "black" in color, and as not having fathers. In books concerned with the pre-Civil War period, Negroes were shown as living only in the rural areas of southern states and they were isolated physically and socially from white characters.

In still other ways, blacks were seen stereotypically: They possessed rolling eyes, flashing teeth, natural musical or rhythmic talent, great superstition, and, not infrequently, bare feet. Black women inevitably wore pigtails or bandanas, were overweight, and were called "Auntie" by white characters. The diet of these characters was, of course, pancakes, chitterlings, fried chicken, and watermelon.

But above all, the self-induced deception presented in these stereotypes was the notion that slaves were contented with their lot.

Between the typical black character book of 1948 and 1970 there is an enormous difference. Currently, there is little evidence that points to a negative stereotype; there is the danger, naturally, that a positive stereotype may emerge as an effort—consciously or unconsciously—to rectify the injustices of the past.

The observation that books ". . . whose Negro, white and Puerto Rican kids always laugh together can be as misleading as portrayal of the ever-grinning slave" is well taken.[3] Some of the present crop of books on the market might be called "brotherhood books" in the sense that they present a black, a white, and an Oriental who, when the chips are down, unite forces to solve the difficulties with which they are confronted. Occasionally, this type of book includes a Jew, a Puerto Rican or an Indian —presumably to touch all possible bases. While the proportion of these books to the total of integrated and black ones available is small, they do exist and they suggest the need for caution. It is important that the image presented of ethnic (and religious) harmony be presented realistically, revealing the diversity of the human condition.

It is important that books which depict all people be presented optimistically but not idealistically. It is important that what the mirror of young people's literature reflects is—like all good literature—truth about human beings and how they live and survive.

In the bibliography which follows, an attempt has been made to provide basic information about the many books for young people which are available and which allow the reader to know individual blacks as they "More often . . . are, people faced with the universal problems of all mankind: earning a living, loving and hating, rejoicing and grieving, ex-

---

3. "Textbooks: Big Dive for Balance," *Time* 88 (August 19, 1966):53.

periencing successes and failures, learning to find their way through a complex world of ideas, and living with other people.[4]

The 202 titles listed here have been selected on the basis of the quality of plot, dialogue, and characterization, on the degree to which blacks are involved in the story—either through description of them or illustrations of them—and, finally, on the contribution the book offers to the total picture of race relations.

The bibliography is arranged according to content related to racial problems, and content not related to racial problems.

annotated bibliography of integrated books for young people: ages 4 to 16

Four to Eight Years Old: Content Related to Racial Problems

Beim, Jerrold. *Swimming Hole.* Illustrated by Louis Darling. New York: William Morrow and Co., 1951. Larry and Bob are two black boys in a group that plays and swims together. Steve, a new boy who doesn't "want to play with anyone "who's colored," plays a mean trick on them. Steve finally discovers skin color is unimportant. One of few simple, muted problem stories for young children.

Burden, Shirley. *I Wonder Why.* Photographs by the author. New York: Doubleday & Co., Inc., 1963. "I like the sea when it wears diamonds . . . and sand when it squeezes through my toes." A black child's catalog of things she likes ends with the question "I wonder why some people don't like me?" Provocative.

Randall, Blossom E. *Fun for Chris.* Illustrated by Eunice Young Smith. Chicago: Albert Whitman and Co., 1956. Jimmy decides to play with Chris and his new black friend instead of taunting them. Chris's mother explains that children look the way they do because it is God's plan that they should look "like their mothers and fathers in some way."

Four to Eight Years Old: Content Not Related to Racial Problems

Alexander, Martha. *The Story Grandmother Told.* Illustrated by the author. New York: The Dial Press, 1969. Lisa, an independent child depicted with an Afro haircut, joins her grandmother in telling the story of Ivan the cat.

Belpré, Pura. *Santiago.* Illustrated by Symeon Shimin. New York: Frederick Warne & Co., 1969. Santiago, a Puerto Rican child, finds his adjustment to a new life made more difficult by the rivalry of Ernie, a black child.

Binzen, Bill. *Miguel's Mountains.* Photographs by the author. New York: Coward-McCann, Inc., 1968. A bulldozer neglects a pile of dirt which becomes transformed by the creative energies of a multiethnic neighborhood. Good photographs of city children at play.

---

4. Rollins, *op. cit.* pp. xi, xiii.

Bonsall, Crosby. *The Case of the Cat's Meow.* Illustrated by the author. New York: Harper & Row, Publishers, 1966. Four boys, one of whom is black, solve the mystery of Mildred, the missing cat.

Barrett, Judith. *Old MacDonald Had an Apartment House.* Illustrated by Ron Barrett. New York: Atheneum Press, 1969. It started out a happily integrated apartment house, but the building superintendent preferred plants to people. Amazingly, Mr. Wrental, the owner, approves of the super's transplants. The incongruities of the pictures will delight children.

———. *The Case of the Dumb Bells.* Illustrated by the author. New York: Harper & Row, Publishers, 1966. Sticking together through thick and thin is difficult when a group of friends (one black) gets in trouble.

———. *The Case of the Hungry Stranger.* Illustrated by the author. New York: Harper & Row, Publishers, 1963. Three older boys (one black) and one little brother become "private eyes" to find the thief who stole a blueberry pie. Good 6-year-old humor.

Brothers, Aileen and Cora Holselaw. *Just One Me.* Illustrated by Jan Balet. Chicago: Follett Publishers, 1967. A black father tells his son he can be anything he wants to be, which sets the boy on an imaginative series of adventures as he feels what it is like to be a tall tree, a long road, a car, merry-go-round, and the wind. He finally decides to be himself because there is "just one me" in the world. The theme is similar to *Magic Michael* by Slobodkin.

Brown, Jeanette Perkins. *Keiko's Birthday.* Illustrated by Jean Martinez. New York: Friendship Press, 1954. The implied theme of this kindergarten tale is that the United States is a union of many cultures. Peter, who came from the Gold Coast, says "I'm American now and I'm a cowboy."

———. *Ronnie's Wish.* Illustrated by Jean Martinez. New York: Friendship Press, 1954. Ronnie, a black child, learns there are sometimes advantages to being young when an adult asks to accompany him to the section of the zoo reserved for children or adults accompanied by children.

Chenery, Janet. *Wolfie.* Illustrated by Marc Simont. New York: Harper & Row, Publishers, 1969. Black and white friends care for a captured wolf spider. Another *Science I Can Read* book like Selsam's *Tony's Birds.*

Cohen, Miriam. *Will I Have A Friend?* Illustrated by Lillian Hoban. New York: The Macmillan Co., 1967. A white child wonders if he will have a friend as he starts out at a new school. The class is integrated and the teacher black. The children are realistically spirited. Shy Jim finally makes one friend and then goes out to play with all the children. This would make an interesting companion piece for Lovelace's *Valentine Box* or Justus' *New Boy in School,* even though the girl and boy in these books are older.

Gill, Joan. *Hush, Jon!* Illustrated by Tracy Sugarman. Garden City: Doubleday & Co., Inc., 1968. Jon is lonesome when his white neighbor friend goes away for the summer. He discovers the value of responsibility by caring for his baby brother.

Greene, Carla. *Railroad Engineers and Airplane Pilots.* Illustrated by Leonard Kessler. New York: Harper & Row, Publishers, 1964. This detailed and factual picture book is sprinkled with a few integrated illustrations.

Grifalconi, Ann. *City Rhythms.* Illustrated by the author. Indianapolis: The Bobbs-Merrill Co., 1965. A black child's father says "This city moves so fast if you don't keep up with it you're left far behind." The boy searches the city for his father's meaning, and gradually he and his interracial friends discover the tempo and sounds of the city too. A good book to stimulate awareness of sights and sounds.

Hall, Elizabeth Starr. *Evan's Corner*. Illustrated by Nancy Grossman. New York: Holt, Rinehart & Winston, Inc., 1966. Evan wants a place of his own in the apartment his eight-member family shares. When he gets his own special corner with a picture, plant and other things, he is still dissatisfied. Perhaps, suggests his mother, he needs to go out of his corner for awhile and help someone else. He follows her advice to his smaller brother's benefit and joy. The lesson is pointed, but the warm family atmosphere in this black family is most appealing.

Hodges, Elizabeth. *Free As a Frog*. Illustrated by Paul Giovanopoulos. New York: Addison-Wesley Press, 1969. Vinnie, a black child, tries to communicate with neighbors by dancing while shy Johnny searches for his own way of communicating with people.

Horvath, Betty. *Hooray for Jasper*. Illustrated by Fermin Rocker. New York: Franklin Watts, Inc., 1966. Jasper, a small black boy, wants to know how to get bigger and his grandfather cryptically tells him he must do something "wonderful" first. After several unsuccessful attempts at wonderfulness, Jasper rescues a neighbor's kitten from a tree—one that is too small for any of the bigger boys to climb. Jasper grows psychologically at least.

Howell, Ruth Rea. *A Crack in the Pavement*. Illustrated by Arline Strong. New York: Atheneum Press, 1970. A crack in the pavement becomes a source of the mystery of life for the wonderfully alive children in this book.

Keats, Ezra Jack. *A Letter to Amy*. Illustrated by the author. New York: The Viking Press, 1968. This time Peter invites a girl to his traditionally all-boy party. The plot illustrates that life can be fun in a smiling, dark-skinned world, too.

———.*Jennie's Hat*. Illustrated by the author. New York: Harper & Row, Publishers, 1966. A little girl's wish that her plain hat turn into an exotic one comes true in a rather extraordinary way. In the background of a church scene, well-dressed, integrated couples are pictured.

———. *Goggles!* Illustrated by the author. New York: Macmillan Co., 1969. Peter goes beyond the protective circle of his black family and is able to hold his own in a not-always-friendly world.

———. *John Henry: An American Legend*. Illustrated by the author. New York: Pantheon Books, 1966. Vibrant pictures accompany this story of the black folk hero, the sledge-hammer expert. It would be a good springboard for discussing changing technology or folk tales.

———. *Peter's Chair*. Illustrated by the author. New York: Harper & Row, Publishers, 1967. In this third of Keats' books about Peter, a tide of jealousy rises in him as he sees his cradle and his crib being painted pink for a new sister. He finally accepts the trade of his baby chair for a big one beside his father.

———. *The Snowy Day*. Illustrated by the author. New York: The Viking Press, Inc., 1962. Race is never mentioned in this 1962 Caldecott Award winning tale of a small black boy's delight in the wonder of snow.

———. *Whistle for Willie*. Illustrated by the author. New York: The Viking Press, Inc., 1964. A black boy tries to learn to whistle so that he can call his dog, Willie, in the same way older boys do.

Kessler, Leonard. *Here Comes the Strikeout*. Illustrated by the author. New York: Harper & Row, Publishers, 1965. "Twenty times at bat and twenty strikeouts" is Bobby's complaint. Even the loan of Willie's lucky cap (Willie is a black teammate) does not help the boy. Finally Bobby asks Willie for help and after much practice, Bobby brings in a run for the Bobcats. This charming story is a *Sports I Can Read* book.

Lewis, Mary. *Halloween Kangaroo*. Illustrated by Richard Lewis. New York: Ives Washburn, Inc., 1964. Jeffrey, a black child, becomes a kangaroo for Halloween and finds himself unable to get back out of his costume. A slight story of a pleasant family and school situation.

Lexau, Joan M. *The Rooftop Mystery*. Illustrated by Syd Hoff. New York: Harper & Row, Publishers, 1968. Albert and Sam, black and white friends, are confronted with the problem of younger sisters. Solid neighbor relationship is depicted between black and white families.

———. *Benjie*. Illustrated by Don Bologneses. New York: The Dial Press, 1964. Benjie is too shy to speak to anyone except his grandmother who raises him. Grandmother drops an earring away from home, and Benjie overcomes his shyness enough to search for this family treasure.

———. *The Homework Caper*. Illustrated by Sydney Hoff. New York: Harper & Row, Publishers, 1966. In this *I Can Read Mystery,* Bill (white) and Ken (black) are buddies who solve a minor mystery as well as the problem of Ken's little sister.

Lexau, Joan. *I Should Have Stayed in Bed!* Illustrated by Sydney Hoff. New York: Harper & Row, Publishers, 1965. Good silly humor! One leading character as well as others are black.

Lipkind, William. *Four-Leaf Clover*. Illustrated by Nicholas Mordvinoff. New York: Harcourt and Co., 1959. Mark, a black child, and his friend, Peter, find a four-leaf clover and consider themselves lucky. They get into a chain reaction of scrapes, but everything ends happily.

McGovern, Ann. *Black is Beautiful*. Photographs by Hope Wurmfeld. New York: Four Winds Press, 1969. Evocative pictures express the beauty of many black things.

Miles, Miska. *Mississippi Possum*. Illustrated by John Schoenherr. Boston: Little, Brown and Co., 1965. The Mississippi River rises higher and higher, forcing a little gray possum as well as Mary and her family to seek higher ground. Hunger and the strange surroundings bring the little black girl and the possum together.

Parker, Bertha. *Wonder of the Seasons*. Illustrated by Eloise Wilkin. New York: Golden Press, 1966. This book captures the fun of the seasons from a child's point of view. Black and white children frolic in the pictures.

Pomerantz, Charles. *The Moon Pony*. Illustrated by Loretta Trezzo. New York: Young Scott Books, 1967. A black father's imaginative response to his young sons' questions, "What is it like on the moon, Daddy?" activates a dream fantasy for the little boy. The family's hot, crowded apartment contrasts with the boy's dream of "a room of his own" and a moon pony.

Rockwell, Anne. *Gypsy Girl's Best Shoes*. Illustrated. New York: Parents' Magazine Press, 1966. A little gypsy girl finds a pair of red dancing shoes. After the grownups in her neighborhood tell her they are much too busy to watch her dance, she meets children in the park who love her dancing and invite her to join them in play. In the picture backgrounds are black firemen, sewer maintenance men, shoppers and schoolchildren.

Rosenbaum, Eileen. *Ronnie*. Photographs by Gloria Kitt Lindauer and Carmel Roth. New York: Parent's Magazine Press, 1969. The promise of a surprise outing with his father causes this black child's feelings to spill over in many directions. The stream-of-thought text and photographs depict a warm family situation.

Scott, Ann. *The Big Cowboy Western*. Illustrated by Richard W. Lewis. New York: Lothrop, Lee and Shepard Co., 1965. Little Martin gets a gun and cowboy outfit on his fifth birthday and becomes Big Cowboy Western, minding the dray horse of a vegetable man. A warm picture of a black family of five girls, a mother, and Martin.

———. *Let's Catch a Monster*. Illustrated by H. Tom Hall. New York: Lothrop, Lee and Shepard Co., 1967. The same family of *Big Cowboy Western*. Martin, who is getting ready for Halloween, decides with his youngest sister to catch a monster. A small tale that is amusing and exciting for children.

———. *Sam*. Illustrated by Symeon Shimin. New York: McGraw-Hill Book Co., 1967. Sam is sent from one family member to another because they are all doing things he is not big enough to do. Once the family realizes Sam is "left out" they find something he is just the right size to do. There is a warm feeling for this black family. Effective illustrations.

Selsam, Millicent. *Tony's Birds*. Illustrated by Kurt Werth. New York: Harper and Brothers, 1961. Although his race is not mentioned in this *Science I Can Read* book, a black boy learns the fun of watching birds which he shares with a white friend.

Showers, Paul. *Look At Your Eyes*. Illustrated by Paul Galdone. New York: Thomas Y. Crowell Co.. 1962. A black boy discovers facts about eyes in this interesting *Let's Read and Find Out* book.

———. *Your Skin and Mine*. Illustrated by Paul Galdone. New York: Thomas Y. Crowell Co., 1965. Another *Let's Read and Find Out* book features a white boy and his black and Oriental friends who discover facts about skin noting pores, hair, sense of touch, fingerprints, melanin, perspiration and the reason for skin covering. Simple and enlightening book that would be useful even in the upper elementary grades. It would complement Korshak's *The Strange Story of Oliver Jones* by giving details of pigmentation suggested in that book.

Stein, R. Conrad. *Steel Driving Man: The Legend of John Henry*. Illustrated by Darrell Woskur. Chicago: Children's Press, 1969. The black folk hero John Henry depicted with many human embellishments. Powerful illustrations accompany the text.

Van Leeuwen, Jean. *Timothy's Flower*. Illustrated by Moneta Barnett. New York: Random House, 1967. Lonely Timothy, on a rare outing with his grandmother, gets a flower which he struggles to care for. Timothy, who is black, wins the friendship of Mrs. Valdez through their interest in plants.

Vogel, Ilse-Margret. *Hello Henry*. Illustrated by the author. New York: Parent's Magazine Press, 1965. A fanciful story about two boys with the same name but with different colored skin.

Wasserman, Selma and Jack. *Moonbeam and the Captain.* Westchester, Illinois: Benefic Press, 1968. A black family's son smuggles a monkey aboard ship causing a series of amusing adventures.

Wasserman, Selma and Jack. *Moonbeam and the Rocket Ride.* Illustrated by George Rohrer. Chicago: Benefic Press, 1965. Dr. Jim, a black, and Scott, his white friend, train for space with an amusing monkey.

———. *Moonbeam Finds a Moonstone.* Chicago: Benefic Press, 1966. More monkey business with Moonbeam the monkey and black Dr. Jim.

Williamson, Stan. *The No-Bark Dog.* Illustrated by Tom O'Sullivan. Chicago: Follett Publishing Co., 1962. This simple picture book does not discuss race, but the black hero shares his concern over his barkless dog with an integrated group of playmates.

Ziner, Feenie and Galdone, Paul. *Counting Carnival.* Illustrated by Paul Galdone. New York: Coward-McCann, Inc., 1962. This simple counting book counts city children, black and white, as they make up a parade.

Eight to Ten Years Old: Content Related to Racial Problems

Bishop, Curtis. *Little League Heroes.* Philadelphia: J. B. Lippincott Co., 1960. Joel is the first black boy to win a place on the Little League team in his Texas town. After much difficulty over race, one of Joel's former white enemies becomes his friend. Even the erring citizens rally round the team at the end.

Burchard, Peter. *Bimby.* Illustrated by the author. New York: Coward-McCann, Inc., 1968. This story of a young black boy's resentment of slavery gives a glimpse of the hierarchy of slaves and overseers on plantations that is both unique and sensitive. See Zagoren.

Caudill, Rebecca. *A Certain Small Shepherd.* New York: Holt, Rinehart & Winston, Inc., 1965. A white mountain boy who has never spoken has frustrating experiences at school. The role of a small shepherd in the Christmas play assumes great significance for him. A snowstorm on Christmas Eve stops the play, but a black baby born in the storm turns the script into life. The marooned couple seeking shelter become a twentieth century parable of the Christmas story.

Gipson, Fred. *The Trail-Driving Rooster.* Illustrated by Marc Simont. New York: Harper and Brothers, Publishers, 1955. All along the trail from Texas to Nevada, the cowboys tease Sam, the black trailcook, about his pet rooster. But the easy-going cameraderie of the cowboys is marred by a saloon keeper's prejudice. The banty, backed up by the cowboys, soon makes him change his ways; however, Dick, the scrappy rooster, is the hero in this series of tall tales. Amusing.

Hughes, Langston. *Black Misery.* Illustrated by Arouni. New York: Paul S. Erickson, Inc., 1969. This posthumous book by the Negro poet suggests the problems of being black in a white culture with a touch of wry humor. The captions might touch off a stream of children's original "Misery is . . ." statements and pictures.

Justus, May. *New Boy in School.* Illustrated by Joan Balfour Payne. New York: Hastings House, Publishers, Inc., 1963. Lennie Lane, a 7-year-old who has recently moved from Louisiana to Tennessee, looks forward with some trepidation to attending an integrated school for the first time. He learns to make friends.

Korschak, Jack. *The Strange Story of Oliver Jones.* Illustrated by Corrine Borja. New York: Mid-America Publishing Co., 1966. Oliver Jones' pride had been that his skin was so white that "not even white milk had such lovely light tones" until he awakens with a black face.

Lawrence, J .D. *Barnaby's Bells.* Illustrated by Michael Lowenbein. New York: The Macmillan Co., 1965. Runaway Felix, who does not know if he is "Negro or Puerto Rican or what," is adopted by a white family, and he and Cliff, a neighbor, become friends. Felix is not the usual oh-so-good black character; he punches a name-calling boy in the nose after much provocation.

Levy, Mimi Cooper. *Corrie and the Yankee.* Illustrated by Ernest Crichlow. New York: The Viking Press, Inc., 1959. A little black girl hides a wounded Union soldier from southern patrollers and later helps him escape. This exciting Civil War story sheds some light on the sometimes diffident treatment of black volunteers in the Union Army, the conversion of the black-and-white run Underground Railroad to wartime uses, underground freedom schools, and the subterfuges blacks resorted to in order to escape detection by Southern whites.

Lovelace, Maud Hart, *The Valentine Box.* Illustrated by Ingrid Fetz. New York: Thomas Y. Crowell Co., 1966. Janice, a shy black fifth grader, fears there will be no valentines for her in her new school. A sudden gust of wind takes a classmate's valentines swirling away but brings a new friend in return.

Neigoff, Mike. *Free Throw.* Illustrated by Fred Orvin. Chicago: Albert Whitman & Co., 1968. The resentment of D. J. Carter, the black hero, toward his newly-integrated junior high school spills over to the basketball court. This is one of the few books for this age level that acknowledges anti-white prejudice.

Norris, Gunilla B. *The Good Morrow.* Illustrated by Charles Robinson. New York: Atheneum Press, 1969. Josie is sent to an interracial camp when her mother recognizes the deep racial wounds within her. A personality conflict with a white child takes on racial connotations for her until she learns the secret of the other girl's problems.

Snyder, Anne. *50,000 Names for Jeff.* Illustrated by Leo Carty. New York: Holt, Rinehart & Winston, Inc., 1969. While Jeff's mama belittles the new open housing project as "not for people like us," her son and daughter yearn to live in the shiny new apartments. The situation seems somewhat dated, but this is one of the few community action plots for this age level.

Tunis, Edwin. *Shaw's Fortune: The Picture Story of a Colonial Plantation.* Illustrated by the author. New York: The World Publishing Co., 1966. A non-fiction presentation of plantation life told through the activities of generations of the Shaw family from 1600 to 1732. Details of colonial living are faithfully portrayed and supplemented by copious illustrations. The author acknowledges that slave-owners may have been oblivious to the morality of slavery but notes that slaves were fully aware of its immorality. Used in conjunction with a book about Harriet Tubman, telling what it felt like to be a slave, would give an excellent overview of both the times and the institution of slavery.

Weiner, Sandra. *It's Wings that Make Birds Fly: The Story of a Boy.* New York: Pantheon Books, Inc., 1968. This story is based on conversations the author had with a young black boy a few weeks before he was killed by an automobile. It is a robust picture of poverty and shifting family structures.

Zagoren, Ruby. *Venture for Freedom: The True Story of an African Yankee.* Cleveland, Ohio: World Publishing Co., 1969. This fictionalized story, based on the autobiography of Broteer, captured in Africa and brought to this country, is similar to Elizabeth Yates' early Newberry winner, *Amos Fortune: Free Man.* Presents in dramatic fashion the black struggle for personal freedom.

Eight to Ten Years Old: Content Not Related to Racial Problem

Abrahams, Robert D. *The Bonus of Redonda.* Illustrated by Peter Bramley. New York: The Macmillan Co., 1969. This first-person story of the Virgin Islands mixes Calypso songs with humor.

Fife, Dale. *Who's in Charge of Lincoln?* Illustrated by Paul Galdone. New York: Coward-McCann, Inc., 1965. The adventures of Lincoln Farnum, a black boy with a reputation for telling whoppers and a passion to see the statue of his namesake in Washington. A desperate bank robber, hiding his stolen money, a deaf baby sitter who breaks her glasses, a new Farnum baby arriving too soon, and his big sister's senior trip combine most miraculously to make Lincoln's wish come true. A believable boy in a modern tall tale.

———. *What's New, Lincoln?* Illustrated by Paul Galdone. New York: Coward-McCann, Inc., 1970. This sequel to *Who's in Charge of Lincoln?* continues his zany misadventures.

Hamilton, Virginia. *Zeely.* Illustrated by Symeon Shimin. New York: The Macmillan Co., 1967. Elizabeth and John Perry visit their uncle on his farm. A neighbor with a tall, silent, mysterious daughter lives nearby and Elizabeth becomes obsessed by the mysterious Zeely. The spell that the author weaves is magnificent, so that it is hard to tell what was real and what imagined.

Horvath, Betty. *Jasper Makes Music.* Illustrated by Fermin Rocker. New York: Franklin Watts, Inc., 1967. Jasper thinks he needs a guitar that costs $30. His mother and father tell him the difference between needing and wanting something. His grandfather shows him a magic shovel and Jasper starts shoveling his way to a shiny new guitar. Duller than the same author's *Hooray for Jasper!*

Konigsburg, Elaine L. *Jennifer, Hecate, MacBeth, William McKinley, and Me, Elizabeth.* New York: Atheneum Press, 1967. It takes a lonesome 10-year-old to believe that Jennifer is a witch. The illustrations show that Jennifer is black, but there is no comment in the book. The story is hilarious and Jennifer a wonderful character. Some elements of stereotyping may mar the story, but it ranks high in reader interest.

Krementz, Jill. *Sweet Pea: A Black Girl Growing Up in the Rural South.* Photographs by the author. New York: Harcourt, Brace & World, Inc., 1969. Wonderful photographs chronicle the pleasures of a little black girl's life in a manner reminiscent of Shackleford's *My Happy Days.* One of the few books depicting blacks in a rural southern setting. The foreward is by Margaret Mead.

Lenski, Lois. *High-Rise Secret*. Illustrated by the author. Philadelphia: J. B. Lippincott Co., 1966. Eight-year-old Pete and his sister Peggy move to a new urban renewal project on Lake Erie. There are descriptions of what it means, good and bad, to live in a low-income project.

Levy, Harry. *Not Over Ten Inches High*. Illustrated by Nancy Grossman. New York: McGraw-Hill Book Co., 1968. Crispus Plunket, a black chimney sweep of colonial Boston, rescues his dog from the law.

———. *Project Boy*. Illustrated by the author. Philadelphia: J. B. Lippincott Co., 1954. Ted Parks lives in the Veterans' Housing Project, a flimsy, barracks-like building. Everyone is poor and the families try to help each other.

Lewis, Mary. *Joey and the Fawn*. Illustrated by H. Tom Hall. New York: Ives Washburn, Inc., 1967. A strong feeling for nature is beautifully conveyed in this story of a black family whose son learns self-confidence.

Lexau, Joan M. *A Kite Over Tenth Avenue*. Illustrated by Symeon Shimin. New York: Doubleday & Co., 1962. Families struggling to survive at the turn of the century. The illustrations are like Hogarth's, showing some blacks. Not the usual light-hearted story for youngsters.

———. *Striped Ice Cream*. Illustrated by John Wilson. Philadelphia: J. B. Lippincott and Co., 1968. Vivid depiction of the day-by-day meaning of black poverty. The family's acceptance of a Good Will bag provides an interesting contrast with the reactions of characters in Baum's *A New Home for Theresa*. Although written for the eight-to-ten age group, sections are rich in detail which could be shared with older ones.

Mann, Peggy. *The Street of the Flower Boxes*. Illustrated by Peter Burchard. New York: Coward-McCann, Inc., 1966. Carlos proves his worth in a story which offers a black policeman as a friend to Puerto Ricans living in a slum.

Martin, Patricia Miles. *Calvin and the Cub Scouts*. Illustrated by Tom Hamilton. New York: G. P. Putnam's Sons, 1964. Calvin borrows a pet for an integrated Cub Scout pet parade.

———. *The Little Brown Hen*. Illustrated by Harper Johnson. New York: Thomas Y. Crowell Co., 1960. A black boy on a farm struggles to find his pet hen and to get his mother a pair of ducks that she wants for her birthday.

Molarsky, Osmond. *Song of the Empty Bottles*. Illustrated by Tom Feelings. New York: Henry Z. Walck, Inc., 1968. Mr. Andrews, a black settlement house worker, encourages young Thaddeus with his music by promising him an inexpensive guitar for completing a song.

Palmer, Candida. *Ride on High*. Illustrated by H. Tom Hall. Philadelphia: J. B. Lippincott and Co., 1966. Tony's big cousin, Charley, gives him a dollar with two passes to the junior high basketball game. An interesting story of two little boys' uncertainties and the confusing monster that a big city sometimes seems. The text makes no comment about the race of the black protagonists.

Peterson, John. *Enemies of the Secret Hide-Out*. Illustrated by the author. New York: Scholastic Book Services, 1965. Sam, Matt and Beany agree to take in two new members, one of whom is black, in this amusing tale.

Prieto, Mariano. *Tomato Boy*. Illustrated by De Lee Smith. New York: John Day Co., 1967. Davy, a black boy from the Bahamas, and his Puerto Rican friend, Paco, solve some personal problems against a background of pictures which provide many details of their poverty.

Renick, Marion. *Ricky in the World of Sports*. Illustrated by Nancy Grossman. New York: Seabury Press, 1967. Blacks and whites pictured in a sports story about a boy who proves himself.

Shotwell, Louisa R. *Roosevelt Grady*. Illustrated by Peter Burchard. Cleveland, Ohio: The World Publishing Co., 1963. The story of a down-and-out family of black migrant workers.

Weiss, Harvey. *Horse in No Hurry*. Illustrated by the author. New York: G. P. Putnam's Sons, 1961. Paul and a black friend, John-Thomas, have assorted comic adventures with their pets.

Woody, Regina. *Almena's Dogs*. Illustrated by Elton C. Fax. New York: Ariel Books, 1954. The black heroine has her hopes realized when her father is asked to operate a kennel.

Ten to Twelve Years Old: Content Related to Racial Problems

Ballard, Martin. *Benjie's Portion*. Illustrated by Douglas Phillips. New York: World Publishing Co., 1969. Ex-slaves living in Canada return to Africa. Benjamin and his family settle in Sierra Leone where the boy learns the circumspection required of a leader.

Baum, Betty. *Patricia Crosses Town*. Illustrated by Nancy Grossman. New York: Alfred A. Knopf, Inc., 1965. Pat is reluctant to go along with Lucy Mae's mother's plan to transfer to an open-enrollment school. Pat is concerned that her black skin will make her less welcome than the light-skinned Lucy Mae. Problems arise but understanding teachers and the children's common interests overcome them.

Bradbury, Bianca. *Undergrounders*. New York: Ives Washburn, Inc., 1966. A white father thinks his 14-year-old son is oblivious to his work in the Underground Railway during the Civil War. When the boy has to take over for his father on a "delivery" he convinces his parents he is growing up.

Brodsky, Mimi. *The House at 12 Rose Street*. Illustrated by David Hodges. New York: Abelard-Schumann, 1966. This story of housing integration, told from a white boys' perspective, offers good contrast with Esther Wier's *Easy Does It*. Bobby Myers' parents, unlike Chip's, offer friendship to the black newcomers and explain some of the facts of blockbusting and myths of property values to their son.

Browin, Frances William. *Looking for Orlando*. New York: Criterion Books, Inc., 1961. An Underground Railroad book told from the point of view of a southern cousin visiting his Pennsylvania Quaker relatives.

Carlson, Natalie Savage. *The Empty Schoolhouse*. Illustrated by John Kaufman. New York: Harper & Row, Publishers, 1965. When the Catholic schools in this bayou town desegregate, Lullah is able to attend school with her best friend, Oralee, for the first time. As outsiders interfere, trouble occurs.

———. *Marchers for the Dream*. Illustrated by Alvin Smith. New York: Harper & Row, Publishers, 1969. The inability of Bethany's family to find a suitable home which they can afford causes her to join the demonstrators in Resurrection City.

Chandler, Ruth Forbes. *Ladder to the Sky*. Illustrated by Harper Johnson. New York: Abelard-Schuman, 1959. Trouble piles on trouble for Chip's black family after they buy and move to a farm.

Coles, Robert. *Dead End School.* Illustrated by Norman Rockwell. Boston: Little, Brown & Company, 1968. Although the book is about sixth-grade boys, they seem much younger because of the large print, simplified story and lifeless hero, Jim. His problems start when his mother, who is too proud to accept welfare, moves to a cheaper apartment in another neighborhood. There the schools are staffed by uncaring teachers and the children are to be bused to an equally dilapidated school nearby to avoid half-day sessions. This becomes the final straw for Jim's mother, and she organizes a successful protest to have them bused to the new under-utilized white schools on the far side of town.

Coombs, Charles. *Young Infield Rookie.* Illustrated by Charles Geer. New York: Lantern Press, 1954. A white Little League player afraid of being hit by a fast ball and a black player afraid of racial prejudice help and are helped by an ex-professional ball player.

Dahl, Mary. *Free Souls.* Boston: Houghton Mifflin Co., 1969. Too many African myths and proverbs, while interesting, interrupt the narrative of this story of the Amistad's revolt. The main character is too ambiguous to be appealing, but the historical paintings and etchings are good.

Douglas, Marjorie Stoneman. *Freedom River.* Illustrated by Edward Shenton. New York: Charles Scribner's Sons, 1953. A slave escapes from slave-catchers with the help of a white boy, and they share hunting adventures with an Indian friend.

Faulkner, Nancy. *The West Is On Your Left Hand.* Illustrated by John Gretzer. Garden City, New York: Doubleday & Co., Inc., 1953. Freed slaves migrate west with their former owners and the psychological aspect of being free is discussed.

Fox, Paula. *How Many Miles to Babylon?* Illustrated by Paul Giovanopoulos. New York: David White Co., 1967. James' daydreams about his identity are shattered by the reality of bigger boys preying upon the weaker in this ghetto story. Surprisingly, the bad boys' motivations are dealt with honestly.

Gates, Doris. *Little Vic.* Illustrated by Kate Seredy. New York: The Viking Press, 1951. Primarily a story of a young boy's belief in the greatness of a horse and his ultimate proof of it, this book deals sensitively with the many barbs the black boy faces.

Graham, Lorenz. *Whose Town?* New York: Thomas Y. Crowell Co., 1969. David's family again tries to protect their seemingly indecisive son from the dangers of city life—this time, from involvement with militant groups.

Hamilton, Virginia. *The House of Dies Drear.* Illustrated by Eros Keith. New York: The Macmillan Co., 1968. Thomas and his black family move to their new home in Ohio, a 100-year-old Underground Railroad relic.

Hodges, Carl G. *Benjie Ream.* Indianapolis: Bobbs-Merrill Co., 1964. After Benjie Ream's older brother sets out for Kansas, to be counted among the abolitionist settlers who will keep the new state free, his father dies and Benjie is bound out to a farmer for 7 years while his mother and sister go to the county farm. Interesting background information on the Kansas-Missouri controversy.

Hoff, Sydney. *Irving and Me.* New York: Harper & Row, Publishers, 1967. Thirteen-year-old Artie moves to Florida to help his father start business and to avoid the warfare of Brooklyn. A fliply told first-person story with two minor discussions of race.

Jackson, G. *Room for Randy.* Illustrated by Frank C. Nicholas. New York: Friendship Press, 1957. Trouble seems imminent when the kids from Tintown, a slum of the neighboring city, have to be bussed to the suburban school for a year. Randy, a black boy who has been fully accepted in the all-white town, is upset because of talk about "spics" and "niggers."

Jones, Ruth Fosdick. *Escape to Freedom.* Illustrated by Dorothy Bayley Morse. New York: Random House, Inc. 1958. An exciting tale of runaway slaves, this book not only sheds light on the Underground Railroad but also quietly mentions some of the not-so-nice aspects of slavery.

Kristof, Jane. *Steal Away Home.* Illustrated by W. T. Mars. Indianapolis: The Bobbs-Merrill Co., Inc., 1969. This Underground Railroad story told from a slave's perspective combines humor, strong characterizations and a sense of the many dangers endured for the love of freedom.

Mantel, S. G. *Tallmadge's Terry.* Illustrated by William Ferguson. New York: David McKay Co., 1965. The anti-slavery Patchens family discovers a runaway slave.

Morse, Evangeline. *Brown Rabbit.* Illustrated by David Stone Martin. Chicago: Follett Publishing Co., 1967. Ceretha Jane Brown, familiarly called Brown Rabbit by her family, is in conflict with her sister and her father who want her to accept people for what they are.

Snow, Donald. *Canalboat to Freedom.* Illustrated by Joseph Cellini. New York: The Dial Press, 1966. Young Ben Lown comes to America from Scotland as an indentured servant and meets black Lundius, a secret conductor on the Underground Railroad. Unique in having a black play a central role in the Underground Railroad. Source notes establish the authenticity of details about the Underground Railroad.

Sterling, Dorothy. *Mary Jane.* Illustrated by Ernest Crichlow. New York: Doubleday & Co., Inc., 1959. Available in paperback by Scholastic. The jeering crowds, unexpected barbs by classmates, and ugly phone calls that have been endemic to many southern scenes of school desegregation are recounted in this story. An interracial friendship develops despite both sets of parents.

Stolz, Mary. *Wonderful, Terrible Time.* Illustrated by Louis S. Glanzman. New York: Harper & Row, Publishers, 1968. Two girls from Harlem have camp experiences and hear reminiscenses from one of their mothers in a warm, believable story.

Sutton, Margaret. *Weed Walk.* Illustrated by Steele Savage. New York: G. P. Putnam's Sons, 1965. Two girls discover the fallacies of racial prejudice as a neighborhood is integrated. There is an interesting contrast between two new neighbors: a slovenly white family and a respectable black one.

Taylor, Theodore. *The Cay.* Garden City: Doubleday & Co., Inc., 1968. An unusual setting—Curacao during World War II. Phillip, who is blinded when his ship is torpedoed, is marooned with an elderly, uneducated black man from the islands. His frustration over his helplessness chips away at the politeness of his race relations until Timothy's psychological astuteness unites the two in a supra-racial human relationship.

Watson, Sally. *Jade.* New York: Holt, Rinehart & Winston, Inc., 1969. A sixteen-year-old redhead, contemptuous of her destiny as a Southern belle, joins pirates to seek her freedom. Several slaves play minor roles with the pirate troupe in quest of their physical as well as spiritual freedom.

Witheridge, Elizabeth. *And What of You, Josephine Charlotte?* Illustrated by
Barbara McGee. New York: Atheneum Press, 1969. The ugliness of slavery is finally brought home to a favored servant and her egalitarian mis-
tress as the white girl's imminent marriage threatens their relationship.
Wier, Esther. *Easy Does It.* Illustrated by W. T. Mars. New York: The Vanguard Press, Inc., 1965. The white hero has recently moved into the
neighborhood and is just beginning to be accepted by the other boys
when a black family moves next door. Chip's sense of fair play, the appealing qualities of the new boy, L. A., and downright stubbornness make
him risk his status in the community to help his new friend.

Ten to Twelve Years Old: Content Not Related to Racial Problems

Bonham, Frank. *Mystery of the Fat Cat.* Illustrated by Alvin Smith. New
York: E. P. Dutton & Co., Inc., 1968. Buddy Williams, a black teenager,
and his street-wise but well-intentioned black and Spanish-American
friends wade deeper and deeper into trouble as they try to find money to
reopen their condemned neighborhood center.
Burch, Robert. *Queenie Peavy.* New York: The Viking Press, 1966. In a depressed rural area of Georgia, a white girl fleetingly envies the better living of the black family next door. The friendliness of the black children
and their father's cooler cordiality tell much about the ingraining of local
racial mores.
Burchardt, Nellie. *Project Cat.* Illustrated by Fermin Rocker. New York:
Franklin Watts, Inc., 1966. Betsy and her younger sister, Jennie, find a
stray cat. Ellen, her white friend, quarrels with her over it. Through caring for the cat, Betsy gains not only a pet but a stronger and more equit-
able relationship with her friend across racial lines. Betsy and her friends
successfully petition for an end to the ban on pets at the project.
Carlson, Natalie Savage. *Ann Aurelia and Dorothy.* Illustrated by Dale Payson.
New York: Harper & Row, Publishers, 1968. The major character is white,
but her black girl friend provides much emotional support as Ann Aurelia
struggles with the problem of a succession of foster homes and a mother
unwilling to assume responsibility for her.
Cooper, Page. *Thunder.* Illustrated by Edward Shenton. Cleveland: World
Publishing Co., 1954. Spud (black) and Peter (white) have adventures
involving the birth and training of a horse.
Hull, Eleanor. *Moncho and the Dukes.* Illustrated by Bernard Case. New
York: Friendship Press, 1964. Johnson, a black boy, lives in an apartment in East Harlem above Moncho. On the edge of trouble in school and
on the streets, they are whisked into a church-sponsored gang trying to
help the local kids by breaking down the walls between people.
Huston, Anne. *Trust a City Kid.* Illustrated by J. C. Kocsis. New York: Lothrop, Lee and Shepard Co., 1966. Twelve-year-old Reggie's social worker
has arranged for him to spend the summer with a Quaker family on a
farm. He has many adjustments to make but he succeeds in adapting to
farm life and a white family of pacifists. Similar to *Joe Bean*.
Jones, Adrienne. *Sail, Calypso!* Illustrated by Adolph Le Moult. Boston: Little,
Brown and Co., 1968. Fascinating book for boys who like sailing! Two
strangers, a black and a white boy, claim a wrecked sailboat as their own
and gradually form a friendship over their forced partnership.

Lewis, Richard. *A Summer Adventure*. Illustrated by the author. New York: Harper & Row, Publishers, 1962. Ross, a black youngster, has summer adventures exploring the woods around his farm home and learning the ways of animals.

Shotwell, Louise. *Adam Bookout*. Illustrated by W. T. Mars. New York: The Viking Press, 1967. Saul takes Adam and a black boy from Alabama, Willie, under his wing at school and the three friends solve a mystery.

Snyder, Zylpha. *Egypt Game*. Illustrated by Alton Raible. New York: Atheneum Press, 1967. April, a Hollywood brat, is left by her flighty mother with her grandmother. She meets Melanie, a lonesome black neighbor her age. They turn their eager minds to developing the mysterious Egypt Game. Outstandingly well written.

Stevenson, William. *The Bushbabies*. Illustrated by Victor Ambrus. Boston: Houghton Mifflin Co., 1965. Jackie, a white child about to leave Africa forever with her gamewarden father, stops off to repatriate her bushbaby pet with the help of their former headman. Much is implied about race relations through the action.

Twelve to Sixteen Years Old: Content Related to Racial Problems

Ball, Dorothy. *Hurricane*. Indianapolis: Bobbs-Merrill Co., 1964. Davey, a white boy, learns that his lifelong black friend suffers from the prejudice of others and their friendship becomes even stronger.

Baum, Betty. *A New Home for Theresa*. Illustrated by James Barkley. New York: Alfred A. Knopf, Inc., 1968. Following her mother's death, Theresa is placed in the foster care of a Negro family. She adjusts to her mother's death and to living with her new family in an integrated cooperative.

Beyer, Audrey White. *Dark Venture*. Illustrated by Leo and Diane Dillon. New York: Alfred A. Knopf, 1968. Demba's misadventures from capture in Africa and transport to New England in the late 1700's.

Blanton, Catherine. *Hold Fast to Your Dreams*. New York: Julian Messner, Inc., 1955. Emmy Lou goes to live with her Aunt and Uncle in Arizona to avoid segregation and continue her dance training only to encounter the less open restriction there. There is a chilling scene in the counselor's office as she attempts to steer the girl into an "acceptable" career for a second-class citizen. The book deals with discrimination in a direct and effective way.

Bonham, Frank. *The Nitty Gritty*. Illustrated by Alvin Smith. New York: E. P. Dutton & Co., Inc., 1969. Charley, a bright ghetto boy, dropping out of school to earn some money, is challenged by a sympathetic English teacher, Mr. Toia, to aim for college. But the boy's down-and-out family and drunken father discourage him as they see other Negroes who have gotten an education discriminated against in employment. Fortunately, Charley makes the central decisions in the plot and Mr. Toia merely shows alternative ways of working toward the boy's goals.

———. *Durango Street*. New York: E. P. Dutton and Co., Inc., 1965. This story of black and Mexican gangs compels interest with its fascinating black hero, Rufus Brown, who leaves reform school to fall heir to the leadership of the gang in a new neighborhood.

Bradbury, Bianca. *Lots of Love, Lucinda.* New York: Ives Washburn, Inc., 1966. Corry Lee's family invites a southern black girl to stay with them to finish high school.

Burchard, Peter. *North by Night.* New York: Coward-McCann, Inc., 1962. Rich detail substantiates this Civil War story of the escape of two white soldiers from a southern prison. Several blacks appear—some friendly to the Union cause and some indifferent. Bibliography provided.

Butters, Dorothy Gilman. *Masquerade.* Philadelphia: Macrae Smith Co., 1961. The reasons for and problems of "passing" are explored in this college friendship book. Exclusion of blacks from the dormitory is the catalyst for three girls', black and white, decision to share a private apartment.

Catton, Bruce. *Banners at Shenandoah.* New York: Doubleday & Co., Inc., 1955. Civil War spying behind Confederate lines and a new-found love for a Southern anti-Secesh girl are the themes. There is interesting information about runaways and freed men in southern swamps, the help freely given the Union by them, and the self-protective reason for the "mumble-jumble accent" of many blacks at that time.

Clarke, Mary. *Petticoat Rebel.* Illustrated by Robert MacLean. New York: The Viking Press, 1964. Dacie, a New England girl of the Revolutionary Period, helps her family prepare some manumitted slaves for independence, teaching them to read and write.

Colman, Hila. *Classmates by Request.* New York: William Morrow and Co., 1964. When a new high school is built on the black side of town, presumably to stop the press for integration, Dan and Carla Monroe and some other white friends decide to integrate the schools in reverse.

Davis, Russell F. and Ashabranner, Brent. *Strangers in Africa.* New York: McGraw-Hill Book Co., 1963. Two Americans, one black, the other white, meet as they travel to West Africa as entomologists. Their friendship develops as the black "discovers" himself.

de Leeuw, Adele. *The Barred Road.* New York: The Macmillan Co., 1954. The white heroine leads her Problems of American Democracy class into community action and greater understanding. The morally vascillating white parents are excellent springboards for provocative discussions of our "American Dilemma." This is one of the earliest books to mention neighborhood integration and the problems associated with the overcrowded ghetto.

Fair, Ronald L. *Hog Butcher.* New York: Harcourt, Brace and World, 1966. Ghetto street language is a hallmark of this book about life in a black slum.

Fritz, Jean. *Brady.* Illustrated by Lynd Ward. New York: Coward-McCann, Inc., 1960. A minister's son shamed by his father's outspoken denunciation of slavery in a slaveless Pennsylvania stumbles onto the secret that his father is a conductor on the Underground Railroad.

Graham, Lorenz. *North Town.* New York: Thomas Y. Crowell Co., 1965. David Williams' suspicious attitude toward white people may be unbelievable for white children who have not read the earlier *South Town.* In the Williams family's desires for a better education for their son who wants to become a doctor, they discover they have traded outright hostility and repression of the South for the subtler restrictions of the North.

Haas, Ben. *The Troubled Summer*. Indianapolis: The Bobbs-Merrill Co., 1966. Clay Williams, in this rather stilted book, longs for the civil rights movement to come to his backwater town. After he and his friend, Andy, are beaten by two white men, Clay is deeply hurt psychologically and has difficulty working with an integrated civil rights group on their target of painting the Baptist church, but his hatred gradually diminishes. There is a didactic review of black history since slavery.

Hentoff, Nat. *Jazz Country*. New York: Harper & Row, Publishers, 1965. Tom, a middle-class white boy almost ready for college, gains acceptance in the world of jazz musicians. In this predominantly black world, he finds himself sometimes rejected on racial grounds. He learns also about the insults flung at his new friends as he searches for a philosophy of life.

Hughes, Langston. *Simple's Uncle Sam*. New York: Hill and Wang Co., 1965. These conversation-type essays are well on their way to becoming classics. With wit and a cynical eye for human error, Hughes writes about integration, "white" religion, gospel singers, welfare, the situation of having light-skinned blacks, being a "passed-around child," fights over home "in the suburbans," reverse integration, the high cost of living in Harlem, fantasies about black political control in Virginia. They are a stylistic cross between the speeches of Mrs. Malaprop and the dialogue of a master comic and his straight man.

Hunter, Kristin. *The Soul Brothers and Sister Lou*. New York: Charles Scribner's Sons, 1968. This black author won the 1968 award of the Council on Interracial Books for Children with this ghetto story for older boys and girls. Louretta, a Negro with the stigma of brownish hair, is distrusted by the other youngsters because of her family's protectiveness and her less-Negroid looks. As she asserts her independence, she realizes her bond with her less fortunate classmates as they face police harassment and as she encounters cruel jibes from her former white friends.

Jackson, Jesse. *Charley Starts From Scratch*. New York: Harper and Brothers, 1958. This third book in the adventures of Charley describes his leaving the white suburb where he had grown up as the son of the live-in maid and butler. Although he had made his way on equal terms in this community, even he and his white buddies together cannot overcome all the barriers for the black there.

———. *Tessie*. Illustrated by Harold James. New York: Harper & Row, Publishers, 1968. Tessie adjusts to the long ride from the exclusive downtown school she is integrating to her home in Harlem.

Lee, Harper. *To Kill a Mockingbird*. Philadelphia: J. B. Lippincott Co., 1960. This perceptive book of the modern South is seen through the eyes of a little white girl. One of the major incidents of the plot is the futile attempt for a black to obtain justice with a false rape charge. The maid in this white home plays an important role, and it is interesting to see how the father teaches his children an attitude toward her quite different from the prevailing mores.

Lipsyte, Robert. *The Contender*. New York: Harper & Row, Publishers, 1965. Much anti-white and anti-Semitic hostility is aired in this story of a boy searching for self-identity in a ghetto.

Marshall, Catherine. *Julie's Heritage*. Illustrated by E. Harper Johnson. New York: Longmans, Green and Company, 1957. Paperback by Scholastic now available. Julie's two white friends become more distant at the start of high school and Julie examines her own and other blacks' racial attitudes.

Mather, Melissa. *One Summer in Between*. New York: Harper & Row, Publishers, 1967. A black college student and her classmates take jobs in the North and agree to compare notes on the treatment of blacks there for their sociology teacher.

McKone, Jim. *Lone Star Fullback*. New York: The Vanguard Press, Inc., 1966. A black high school athlete on an all-white team proves himself stronger than his antagonizers.

Means, Florence Crannell. *Tolliver*. Boston: Houghton Mifflin Co., 1963. A poor girl from St. Helena Island and her even poorer boyfriend at Fisk are the chief characters. Determined to become a doctor although he is only a marginal student because of his poor former schooling, he is caught cheating on a final exam and expelled.

Miller, Warren. *The Siege of Harlem*. Illustrated by John Schoenherr. New York: McGraw-Hill Book Co., 1964. Modeled after Uncle Remus's tales, this is the story of a grandfather relating to his sophisticated African-named grandchildren how Harlem seceded from the Union when blacks were denied equality in the nation.

Newell, Hope. *A Cap for Mary Ellis*. New York: Harper and Brothers, 1953. Two black friends from Harlem help desegregate a nursing school.

Quigley, Martin. *Today's Game*. New York: The Viking Press, Inc., 1965. Barney, the team manager, trades his long-time friend and neighbor, Jerry Adams, for an up-and-coming black player. Barney finds his team in a long losing slump as the team comes up against Jerry's pitching. The problems of a major league baseball player finding adequate housing and the fierce determination of some players to break out of the black minor leagues to show what they can do are beautifully described.

Rodman, Bella. *Lions in the Way*. Chicago: Follett Publishing Co., 1966. Robert Jones looks forward with some uncertainty to being among the first to desegregate the local high school in this border town. It takes violence to bring the town to its senses.

Sprague, Gretchen. *A Question of Harmony*. New York: Dodd, Mead and Co., 1966. Jeanne meets Dave and another music-loving friend, black Mel Johnson, and their friendship deepens as they play string trios Sundays. Jeannie's slow realization that they are being snubbed because of Mel turns into fury over this abridgement of her own civil rights and makes the three of them determined to protest.

——. *White in the Moon*. New York: Dodd, Mead and Co., 1968. A sequel to *A Question of Harmony* that stands on its own. The problem presented is that of the propriety of being too solicitous of Negro friends.

Vroman, Mary. *Harlem Summer*. Illustrated by John Martinez. New York: G. P. Putnam's Sons, 1967. John, a high school student from Montgomery, Alabama, comes to Harlem where he learns many things about ghetto life and about himself.

Whitney, Phyllis. *A Step to the Music*. New York: Thomas Y. Crowell Co., 1953. The scene is Staten Island during the Civil War and two white heroines quarrel over sweethearts and divided wartime loyalties. During the vividly described anti-black draft riots in the city, the girls help a black escape the mob's wrath.

Young, Jefferson. *A Good Man.* Indianapolis: Bobbs-Merrill Co., Inc., 1952. When a tenant farmer decides to paint his house white, it becomes not only a symbol for him to work for but one for all the whites of the area to unite against. The story vividly describes the economic pressure on southern blacks.

Twelve to Sixteen Years Old: Content Not Related to Racial Problems

Barrett, William. *Lilies of the Field.* Illustrated by Burt Silverman. New York: Doubleday & Co., Inc., 1962. Homer Smith, a black newly discharged from the Army, working his way across country with his station wagon home, agrees to work for some German nuns on their building for a day. But one day stretches into another as he discovers the sisters are counting on him to build a church for them singlehandedly. Homer's irritation with the Mother Superior's imperious manner melts as his pride in accomplishment grows and as he proves to himself that he can be his own boss.

Bontemps, Arna. *Lonesome Boy.* Illustrated by Feliks Topolski. Boston: Houghton Mifflin Co., 1955. Grandpa warns Bubber to mind where he blows his horn because he might get into devilment. But the boy's fascination with his horn is too much. He runs away to New Orleans to be caught up in the frenzy of the world of jazz.

Butters, Dorothy Gilman. *Heartbreak Street.* Philadelphia: Macrae Smith Co., 1958. With the help of the staff of the Community Center, Kitty, an upwardly mobile white girl from the wrong side of town, changes her values from the purely personal. Clovis, a black social worker, helps inspire Kitty's family to fix their house by displaying her own do-it-yourself attractive apartment on the same street.

Dahl, Borghild. *Good News.* New York: E. P. Dutton & Co., 1966. A pre-depression multi-ethnic community is the setting of this book. Two college journalism students, one black and the other white, decide to publish a weekly paper as their term project. In addition to learning the newspaper business through their venture, they spark a revitalization of their town by learning much about their neighbors.

Emerson, Donald. *Court Decision.* New York: David McKay Co., 1967. Ken, a new white boy in the neighborhood, is soon in trouble with everyone. There are different characters from those in *Span Across the River* by the same author, but Wally Carson, the black ballplayer, appears again. The plot is similar to the earlier book but Wally's character is described with more detail, including comments about his mother's hurting her wrist in a civil rights demonstration.

Friermood, Elizabeth H. *Whispering Willows.* New York: Doubleday & Co., 1964. Tess, a white orphan growing up in Indiana at the turn of the century, is friendly with the Washington family, her black neighbors. She longingly shares the many joys and sorrows of this large family, a family struggling to survive economically but rich in spirit.

Means, Florence Crannell. *Reach for a Star.* Boston: Houghton Mifflin Co., 1957. Toni, the daughter of a black druggist, goes to Fisk instead of to a more expensive integrated school. At college she learns to be less class-conscious and more tolerant of people's differences.

Newell, Hope. *Mary Ellis, Student Nurse.* New York: Harper and Brothers, 1958. Mary Ellis's years at her nursing school result in an increasing maturity in outlook. A minor note of discord occurs when a new freshman seems to be a kleptomaniac and Mary Ellis hopes it is not a new black freshman. It was not. Good girls' career story.

Norton, Andre. [Alice Mary]. *Quest Crosstime.* New York: The Viking Press, Inc., 1965. A gripping science fiction story with the hero, a brown-skinned survivor from Earth who becomes a member of the elite Wardsmen on the planet Vroom.

Weik, Mary. *The Jazz Man.* Illustrated by Ann Grifalconi. New York: Atheneum Press, 1966. A gripping picture of a little boy caught in the chaos of Harlem poverty. This eerie tale is about a lame 9-year-old boy isolated in a top floor apartment, his only bonds to the larger world being his parents whom he sees only at night and a musician he sees through a window across the courtyard.

Sixteen Years Old and Up: Content Related to Racial Problems

Armstrong, William H. *Sounder.* Illustrated by James Barkley. New York: Harper & Row, Publishers, 1969. A fierce will to live keeps a family from being crushed by southern racial violence. Winner of the 1969 Newberry Medal.

Baldwin, James. *Go Tell It on the Mountain.* New York: The Dial Press, 1963. A story of John's struggle for salvation and survival in the harsh world of Harlem. John is torn between his desire to please his mother plus the historical pull of his church over his soul and his shrinking from the meanness of his foster father. The lives of John's closest relatives are reviewed in a series of flashbacks as they watch his coming through to glory.

Ball, John. *In the Heat of the Night.* New York: Harper and Brothers, 1965. Virgil Tibbs, visiting police detective, is seized upon as a suspect when a murder occurs in this sleepy southern town—a suspect because he is black and is carrying a large sum of money in his wallet. When Virgil's identity is established and he is loaned to the local police because of his expertise in homicide cases, he finds himself in the position of being the person who is actually in charge in a situation where his race had always been subordinated.

Corder, Eric. *Slave Ship.* New York: David McKay Co., 1969. The barbarous practices of the slave traders are related in detail.

Fair, Ronald. *Many Thousand Gone.* New York: Harcourt, Brace and World, 1965. In a Faulknerian manner the story of Jacobs County, Mississippi, from pre-Civil War days to the present is unfolded with its details of white duplicity, violence and rape. Jesse is the last pure-blooded black to be born in the county, a private armed camp from which no brothers escape alive or find out about the outside world. He is hidden by Granny, but the white men finally catch her. U. S. marshals, responding to a smuggled S. O. S. from the rebelling blacks, fresh in their innocence of southern ways, find themselves jailed. The black youths burn the white town and set their "emancipators" free. This is a grim picture of white barbarity, which Fair calls "a fable." The story of the "first-borns" is sardonically humorous, but the second half of the story is murderously chilling.

Ford, Jesse Hill. *Liberation of Lord Byron Jones.* Boston: Little, Brown and Co., 1965. The all-pervasive web that southern mores weave to degrade black people is convincing in this novel. The story is told in a series of scenes narrated by a dozen or so characters—each in the style appropriate to the particular narrator.

Grau, Shirley Ann. *The Keepers of the House.* New York: Alfred A. Knopf, Inc., 1964. This wonderful historical account of a family with both black and white ancestors is told by the granddaughter about the man who not only had relations with a black housekeeper, but also secretly married her.

Smith, William. *The Stone Face.* New York: Farrar, Strauss and Young, 1963. Simeon Brown, a black American, flees to Paris to keep him from murder and its consequences. Flashbacks reveal the lustful games of summer nights, the horrors of slum dwellings, violence, police beatings, seeing Algerians become the despised minority with blacks now respectable "white" men.

———. *South Street.* New York: Farrar, Strauss and Young, 1954. Fascinating characters: Phillip, Michael and Claude, brothers who had announced a vendetta against whites when a white man murdered their father; Kristin, a richly alive white violinist Claude meets; Slim, a numbers runner. Race hatred in both directions versus love of humanity are deftly explored.

Walker, Margaret. *Jubilee.* Boston: Houghton Mifflin Co., 1966. Jubilee is the equivalent of *Gone With the Wind,* both in plot and fascination, told from the point of view of golden haired Vyry, the daughter of a slave sired by the plantation master.

Warren, Robert Penn. *Band of Angels.* New York: Random House, Inc., 1955. A girl raised as white discovers her true racial identity at her father's death and is stripped of her inheritance although she had been raised as his daughter.

Williams, Edward G. *Not Like Niggers.* New York: St. Martin's Press, 1969. A pathetic family is split between a mother obsessed by her attempt to act "not like niggers" and a father increasingly frustrated by life.

Wright, Charles. *The Wig.* New York: Farrar, Straus & Giroux, Inc., 1966. Far-out humor about a black who uses the perfect hair straightener and then tests how everyone, including himself, reacts to it.

Sixteen Years Old and Up: Content Not Related to Racial Problems

Ball, John. *The Cool Cottontail.* New York: Harper & Row, Publishers, 1966. In the fictional time interval between Virgil Tibbs' solution of the murder in *In the Heat of the Night* and the discovery of a body floating in the pool of the nudist resort, the black inspector has matured considerably. Or, perhaps, it is because the setting is no longer the Deep South but California. The inspector is still sensitive to the different reactions his skin arouses, but he is not as solicitous about deferring to people's prejudices. This makes him a more human character. He is still, however, inhumanly clever at deducing the logic of crime. The bad guy is also black, a man trained in street fighting by a militant group formed after the Watts riot, who is willing to kill for money when racial retribution is involved.

What People Read: A Bibliography of Research and Commentary on the Contents of Textbooks and Literary Media

Jean Dresden Grambs

introduction

Throughout the previous chapters one constant theme has been evident: that books and textbooks have been subject to the vagaries of the market place, with only moderate regard for accuracy or awareness of distortion or bias. In several instances it has been noted that research was lacking regarding the impact of instructional and reading materials. What research is available has been cited.

The bibliography that follows attempts to bring together research studies and scholarly commentary about the content of reading materials, text and otherwise. Unpublished material is not included. The bibliography goes beyond the major focus of this volume, *Black Image*, primarily in the interest of research. The variety of studies that have been done on literary and textbook content is interesting; of further interest is the variety of research approaches employed. The serious student, therefore, who wishes to pursue some of the ideas and issues raised in this volume can find, in this bibliography, models of research approaches. He may also, of course, find further studies about the way in which different topics have been handled by text or trade book authors.

The bibliography does not include those mountains of criticism which pour forth from academic departments of English, though undoubtedly the best of these could also be utilized as critical models for further study. Nor does the bibliography include data from the area of bibliotherapy although there is a fine line between the affective influence of text and literary materials, and books utilized in therapy.

It is hoped that this volume, and this bibliography particularly, will encourage others to do more critical reading, reviewing, and careful writing of and about materials for use in and out of school.*

historical

A. Published Research: Books and Monographs

Altschal, Charles. *The American Revolution in Our School Books.* New York: George H. Doran Co., 1917.

Barry, F. U. A. *A Century of Children's Books.* New York: George H. Doran Co., 1932.

Elson, Ruth Miller. *Guardians of Tradition: American Schoolbooks of the Nineteenth Century.* Lincoln: University of Nebraska Press, 1964.

Hazlitt, W. Carey. *Schools, Schoolbooks and Schoolmasters,* 2nd ed. New York: Stetchert and Co., 1905.

James, Phillip. *Children's Books of Yesterday.* London: The Studio Publication, 1933.

Johnson, Clifton. *Old Time Schools and Schoolbooks.* New York: Dover Publishing Co., 1963 (reprint of 1904 ed.).

Keiser, Albert. *The Indian in American Literature.* New York: Oxford University Press, 1933.

Kiefer, Monica. *American Children Through Their Books—1790-1835.* Philadelphia: University of Pennsylvania Press, 1948.

Meigs, Cornelia, et al. *A Critical History of Children's Literature.* New York: The Macmillan Co., 1953.

Minnich, Harvey C. *William Holmes McGuffey and His Readers.* New York: American Book Co., 1936.

Mosier, Richard D. *Making the American Mind: Social and Moral Ideas in the McGuffey Readers.* New York: King's Crown Press, Columbia University, 1947.

Roselle, Daniel. *Samuel Griswold Goodrich: Creator of Peter Parley.* New York: The State University of New York Press, 1968.

Rosenbach, A. S. W. *Early American Children's Books.* Portland: Southworth Press, 1933.

Schlesinger, Arthur. *Learning How to Behave: A Historical Study of American Etiquette Books.* New York: The Macmillan Co., 1946.

Smith, Dora V. *Fifty Years of Children's Books: 1910-1960.* Champaign, Ill.: National Council of Teachers of English, 1963.

---

*An earlier version of this bibliography included unpublished research studies, and was restricted primarily to school textbooks and children's books in the social sciences. See: Barbara Finkelstein, Loretta Golden and Jean D. Grambs, "A Bibliography of Research and Commentary on Textbooks and Related Works," *Social Education* 29 (March, 1969): 331-336.

Spieseke, Alice Winifred. *The First Textbooks in American History, and Their Compiler, John McCulloch*. New York: Teachers College Press, Columbia University, 1938.

Sunley, Robert. "Early Nineteenth-Century American Literature on Child Rearing" in *Childhood in Contemporary Cultures*, edited by Margaret Mead and Martha Wolfenstein, pp. 150-167. Chicago, Ill.: University of Chicago Press, 1955.

Weeks, Stephen B. *Confederate Textbooks, 1861-1865*, in *Report of The United States Commissioner of Education for 1898-899*. Washington, D. C.: Government Printing Office, 1900.

Warfel, Henry R. *Noah Webster, Schoolmaster to America*. New York: The Macmillan Co., 1936.

B. Articles

Belock, M. V. "Courtesy Tradition and Early Schoolbooks." *History of Education Quarterly* 8 (Fall, 1968): 306-318.

Belock, M. V. "Noah Webster's Speller and the Way to Success." *Phi Delta Kappan* 49 (October, 1967): 85-87.

Brown, Ralph. "The American Geographies of Jedidiah Morse." *Annals of the Association of American Geographers* 30 (September, 1941): 145-267.

Deane, Paul C. "The Persistence of Uncle Tom: An Examination of the Image of the Negro in Children's Fiction Series." *Journal of Negro Education* 37 (April, 1968): 140-145.

Elson, Ruth Miller. "American Schoolbooks and 'Culture' in the Nineteenth Century." *Mississippi Valley Historical Review* 46 (December, 1959): 411-434.

England, Merton J. "The Democratic Faith in American Schoolbooks, 1783-1860." *American Quarterly* 15 (Summer, 1963): 191-199.

England, Merton J. "England and America in the Schoolbooks of the Republic, 1783-1861." *University of Birmingham Historical Journal* 9 (1963): 92-111.

Franklin, John Hope. "Rediscovering Black America: A Historical Roundup." *New York Times Book Review*, 8 September 1968, 1+.

Gross, Theodore L. "The Negro in the Literature of Reconstruction." *Phylon* 22 (1961): 5-14.

Sahli, J. R. "Slavery Issue in Early Geography Textbooks." *History of Education Quarterly* 3 (September, 1963): 153-158.

Sanford, Charles L. "Classics of American Reform Literature." *American Quarterly* 10 (Fall, 1938): 295-311.

Shankland, Rebecca H. "The McGuffey Readers and Moral Education." *Harvard Educational Review* 31 (Winter, 1961): 60-72.

Shurter, Robert L. "The Utopian Novel in America, 1888-1900." *South Atlantic Quarterly* 34 (April, 1935): 137-144.

Suhl, Isabelle. "The Real Doctor Doolittle." *Inter-racial Books for Children* 2 (Spring, Summer 1969): 1-2.

Tyack, David. "Forming the National Character: Paradox in the Educational Thought of the Revolutionary Generation." *Harvard Educational Review* 34 (November, 1963): 71-78.

Younker, Donna Lee. "The Moral Philosophy of William Holmes McGuffey." *Educational Forum* 27 (November, 1963): 71-78.

Zimet, Sara F. "American Elementary Reading Textbooks: A Sociological Review." *Teachers College Record* 70 (January, 1969): 331-340.

contemporary

A. Published Research: Books and Monographs

American Council on Education. *Intergroup Relations in Teaching Materials.* Washington, D.C.: American Council on Education, 1949.

American Management Association. "The Executive in Fiction: A Symposium." In *People at Work: The Human Element in Modern Business.* pp. 178-195. Management Report No. 1. New York, 1957.

Armens, Sven. *Archetypes of the Family in Literature.* Seattle: University of Washington Press, 1966.

Billington, Ray Allen, et al. *The Historian's Contribution to Anglo-American Misunderstanding: Report of a Committee on National Bias in Anglo-American History Textbooks.* New York: Hobbs, Dorman and Co., Inc., 1966.

Blotner, Joseph. *The Political Novel.* Garden City, N. J.: Doubleday & Co., Inc., 1955.

Books for Schools and the Treatment of Minorities. Hearings before the Ad Hoc Subcommittee on De Facto School Segregation of the Committee on Education and Labor, House of Representatives, Eighty-Ninth Congress, Second Session, on Books for Schools and the Treatment of Minorities. Washington, D. C.: U. S. Government Printing Office, 1966, p. 1-828.

Carpenter, Marie E. *The Treatment of the Negro in American History School Textbooks.* Menasha, Wis.: George Banta Publishing Co., 1941.

Committee for Economic Development. *Economic Education in the Schools.* New York: The Committee for Economic Development, 1961.

Cronbach, Lee J., ed. *Text Materials in Modern Education.* Champaign, Ill.: University of Illinois Press, 1955.

Darten, F. J. Harvey. *Childrens' Books in England: Five Centuries of Social Life.* Cambridge: Cambridge University Press, 1960.

Deegan, Dorothy Yost. *The Stereotype of the Single Woman in American Novels.* New York: King's Crown Press, Columbia University, 1951.

Deiulio, Anthony M. "Youth Education: A Literary Perspective." *Youth Education: Problems, Perspectives, Promises,* edited by Fred T. Wilhelms, pp. 58-83. Washington, D. C.: Association for Supervision and Curriculum Development, 1967 Yearbook.

Doherty, Robert E. *Teaching Industrial Relations in High Schools.* Ithaca, N.Y.: State Industrial and Labor Relations, Cornell University, 1964.

Foff, Arthur. "The Teacher as Hero." In *Readings in Education,* edited by Arthur Foff and Jean D. Grambs, pp. 19-21. New York: Harper & Row, Publishers, 1956.

Green, Philip, and M. Walzer, eds. *The Political Imagination in Literature.* New York: The Free Press, 1959.

Hart, James. *The Popular Book: A History of America's Literary Taste.* Berkeley: University of California Press, 1961.

Harlan, Louis R. *The Negro in American History.* Washington, D. C.: American Historical Association, 1965.

Harris, Judah. *The Treatment of Religion in Elementary School Social Studies Textbooks.* New York: Anti-Defamation League of B'nai B'rith, 1963.

Himelatein, Morgan X. *Drama as a Weapon.* New Brunswick, N. J.: Rutgers University Press, 1963.

Holland, Henry M. *Politics Through Literature.* Englewood Cliffs, N. J.: Prentice-Hall, Inc., 1968.

Howe, Irving. *Politics and the Novel.* New York: Horizon Press, 1957.

Indians in Literature. Minneapolis: University of Minnesota Press, n.d.

Kane, Michael B. *Minorities in Textbooks.* Chicago: Quadrangle Books, 1970.

Lively, Robert A. *Fiction Fights the Civil War.* Chapel Hill: University of North Carolina, 1957.

Lorang, Sister Mary Corde. *Burning Ice: The Moral and Emotional Effects of Reading.* New York: Charles Scribner's Sons, 1968.

Lynch, James J. and Evans, Bertrand. *High School English Textbooks: A Critical Examination.* Boston, Mass.: Little, Brown and Co., 1963.

Marcus, Lloyd. *The Treatment of Minorities in Secondary School Textbooks.* New York: Anti-Defamation League of B'nai B'rith, 1961.

Margolies, Edward. *Native Sons: A Critical Study of Twentieth-Century Negro American Authors.* Philadelphia: J. B. Lippincott Company, 1968.

Martin, Helen. *Nationalism in Children's Literature.* Chicago: University of Chicago Press, 1934.

Mayer, Martin. *The Schools.* New York: Harper & Row, Publishers, 1961. pp. 378-383.

Meyer, Row W. *The Middle Western Farm Novel in the Twentieth Century.* Lincoln: The University of Nebraska Press, 1964.

Michigan Department of Education. *A Report on the Treatment of Minorities in American History Textbooks.* Lansing, Mich., 1968.

National Society for the Study of Education. *The Text Book in American Education.* Thirtieth Yearbook, Part II. Chicago: University of Chicago Press, 1931.

Nolen, Claude H. *The Negro's Image in the South.* Lexington: University of Kentucky Press, 1967.

Olson, Bernhard E. *Faith and Prejudices: Intergroup Problems in Protestant Curricula.* New Haven, Conn.: Yale University Press, 1963.

Peacock, Fletcher and Edmonston, James. *A Study of National History Textbooks Used in the Schools of Canada and the United States.* Canada-United States Committee on Education, Washington, D. C.: American Council on Education, 1949.

Pierce, Bessie. *Civic Attitudes in American Textbooks.* Chicago: University of Chicago Press, 1930.

Plank, Robert. *The Emotional Significance Between Beings, A Study of the Interaction Between Psychopathology, Literature and Reality in the Modern World.* Springfield, Ill.: Charles C. Thomas, Publisher, 1968.

Quillen, I. James. *Textbook Improvement and International Understanding.* American Council on Education, 1948.

Robinson, Cecil. *With the Ears of Strangers: The Mexican in American Literature.* Tempe: University of Arizona Press, 1963.

Rogers, Katherine M. *The Troublesome Helpmate: A History of Misogyny in Literature.* Seattle: University of Washington Press, 1966. pp. 265-277.

Root, Merrill E. *Brainwashing in the High Schools.* New York: The Devin-Adair Co., 1958.

Shepard, Jon P. *The Treatment of Characters in Popular Children's Fiction.* Berkeley: University of California Press, 1958.

Sloan, Irving. *The Negro in Modern American History Textbooks,* 2nd ed. Chicago: American Federation of Teachers, 1967.

Stewart, Maxwell. *Prejudice in Textbooks.* New York: Public Affairs Pamphlets, 1950.

Waldo, Dwight. *The Novelist on Organization and Administration: An Inquiry into the Relationship Between Two Worlds.* Berkeley, Institute of Governmental Studies, June, 1968.

Walworth, Arthur. *School Histories at War—Study of the Treatment of Our Wars in the Secondary School History Books of the United States and in Those of Its Former Enemies.* Cambridge, Mass.: Harvard University Press, 1938.

Wilson, Harold E. *Latin America in School and College Teaching Materials.* Report of the Committee on the Study of Teaching Materials on Inter-American Subjects. Washington, D. C.: American Council on Education, 1946.

Wilson, Logan. *The Academic Man.* New York: Oxford University Press, 1942.

B. Articles

Abramowitz, Jack. "Textbooks and Negro History." *Social Education* 33 (March, 1969): 306-309.

Adams, Robert. "Books: The Girl Scout Handbook, Revised Edition." *Esquire* (February, 1964): 38-42.

Alilunas, Leo J. "The Image of Public Schools in Roman Catholic American History Textbooks." *History of Education Quarterly* 3 (September 3, 1963): 159-165.

"Are Our Children Learning History with a Slant?" *UNESCO Courier* 9 (May, 1956): 1-3.

Arnold, James. "Religious Textbooks . . . Primers in Bigotry." Reprint from *Ave Maria.* Available from American Jewish Committee, New York, 1964.

Arnsdorf, Val E. "Readability of Basal Social Studies Materials." *Reading Teacher* 16 (1963): 243-246.

———. "Study of Intermediate Grade Children's Understanding of Basal Social Studies Materials." *California Journal of Educational Research* 14 (March, 1963): 67-73.

Banks, James A. "A Content Analysis of the Black American in Textbooks." *Social Education* 33 (December, 1969): 954-957.

Belok, Michael V. "The Fictional Academic Woman." *Educational Forum* (January, 1962): 197-203.

Bennett, Lerone, Jr. "The Negro in Textbooks: Reading, 'Riting, and Racism." *Ebony* 22 (March, 1967): 130-138.

Billington, R. A. "History is a Dangerous Subject." *Saturday Review* 49 (January 15, 1966): 59-61, 80-81.

Black, Hillel. "What Our Children Read." *Saturday Evening Post* 240 (October 7, 1967): 27-29+.

Black, Isabella. "Race and Unreason: Anti-Negro Opinion in Professional and Scientific Literature since 1954." *Phylon* 26 (Spring, 1965): 65-79.

Blatt, Gloria T. "Mexican-Americans in Children's Literature." *Elementary English* 45 (April, 1968): 446-451.

Blom, G. E. "Content of First Grade Reading Books." *Reading Teacher* 21 (January, 1968): 317-323.

Blom, Gaston E., Waite, Richard R., and Zimet, Sara F. "Ethnic Integration and Urbanization of a First Grade Reading Textbook: A Research Study." *Psychology in the Schools* 4 (April, 1967): 176-184.

Blythe, Irene T. "The Textbooks and the New Discoveries, Emphasis and Viewpoints in American History." *Historical Outlook* 23:395-402.

Bovyer, George G. "Stories and Children's Concepts of Sportsmanship in the Fourth, Fifth, and Sixth Grades." *Elementary English* 39 (December, 1962): 762-765.

Bragdon, Henry W. "The New Curricula in Social Studies." *American Behavioral Scientist* 6 (1962): 32-34.

Burkhardt, R. W. "The Soviet Union in American Textbooks." *Progressive Education* 28 (October, 1950): 20-23.

Carpenter, Frederic I. "The Adolescent in American Fiction." *English Journal* 46 (September, 1957): 313-319.

Child, Irvin L., et al. "Children's Textbooks and Personality Development: An Exploration in the Social Psychology of Education." *Psychological Monographs* 60 (1946): 1-53.

Childress, Alice, et al. "The Negro Woman in American Literature." *Freedomways* 6 (April, 1966): 9-25.

Clyse, Juanita. "What Do Basic Readers Teach about Jobs?" *Elementary School Journal* 60 (May, 1959): 446-460.

Collier, Marilyn. "An Evaluation of Multi-Ethnic Basal Readers." *Elementary English* 44 (February, 1967): 152-157.

Cousins, Norman. "The Environment of Language." *Saturday Review* 50 (April 8, 1967): 36.

Cunningham, George E. "Derogatory Image of the Negro and Negro History." *Negro History Bulletin* 28 (March, 1965): 26-27+.

du Charms, Richard, and Moeler, Gerald H. "Values Expressed in American Children's Readers." *Journal of Abnormal and Social Psychology* 64 (1962): 136-142. Also reprinted in *Psychological Studies of Human Behavior*, edited by Kuhlen and Thompson. New York: Appleton-Century-Crofts, 1963.

Egger, Rowland. "The Administrative Novel." *American Political Science Review* 53 (June, 1959): 448-455.

Elkin, S. M. "Minorities in Textbooks: The Latest Chapter." *Teachers College Record* 66 (March, 1965): 502-508.

Epstein, Jason. "Good Bunnies Always Obey; Books for American Children." *Commentary* 2 (February, 1963): 112-122.

Evans, Eva Knox. "The Negro in Children's Fiction." *The Publishers Weekly* 140 (October 18, 1941): 650.

Evarts, Peter. "Suburbia: The Target Area." *Wilson Library Bulletin* 41 (October, 1966): 173-185.

Fisher, Walter R. "Philosophic Perspective and Beginning Public Speaking Texts." *The Speech Teacher* 19 (September, 1970): 206-210.

Fitch, Robert M. and Van Ness, James S. "The Historian's Contribution?" *Social Education* 30 (November, 1966): 502-506.

Frank, Libby. "My Weekly Reader Re-Read." *Changing Education* 4 (Spring, 1968): 60-62.

Friedsam, H. J. "Bureaucrats as Heroes." *Social Forces* 32 (March, 1954): 269-274.

Gast, E. K. "Minority Americans in Children's Literature." *Elementary English* 44 (January, 1967): 12-23.

Golden, Loretta. "The Treatment of Minority Groups in Primary Social Studies Textbooks." *Interracial Review* 39 (September, 1966): 150-154.

Groff, Patrick. "The Abolitionist Movement in High School Texts." *Journal of Negro History* 32 (1963): 45+.

Hanvey, Robert. "Augury for the Social Studies." *School Review* 69 (1961): 11-24.

Harris, Nelson H. "The Treatment of Negroes in Books and Media Designed for the Elementary School." *Social Education* 33 (April, 1969): 434-437.

Henry, Jeanette. "Our Inaccurate Textbooks." *The Indian Historian* 1 (December, 1967).

Hughes, Stuart H. "The Historian and the Social Scientist." *American Historical Review* 66 (1960): 20-46.

Johnson, J. C., and Geoffrey, K. E. "Value Reflected in Behavioral Modes: A Theoretical Construct." *Journal of the Reading Specialist* 7 (March, 1968): 114-121.

Kaiser, Ernest. "The History of Negro History." *Negro Digest* 7 (March, 1968): 10-15.

Keukel, William F. "Marriage and the Family in Modern Science Fiction." *Journal of Marriage and the Family* 31 (1969): 6-14.

Kidd, Virginia. " 'Now You See,' Said Mark." *New York Review of Books* 15 (September 3, 1970): 35-36.

Klineberg, Otto. "Life is Fun in a Smiling, Fair Skinned World." *Saturday Review* 46 (February 16, 1963): 75+.

Koelsch, George J., III. "Readability and Interests of Five Basal Reading Series with Retarded Students." *Exceptional Children* 35 (February, 1969): 487-488.

Krug, Mark M. "Distant Cousins: A Comparative Study of Selected History Textbooks in England and in the United States." *School Review* 71 (Winter, 1963): 425-441.

———. "Freedom and Racial Equality: A Study of 'Revised' High School History Texts." *School Review* 78 (May, 1970): 297-344.

———. "On Rewriting the Story of Reconstruction in the United States History Textbooks." *The Journal of Negro History* 46 (April, 1961): 133-153.

———. "Safe Textbooks and Citizenship Education." *School Review* 68 (1960): 463-480.

Landes, David. "The Treatment of Population in History Textbooks." *Daedalus* 97 (Spring, 1968): 363-384.

LaNoue, George R. "The National Defense Education Act and 'Secular Subjects.'" *Phi Delta Kappan* 43 (June, 1962): 380-388.

Larrick, Nancy. "The All-White World of Children's Books." *Saturday Review* 48 (September 11, 1965): 63-66.

Lowi, Theodore J. "American Government, 1933-63: Fission and Confusion in Theory and Research." *American Political Science Review* 58 (September, 1964): 589-599.

Lowry, Heath W. "A Review of Five Recent Content Analyses of Related Sociological Factors in Children's Literature." *Elementary English* 46 (October, 1969): 736-740.

Mandel, R. L. "Children's Books; Mirrors of Social Development." *Elementary School Journal* 65 (January, 1964): 190-199.

McClelland, David C. "Values in Popular Literature for Children." *Childhood Education* 40 (November, 1963): 135-138.

McPherson, James. "The 'Saga' of Slavery; Setting the Textbooks Straight." *Changing Education* 2 (Winter, 1967): 26-33+.

Morgan, Edmund S. "An Anglo-American Contribution to Historical Misunderstanding." *Social Education* 30 (November, 1966): 499-502.

Moore, John R. "State History Textbooks: Essays in Ethnocentrism." *Social Education* 33 (March, 1969): 267-276.

Noah, Harold J., Prince, Carl E., and Riggs, C. Russell. "History in High School Textbooks: A Note." *School Review* 70 (1962): 415-436.

Palmer, John R. "History Textbooks and Social Change." *Social Education* 25 (March, 1961): 135-136.

Patterson, Franklin K. "Social Science and the Curriculum." *American Behavioral Scientist* 6 (1962): 28-32.

Preer, Bette B. "Guidance in Democratic Living Through Juvenile Fiction." *Wilson Library Bulletin* 22 (May, 1948): 679-681.

Reddick, Lawrence D. "Racial Attitudes in American History Textbooks of the South." *Journal of Negro History* 19 (July, 1934): 225-265.

Roberts, Launey F., Jr. "Ethnocentric Identification: A Survey of the Pictorial Content of Selected Current Elementary School Textbooks." *Negro History Bulletin* 30 (December, 1967): 6-10.

Robbins, John. "The New Asia and American Education." *Teachers College Record* 62 (1961): 339-347.

Ross, Raymond. "Cultivating Taste in Children's Literature." *Education* 86 (September, 1965): 22-26.

Saveth, Edward N. "Good Stocks and Lesser Breeds: The Immigrant in American Textbooks." *Commentary* 7 (May, 1949): 494-498.

Shaver, James P. "Diversity, Violence, and Religion: Textbooks in a Pluralistic Society." *School Review* 75 (August, 1967): 311-327.

———. "Reflective Thinking, Values, and Social Studies Textbooks." *School Review* 73 (Autumn, 1965): 226-676.

Shepard, J. P. "The Treatment of Characters in Popular Children's Fiction." *Elementary English* 39 (November, 1962): 672-676.

Sledd, James. "Essay Review: As in Itself it Really Is." *School Review* 74 (Autumn, 1966): 341-352.

Sletkin, Aaron. "The Treatment of Minorities in Textbooks: The Issues and the Outlook." *Strengthening Democracy*. New York: New York City Board of Education, May, 1964.

Soares, Anthony J. and Simpson, Ray H. "Interest in Recreational Reading of Junior High School Students." *Journal of Reading* 11 (October, 1967): 14-21.

Stampp, Kenneth, et al. "The Negro in American History Textbooks." *Integrated Education* 2 (October-November, 1964): 9-25.

Stoer, M. W. "A Second Look: The Treatment of Characters in Popular Children's Fiction." *Elementary English* 40 (February, 1963): 172-173.

Strickland, Ruth G. "Language of Elementary School Children: Its Relationship to the Language of Reading Textbooks and the Quality of Reading of Selected Children." Indiana University School of Education *Bulletin* 38 (July, 1962): 1-129.

Tannenbaum, Abraham. "Family Living in Textbook Town." *Progressive Education* 31 (March, 1954): 133-141.

Textbook Committee of the Committee on Economic Education of the American Economic Association. "Economics in the Schools." *American Economic Review* 53 (1963): 1-27 (part 2 supplement).

Trecker, Janice Law. "Women in U. S. History High School Textbooks." *Social Education* 35 (March, 1971): 249-260+.

Trezise, Robert L. "The Black American in American History Textbooks." *Social Studies* 60 (April, 1969): 164-167.

Tucker, E. P. "Anti-Evolutionists of 1964: Opposition by Church of Christ in Texas." *Science Education* 51 (October, 1967): 371-378.

Twyford, Loran C., et al. "Behavioral and Factual Analysis." *Audio-Visual Communication Review* 7 (1959): 182-192.

Vogel, Virgil J. "The Indian in American History Textbooks." *Integrated Education* 33 (May-June, 1968): 16-22.

_____. "The Indian in American History." *Social Education* 33 (February, 1969): 200-203.

Waite, Richard R. "Further Attempts to Integrate and Urbanize First Grade Reading Textbooks: A Research Study." *Journal of Negro Education* 37 (Winter, 1968): 62-69.

Waite, Richard R., et al. "First-Grade Reading Textbooks." *Elementary School Journal* 67 (1967): 366-74.

Walton, Jeanne. "The American Negro in Children's Literature." *Eliot-Pearson School News,* Tufts University, February, 1964.

Wargny, Frank O. "The Good Life in Modern Readers." *Reading Teacher* 17 (November, 1963): 88-93.

Wiberg, J. Lawrence, and Blom, Gaston E. "A Cross-National Study of Attitude Content in Reading Primers." *International Journal of Psychology* 5 (1970): 109-122.

Wiberg, John L. and Trost, Marion. "A Comparison Between the Content of First Grade Primers and the Free Choice Library Selections Made by First Grade Students." *Elementary English* 47 (October, 1970): 792-799.

Wolfenstein, Martha. "Fun Morality: An Analysis of Recent American Child-Training Literature." *Journal of Social Issues* 7 (1951): 15-25.

Wood, Herbert J. "The Far East in World History." *Social Education* 15 (April, 1951): 155-159.

Worley, Stinson E. "Developmental Task Situations in Stories." *Reading Teacher* 21 (November, 1967): 145-148.

Zimet, Sara F. "American Elementary Reading Textbooks: A Sociological Review." *Teachers College Record* 70 (January, 1969): 331-340.
_____. "Children's Interests and Story Preferences: A Critical View of the Literature." *Elementary School Journal* 67 (1967): 366-374.
Zuercher, Roger. "The Treatment of Asian Minorities in American History Textbooks." *The Indiana Social Studies Quarterly* 22 (Autumn, 1969): 19-27.

C. General Commentary

Alexander, Albert. "Does the American History Textbook Still Wear a Gray Flannel Cover?" *Social Education* 33 (March, 1969): 300-305.
———. "The Gray Flannel Cover on the American History Textbook." *Social Education* 24 (January, 1960): 11-14.
Aptheker, Herbert. "Integrated Education Requires Integrated Texts." *Political Affairs* 43 (June, 1964): 47-52.
Bonham, Frank. "Return to Durango Street." *Library Journal* 91 (September, 15, 1966): 36-39.
Brazziel, William F. "Negro History in the Public Schools: Trends and Prospects." *Negro History Bulletin* 28 (November, 1965): 36, 38.
Busch, Fred. "Basals Are Not for Reading." *Teachers College Record* 72 (1970): 25-30.
Cianciolo, P. J. "Children's Literature Can Affect Coping Behavior." *Personnel and Guidance Journal* 43 (1965): 897-903.
Cook, Clea A. H. "Multi-Cultural Textbook Series." *California Journal for Instructional Improvement*, May, 1966: 95-110.
Cronbach, Lee J., ed. *Text Materials in Modern Education.* Urbana: University of Illinois Press, 1955.
Cousins, Norman. "The Environment of Language." *Saturday Review* (April 8, 1967): 36.
Davis, Lucian. "Current Controversy: Minorities in American History Textbooks." *Journal of Secondary Education* 41 (November, 1966): 291-94.
Egoff, Sheila. "Precepts and Pleasures: Changing Emphases in the Writing and Criticisms of Children's Literature." In *Only Connect: Readings on Children's Literature,* edited by Sheila Egoff, G. T. Stubbs, and L. F. Ashley. New York: Oxford University Press, 1969.
Ferkiss, Victor C. "The Literary Approach to Politics." *Thought: Fordham University Quarterly* 31 (Autumn, 1956): 350-364.
Franklin, John Hope. "Whither Reconstruction Historiography." *Journal of Negro Education* 17 (1948): 446-461.
Gibson, Emily Fuller. "The Three D's: Distortion, Deletion, Denial." *Social Education* 33 (April, 1969): 405-409.
Glancy, Barbara. "The Beautiful People in Children's Books." *Childhood Education* 46 (April, 1970): 365-70.
Henry, Jules. "Reading for What?" *Teachers College Record* 65 (October, 1963): 35-49.
Hersey, John. "Why Do Students Bog Down on First 'R'?" *Life* 36 (May 24, 1954): 136-140+.
Hicks, Granville. "Fiction and Social Criticism." *College English* 65 (April, 1952): 355-361.

Joyce, William W. "Minority Groups in American Society: Imperatives for Education. *Social Education* 33 (April, 1969): 429-433.

Kaiser, Ernest. "Trends in American Negro Historiography." *Journal of Negro Education* 31 (1962): 468-479.

Kroll, Morton. "Administrative Fiction and Credibility." *Public Administration Review* 25 (March, 1965): 80-84.

Lewis, Wyndham. "The Propagandist in Fiction." *New York Times Current History* 40 (August, 1934): 567-572.

Lynn, Kenneth S. "Authors in Search of the Businessman." *Harvard Business Review* 34 (September-October, 1956): 116-124.

Margolis, Richard J. "The Well-Tempered Textbook." *Education Digest* 31 (December, 1965): 24-27.

Massialas, Byron G. "Selecting a Social Studies Textbook." *Social Education* 25 (1961): 237-238.

Maurice, Sister Mary. "Awakening to Human Values in Children's Literature." *Catholic School Journal* 68 (March, 1968): 41-43.

Mayer, Martin. "The Trouble with Textbooks." *Harper's* 205 (July, 1962): 65-71.

Meyer, Howard N. "Overcoming the White Man's History." *Massachusetts Review* 7 (1966): 569-578.

Polos, N. C. "Textbooks and the Invisible Man." *Educational Forum* 31 (May, 1967): 477-480.

"A Realistic Children's Book . . . Realistic Children." *Mad Magazine*, September, 1961.

Reid, James M. *An Adventure in Textbooks*. New York: R. R. Bowker Co., 1969.

Rogers, Vincent R. and Muessig, Raymond H. "Needed: A Revolution in the Textbook Industry." *Social Studies* 54 (October, 1963): 169.

Rose, Lois, and Rose, Stephen. *The Shattered Ring: Science Fiction and the Quest for Meaning*. Richmond, Virginia: John Knox, Publisher, 1970.

Roth, Joel A. "Dick and Jane Make Some New Friends." *Book Production Industry* 41 (June, 1965).

Scully, Malcolm G. "Campus Novels Said to Take a Dim View of Teachers and Administrators." *Chronicle of Higher Education* 5 (February 8, 1971): 1, 8.

Shrag, Peter. "The Emasculated Voice of the Textbook." *Saturday Review* 50 (January 21, 1967): 74.

Sloan, Irving. "Balance and Imbalance: 'New' History Texts and the Negro." *Changing Education* 1 (Fall, 1966): 14-19.

Stewart, Charles E. "Correcting the Image of Negroes in Textbooks." *Negro History Bulletin* 28 (November, 1964): 29-30+.

"The Writing and Teaching of American History in Textbooks." *AHA Newsletter* 4 (April, 1969): 7-10.

Zimet, Sara Goodman. "Little Boy Lost." *Teachers College Record* 72 (September, 1970): 31-39.

Index